1990

METAPHYSICS OF KNOWLEDGE

AN INTRODUCTION TO
METAPHYSICS
OF KNOWLEDGE

YVES R. SIMON

Translated by
Vukan Kuic *and* **Richard J. Thompson**

Fordham University Press
New York
1990

Translated from *Introduction à l'ontologie du connaître* (Paris: Desclée
De Brouwer, 1934).

Printed in the United States of America

Contents

Translators' Preface

THE PRESENT VOLUME is the product of several years of collaboration at a distance between two people who both knew Yves R. Simon personally and admired his work. Vukan Kuic, of the University of South Carolina, was Simon's student at The University of Chicago from 1954 to 1956, and has edited three of Simon's posthumous volumes. Richard J. Thompson, of the University of Notre Dame, first read this book in a graduate course at the Pontifical Institute of Mediaeval Studies at Toronto, and came to know Simon as a neighbor and a friend when he moved to South Bend in 1948.

Thompson began to translate this book in 1981, on the suggestion from another friend of Simon's, Frederick J. Crosson, then Dean of the College of Arts and Letters at the University of Notre Dame, and with further encouragement from Anthony O. Simon, director of the Yves R. Simon Institute, completed the first draft in the summer of 1982. While Thompson was in London with the Notre Dame Arts and Letters program, Kuic read the manuscript and suggested a number of stylistic changes. The question was the choice between a more literal and a more idiomatic rendering of the text, which arises with any translation but presents special difficulties in the case of a technical philosophical treatise such as this one. Kuic and Thompson met for a few days at the Jacques Maritain Center at Notre Dame (where most of the Simon papers are kept), and produced a second, joint draft of the text in late 1983. After some additional work by Thompson, the manuscript was put on disks and forwarded to Kuic for final editing in 1984. For a number of extraneous reasons, this took more than two years, and it was then decided that while the anonymous reader at Fordham University Press reviewed the manuscript, Thompson should also have another go at it. Consequently, the present text incorporates most of Thompson's final recommendations as well as the corrections and changes suggested by the outside reader.

The numerous and extensive quotations in the footnotes, which in the French volume are given in the original Latin, Greek, or German, have here all been translated into English. Because of the non-existence, or inaccessibility, of English versions of many of these sources, these are original translations by Thompson and Kuic except in the following cases. The quotations from the second part of *Ars logica* by John of St. Thomas are from *The Material Logic of John of St. Thomas*, edited and translated by Yves R. Simon, John J. Glanville, and G. Donald Hollenhorst (Chicago: The University of Chicago Press, 1955). Simon was particularly proud of their having succeeded in rendering this scholastic treatise into readable English, and the present translators have used this text as a model for translating from the rest of John of St. Thomas' work. Similarly, quotations from the work of Cajetan have been matched as much as possible with the passages that Simon himself translated for "An Essay on Sensation" in *The Philosophy of Knowledge*, edited by Roland Houde and Joseph Mullally (Chicago: Lippincott, 1960; pp. 55–95). Quotations from the *Summa theologica* by Thomas Aquinas have been adapted from the translation by the Fathers of the English Dominican Province, revised by Daniel J. Sullivan and published as Volumes 19 and 20 of *The Great Books of the Western World* (Chicago: Encyclopaedia Britannica/Benton, 1952). Quotations from St. Thomas' *De veritate* have been adapted from *The Disputed Questions on Truth*, translated by Robert W. Mulligan (Chicago: Regnery, 1952), and those from *In Metaphysica* from the *Commentary on the Metaphysics of Aristotle*, translated by John P. Rowan (Chicago: Regnery, 1961). All quotations from Aristotle are from *The Basic Works of Aristotle*, edited by Richard McKeon (New York: Random House, 1941). Finally, quotations from Jacques Maritain's *Les Degrés du savoir* are from *The Degrees of Knowledge*, translated under the supervision of Gerald B. Phelan (New York: Scribner's, 1959). In form, the references in the present volume follow on the whole the Chicago *Manual of Style*. But while this has required in many instances supplementing the original citations with more complete publication data from various library catalogues, these additions are not specially marked in the text.

When *Introduction à l'ontologie du connaître* was first published more than half a century ago, one noted reviewer introduced his evaluation as follows:

> Works dealing with the ontological problems of knowledge are very rare these days. Questions of epistemology and of critique seem to have usurped all attention. Though every once in a while someone dares to enter the domain of philosophical psychology proper, the sector of the ontology of knowledge is carefully avoided. Yves Simon has opened it again for discussion with remarkable assurance. He boldly recognizes its many difficulties, and one cannot but admire both the precision of his formulation of its problems and the tight dialectic of his exposition and justification of his interpretation [Louis de Raeymaeker, *Revue Néoscholastique de Philosophie*, 38 (1935), 509–10].

The questions raised by Simon are not just still with us; they appear to be pursued rather more directly: "What is the nature of knowledge? What kind of activity is it—to know? And what is involved in the development of human knowledge?" Amidst the confusion of current debates, the present reader may find useful the following summary of Simon's treatment by this early reviewer:

> To answer the first question, the author develops the theory of "intentional" existence and its conditions. To solve the second problem, he explains at length the nature of immanent action and the sense in which knowledge is an activity and a quality. And with regard to the third question, he does not hesitate to face its many difficulties, including the necessity and the role of experimental knowledge, the role of material things in producing sensation, the contribution of sensible knowledge in the formation of concepts, the nature and role of concepts, the significance of judgments in the knowledge of truth, and the various forms of the active development of the mind [ibid., 510].

But if one had to describe Simon's accomplishment by reducing it to a single point, what Simon succeeded in showing, in this reviewer's opinion, was that an ontology of knowledge based on common experience disproves all idealism and leads to realism by strictest necessity.

How well Simon establishes this thesis will today inevitably also be interpreted in different ways by different readers, largely according to their understanding of what philosophy is all about. Thus one suspects that, glancing at the footnotes, some will see this work as a learned latter-day commentary on Scholastic teaching about creaturely knowledge and related subjects. But this would be a most superficial view because this book deals not with the history but with the ever-present problems of ontology and epistemology. Moreover, as Simon liked to point out, there is no such thing as a uniform Scholastic philosophy. Medieval writers did have a common *Problematik* and a common way of treating their subjects, but they more often than not also sharply disagreed in their substantive interpretations. Nor can one argue that Simon simply chose to side with Aquinas and his school, for, as the reader will find out, Simon has to be convinced by argument before he accepts any position. Of course, Simon would not object to being called a Thomist philosopher. But for him truth had no labels, and he was keenly aware that "access to rare truth is the most undeserved of all privileges." Accepting the Cardinal Spellman–Aquinas Medal from the American Catholic Philosophical Association in 1958, he put it this way:

This is really what is strangest in the philosopher's calling: this duty of fighting an often solitary fight against learned and dignified persons, against Descartes and Spinoza and Berkeley and a few others, with the inescapable implication that he, the solitary fighter, knows better about the really important issues than most of the greatest among the philosophical geniuses. It looks as if a painter of fair talent went to war against Leonardo da Vinci, Michelangelo and Rubens. How can the philosopher convince people that he is not yielding to insane pride? The audacity with which he discusses, criticizes and refutes genius bears all the appearances of the worst kind of conceit. Can anything be done to remove these damaging appearances? Much can be done indeed, but to conceal certainty by proposing truth under the externals of socially acceptable opinion is not always the right method. The job has to be done through things that are much more difficult to acquire than good social manners. These things are virtues, and accordingly they are hard to get. In the fulfillment of the philospher's duty there is no substitute for the fearless love of truth, for selflessness, fortitude and humility [*Proceedings*, 32, 33].

Those who knew Simon and those familiar with his work recognize that these remarks express his deepest convictions. He
understood well that in addition to whatever social problems he
may encounter, the main reason why the philosopher needs an
excess of courage is the weight of past failure brought about by
the fact that the philosophical enterprise pushes at the limit of
the human mind's possibilities. Therefore, an unwavering determination to approach the philosophical enterprise as the supreme rational discipline, or, as he insisted, scientifically, was in
Simon's opinion the exclusive condition of the possibility of its
progress.

"From a philosophical standpoint," Simon explained,

> one major characteristic of our time is a deepened split between
> man's concern for mystery and the forms of scientific thought.
> Referring to well-known propositions of Maritain in *A Preface to
> Metaphysics*, let us say that a question can be predominantly a
> problem or predominantly a mystery. A problem is a question the
> true answer to which leaves no room for further elaboration. Des-
> cartes was praising the handiness of problems when he pointed
> out that a child who has performed a multiplication according to
> the rules of arithmetic knows as much about the product as any
> mathematical genius in the world. But a mystery is a question of
> such character that an answer unqualifiedly true and sound and
> appropriate not only admits of but also urgently demands fur-
> ther inquiries into inexhaustible intelligibility. The mystery aspect
> predominates in religion, in metaphysics, in philosophy gener-
> ally, and in human affairs. The problem aspect predominates in
> the disciplines called the *sciences* by common usage, in techniques,
> and generally in the fields where the pattern of positive science
> exercises a strong influence. Interest in philosophy, religion, the-
> ology, human sciences, and humane studies is no less today than
> in celebrated periods of intellectual greatness. But it is impossi-
> ble not to be struck by a widespread aversion to scientific forms in
> philosophy, theology, and human affairs—briefly, in the realms
> characterized by the predominance of mystery. . . . What is lack-
> ing in our relation to mystery is neither earnestness nor abun-
> dance of ideas, it is the rigor of the scientific spirit. There are
> things which will never be accomplished by "the tragic sentiment
> of life," "immersion in history," "experience of death," "esprit de
> finesse," "cultural refinement," "esthetic sophistication," "our cul-
> tural heritage," etc. Those things are clarity in the statement of

questions and principles, firmness in inference, rational evidence of conclusions, appropriateness in prediction, integral preservation of past developments, lucid order, and the unique defense against error that rational forms alone can provide [*Material Logic of John of St. Thomas*, pp. xxii–xxiii].

Lest these remarks on the rigors of the philosophical enterprise convey the impression that Simon was cold and aloof, we must conclude with a final quotation from his Medalist Address that in a way sums up the man and his work, including perhaps especially this book. Philosophical work, Simon recognized, has to be done, for the most part, in solitude. But something wonderful happens

when the philosopher breaks out of his solitude and succeeds in communicating, together with a particle of truth, something of the aspiration, something of the dedication, something of the hope and the love that keep him going through never-ending difficulties. . . . A philosopher who has ever succeeded in communicating his inspiration together with his demonstration, and who has experienced the joy of friendship born of such communication, will always feel that if he had to choose again, philosophy would again be his calling.

Vukan Kuic
Richard J. Thompson

1

Nature and Cognition

To Be and to Know

WHENEVER WE BEGIN to reflect seriously on the problem of cognition, we inevitably find ourselves baffled by outrageous paradoxes. To reassure ourselves, we put aside all abstractions to concentrate on things most familiar to us. We tell ourselves that, regardless of the problems it presents, cognition is a fact and must, therefore, be possible. If there is anyone who has not felt this anguish, this need to return to the commonplace and to take hold of what is certain in it, we can be sure that he has not recognized the problem. For it is only those who cannot distinguish between the things of nature and the things of the mind who find nothing "unnatural" in the phenomenon of cognition.

A sound metaphysics of knowledge must, therefore, take for its experimental starting point what common sense has never doubted: namely, that *some beings are capable of cognition and some are not.* In our daily lives, we take this twofold fact for granted and act accordingly. And yet, this fact has not prevented a philosophy as old as the world from contending that there does not exist—that there cannot exist—anything completely lacking in cognition. According to this school, cognition is a necessary property of being, perhaps even identical with it (which would indeed eliminate quite a few difficulties). To meet this challenge of a philosophy's denying facts of experience, we need to show that they are also philosophical facts.[1]

---

[1] Though the word is not perfect, we shall call *hylozoism* any doctrine that extends the power of cognition beyond what we call the animal kingdom. In the history of thought, hylozoism sometimes includes only living things, but at other times it embraces all things, and then it may also be called *panpsychism.* The main reason why some thinkers have deemed it necessary to invoke cognition to explain vital phenomena, and at the same time deny that inorganic things have that power, is simply that finality is so much more obvious in the

The theory that attributes both cognition and desire to all things seems to have its principal source in the concern for a satisfactory explanation of the phenomenon of finality, which the universe reveals in all its parts, or, better still, which our intelligence observes in every nature. We see plants responding to stimuli. We count on chlorine and silver to make silver chloride. Indeed, we confidently expect finality wherever there is activity, and we know only things that are active. But does this universal finality not presuppose universal cognition? What we seem to have here is a pre-established relation between a cause and the effect that will issue from it. Yet the effect is not given with the cause in any determinate way and will be something new and additional in relation to it. In other words, finality implies a kind of predetermination of the present by the future, of what exists actually by what exists only potentially. But that which exists only potentially can never as such determine or influence anything. For it to predetermine the present in any way, this future must have actuality somewhere, and that can only be in someone's knowledge.

---

behavior of things that are alive. But since the obscurely purposive activity of inanimate agents calls for every bit as much explaining, as soon as one assumes that every activity pointing to an end presupposes some kind of knowledge on the part of the agent itself, the panpsychist position seems to be the only logical one.

We also note that, since Descartes, the psychic interpretation of vital phenomena has been for many writers the only way to distinguish and identify living beings. For if there is nothing in the universe but extension and thought, the only way a living thing can be distinguished from mere extension is by endowing it with thought. This is how vitalism gets embroiled with hylozoism and generates interminable debates over a wrongly stated problem.

But we must not fail to mention also another source and foundation of panpsychism, namely, materialist philosophies. Materialists tend to attribute thought to all matter because they reject the hierarchy of essences with irreducible ontological values, which precludes explaining the attributes of an essence of a higher order by the attributes of an essence from a lower order. Thus, if thought is postulated in any corporeal being, it must be postulated in all. Cf. Albert Dastre, *La Vie et la mort* (Paris: Flammarion, 1920), pp. 236–37.

On ancient hylozoism, see Adolf Stöhr, *Der Begriff des Lebens* (Heidelberg: Winter, 1909), p. 4. As its principal representatives Stöhr cites Thales, Anaximander, Heraclitus, and Empedocles. Among the modern spokesmen for hylozoism (either in a restricted or, more often, in its broadest sense) we may point to Campanella (ibid., p. 50); Francis Glisson, the founder of the theory of irritability (*Tractatus de ventriculo et intestinis* [1677]; cf. H. Marion, *Revue*

Metaphysical reason affirms no more than this. It is the pan-psychist philosophy that goes further and claims that cognition is necessarily joined to all activity and that every tendency in any active thing proceeds from knowledge possessed by that thing itself. This interpretation we believe to be arbitrary.[2] For although it is true that for an action to be directed toward its end that end must be known, it is not necessary that it be known by the agent itself; it is enough that this end be known by someone or some-thing that holds the agent in its power. The arrow does not know where it is headed, but the archer does. Indeed, even with regard to animate beings, we cannot always be sure whether they move by their own desire and knowledge. Thus scientists are by no means agreed on whether, say, an amoeba possesses images and feels emotions. Perhaps they will eventually figure it out experi-mentally, but it is also possible that we may never know for certain.

We shall find it useful, then, to distinguish between *psychic* tendencies[3] of subjects who are fully aware of them and *natural* or *apsychic* tendencies that spring from the constitutions placed in every existing thing by the creative thought and will.[4] Inter-estingly enough, though this notion of a natural tendency imme-diately destroys the basic hypothesis of panpsychism, panpsych-

---

Philosophique, 14 [1882], 140); Claude Perrault, *Essai sur le bruit* (1680); Leibniz; Ernest Haeckel, *Essais de psychologie cellulaire* (Paris: Baillière, 1880), p. 156, and *Enigmes de l'univers* (Paris: Schleicher, 1905), pp. 253, 258 (Oliver J. Lodge, *Life and Matter* [New York: Putnam, 1912], p. 42, after quoting from Haeckel, writes: "Thus, in order to explain life and mind and consciousness by means of matter, all that he does here is to assume that matter possesses these unex-plained attributes."); Gustave T. Fechner, *Nanna, oder über das Seelenleben der Pflanzen* (5th ed. [Leipzig: Voss, 1921]) and *Zendavesta, oder über die Dinge des Himmels und des Jenseits* (Leipzig: Voss, 1922); cf. Stöhr, pp. 57–58: "He asks, 'How does consciousness get into the living organism?' And his answer is that consciousness was always there." Pierre Jean's *Psychologie organique* (Paris: Alcan, 1925), p. 289, is also full of interesting suggestions.

[2] It may be said that Schopenhauer's position is perfectly contrary to pan-psychist finalism. For Schopenhauer, it is the will that is present everywhere, making every tendency an expression of volition. Whether the will is con-scious or not is accidental (*The World as Will and Idea*, trans. R. B. Haldane and J. Kemp, 3 vols. [London: Routledge & Kegan Paul, 1883], I, §19, II, § 83).

[3] We shall regularly use *psychism* and its derivatives not in the broad sense in which some apply it to everything that is alive, but in the restricted and more acceptable sense in which it is essentially related to cognition.

[4] Thomas Aquinas, *In Phys.* I, lect. 15; *De ver.*, q. 25, a. 1; *Sum. th.* I, q. 6, a.

ism is not necessarily saved by its rejection. When panpsychism totally rejects the notion of natural or apsychic finality, it also finds itself unable to justify its own position. For even if it were true that every single being is endowed with the power of cognition, one would still have to concede the existence of apsychic finality precisely in order to explain this universal cognitive endowment. For where else could a plant's knowing response to stimuli come from? Unless we assume that for this plant *to be is to know*, the very first such allegedly cognitive response could not be anything else but an expression of a natural and apsychic tendency incorporated in the plant's constitution. The will wills the intellect to know but only upon being previously enlightened by the intellect. The first act of understanding is not commanded by the will. It is determined by the natural tendency of the intellect toward its perfection—or it never takes place.[5]

Consequently, unless we hold that nothing exists except thought in pure act, we see that, no matter how far panpsychism is extended, it does not allow us to dispense with the role of natural tendencies or to get along without a transcendent principle of order in the universe. The effort to argue against experience and to try to prove that every natural tendency is psychic is both gratuitously pretentious and impossible to maintain. Perhaps people would not be so tempted to attribute emotions to plants and atoms if they simply realized that natural tendencies are to be found aplenty even in intelligent beings. In agreement with common sense, they would then be able to accept the fact that some things lack cognition, and that between these things and those beings that have that power there is a radical difference.

To pursue this difference and draw the first lines of an intelligible sketch of a metaphysics of knowledge, let us begin by noting how closed, how restricted, a thing lacking in cognition appears compared with the openness of beings endowed with knowledge. *The subject possessing knowledge has an ampli-*

1, ad 2; q. 19, a. 1; q. 59, a. 1; q. 78, a. 1, ad 3; q. 80, a. 1; q. 81, a. 2; q. 87, a. 4; I–II, q. 1, a. 2; q. 8, a. 1; q. 17, a. 8; q. 26, a. 1; q. 35, a. 1; q. 40, a. 3; Cajetan, *In De an.* II, 3 (Bologna, 1617 [hereafter cited as B], 91A); *In Ia,* q. 19, a. 1; q. 78, a. 1; *In IaIIae,* q. 30, a. 4.

[5] Roland Dalbiez, "Saint Jean de la Croix d'après M. Baruzi," offprint from *La Vie Spirituelle* (October–November 1928), 14.

tude clearly denied to the other things of nature.[6]

Amplitude and openness—like most terms of human language, these notions have a spatial origin, but they are easily transferred to the intelligible order by the spontaneous activity of analogical thought. When a small child begins to recognize the people and things that surround him, we say that his mind is opening up. To say that someone is of limited intelligence is a grave insult, since it is so contrary to the nature of the mind to be limited. One hesitates to call intelligent a man who is at home in financial affairs, but who has no understanding of the fine arts or the moral life; we suspect him of having a closed mind. When a professor continues to teach from notes that he has used for years, we may say that he is treasuring the knowledge that he had acquired in his youth, but we cannot avoid the implication that his understanding of the subject is deficient. Indeed, there is nothing that suggests to a child more vividly the idea of the divine immensity than God's omniscience: God must be infinitely great because He knows everything.

Read again the famous page in which Pascal rises to the heights of the greatest metaphysicians:

Man is but a reed, the most feeble thing in nature; but he is a thinking reed. The entire universe need not arm itself to crush him. A vapour, a drop of water suffices to kill him. But if the universe were to crush him, man would still be more noble than that which killed him because he knows that he dies and the advantage which the universe has over him; the universe knows nothing of this.

All our dignity consists, then, in thought. By it we must elevate ourselves, and not by space and time which we cannot fill. Let us endeavour, then, to think well. . . .

It is not from space that I must seek my dignity, but from the government of my thought. I shall have no more if I possess worlds. By space the universe encompasses me and swallows me up like an atom; by thought I comprehend the universe.[7]

---

[6] Aristotle, *On the Soul* III, 8, 431B20: "Let us now summarize our results about the soul and repeat that the soul is in a way all existing things"; Thomas Aquinas, *De ver.*, q. 2, a. 2; *Sum. th.* I, q. 14, a. 1; q. 54, a. 2.

[7] *Pensées*, trans. W. F. Trotter (New York: Dutton, 1958), 6.347–48.

Here we are confronted with a formidable challenge hurled at the principle of identity, and whatever chance we have of advancing in our understanding of the nature of cognition will clearly depend on our awareness of the strength of this challenge. Thus Professor Bergson argues that even by his body man occupies more than just the tiniest space which is ordinarily allotted to him, and with which Pascal contented himself when he reduced the "thinking reed" to being, materially, only a reed. For if it is our body that supports our consciousness, the two are co-extensive, and the body thus comprises all we perceive, including our grasp of the stars.[8] Clearly Bergson exaggerates, and we must protest. After all, I measure my height not in billions of miles but in feet and inches. Still, what I know is present to me, is within me—including the stars. What I know, I am.[9]

That knowing is a way of being, that one is what one knows, is a thesis basic to critical realism, and if it seems to resist any sort of direct demonstration, this is because it expresses something logically prior to demonstration. What we have here is the very essence, the intelligible nucleus, of the object in question, to which properties can be attached by demonstration, but which itself is grasped intuitively. Just as the fact of cognition represents its experimental starting point, so this intuitive *Wesenschau* constitutes the noetic starting point of a sound metaphysics of knowledge, regardless of how many arguments from absurdity may be produced against it. This is why, rather than arguing points with those who happen not to grasp it, our major concern will be to indicate a method for arriving at this intuition.

Confronted with an object of cognition, we may consider and describe its content, or we may consider and describe its *form as an object*.[10] From the first point of view, we speak of its colors, its

---

[8] Henri Bergson, *The Two Sources of Morality and Religion*, trans. R. A. Audra and C. Brereton (Garden City, N.Y.: Doubleday Anchor, 1954), p. 258. See also Jacques Maritain, *La Philosophie bergsonienne*, 2nd ed. (Paris: Rivière, 1930), p. 269.

[9] Aristotle, *On the Soul* III, 4, 430A4: "For speculative knowledge and its object are identical"; ibid., 7, 431B16: "In every case the mind which is actively thinking is the objects which its thinks"; ibid., 8, 431B22: "Knowledge is in a way what is knowable and sensation is in a way what is sensible."

[10] John of St. Thomas, *Phil. nat.* III, q. 2, a. 3 (ed. B. Reiser, 3 vols. [Turin: Marietti, 1937]—hereafter identified as R—III, 76B38): "The mate-

hardness, its shape, its genus, and its specific difference; such descriptions are given by the sciences, by the philosophy of nature, and by the metaphysics of being. The ontology of knowing adopts the second point of view: it brackets the content of the object and considers strictly the form that makes of it an object of knowledge. And just as, when considered in its content, this object makes known to us the thing that is manifested in it and by it, so considered in its form, the object of cognition ought to reveal to us what it means, or what it is, to *know*. The content of the object perceived (the green of the grass, the gray of the highway, the notes of the melody) is what makes its perception the particular act that it is (i.e., an act of sight or an act of hearing). Similarly, the form of the object of cognition makes the act of knowing an act of knowing, and not some other kind of act. It is this form that makes the faculty of knowing what it is. It is clear, however, that the form of the object (here we take the word *object* in a very general sense as the *end that specifies an activity*, whatever that may be)[11] belongs among those realities that can be defined only in the language of relations and by the expression of a relation. Just as an effect, as effect, is definable only in relation to a cause, so an object of cognition, as object and in its form of object, can be defined only in relation to the subject that it confronts, or, even better, in relation to the faculty whose act it causes to be a particular kind of act.[12] Thus describing the object of knowledge *in its form as object* is equivalent to revealing the nature of its relation with the knowing subject or the cognitive faculty.[13]

This is the only way to approach the intuitive act that lets us grasp the essence of knowing, which is inaccessible to any dis-

---

rial content of an object is one thing, but its form, by reason of which it pertains to a particular power and act and specifies or distinguishes that act, is another."

[11] Additional considerations of the notion of *object in general* will be found below, p. 76.

[12] The analogy is incomplete. The case of divine causality aside, the relation of causality is a real relation both in the cause and in the effect; the relation of objectivity is real only in the subject.

[13] John of St. Thomas, *Phil. nat.* III, q. 2, a. 3 (R, III, 76в39): "And this formality (of the object) is nothing but that very proportion or adaptation to a particular act or potency; the proportion is a relation."

course. We are looking at the relation of the object of knowledge to the faculty of knowing. What kind of relation is it? Well, it is a relation of *pure qualitative determination*, innocent of everything involved in the order of movement, effectuation, or desire. The relation that defines the object of knowledge is not like that between an effect and its efficient cause. Knowing is not making, creating, or transforming; we could say that in knowing we touch the object, but we never interfere with it. Nor does our relation with objects of knowledge resemble that between the lover and the beloved. Desire is a like a weight, and it sets things in motion. But the one who knows, the knower as such, the contemplative, is completely at rest in relation to the object of knowledge.[14] Indeed, to conceive knowledge either as some sort of making or as the result of some sort of desire is to misconstrue its nature and turn it into what it is not.

Again, though it is true that the notion of object is used properly in explaining such activities as love or work, it is only in knowledge that the *object* enjoys a state of absolute purity. As an extrinsic formal cause, the object makes the action and the faculties what they are, and ultimately determines the nature of the act and of the faculty. Thus the abstract notion of object conveys nothing other than formal determination; it is a pure principle of specification. In the case of transitive action, however, as well as in the case of desire, the usefulness of the notion of *object* depends essentially on its being incorporated into realities whose primary intelligible function is not that of specification. For instance, an object of desire plays a specifying role only by assuming the aspect of an end, by being wrapped up, so to speak, into something perceived as a good. But the primary function of the good or the final cause is not specification but motion; and so, what is at issue here, rather than the nature of the act, is the actual placing of that act into existence. Similarly, an object of transitive action plays its specifying role only by assuming the

---

[14] Ibid., q. 4, a. 1 (R, III 102B9ff.): "Cognition deals with objects by drawing them to itself in a kind of union or assimilation with them; it leaves them absolutely intact. Thus a person is not altered in any way just by being seen. Nor does cognition incline or tend toward objects as by weight, which is the way of the will. Cognition relates to objects by assimilation and union, which is within its power."

aspect of an effect, which has to do far more with results and realization than with specification. By contrast, an object of knowledge remains always a pure object. Its specific role as the object of knowledge, rather than adding something to its general role as object [understood also as purpose or effect], calls, on the contrary, for the exclusion of all other functions. In other words, the relation that defines the object of knowledge is the relation of a form that does nothing else but specify that a particular thing will be what it is within the subject who perceives it. Thus to know an object of a certain kind is to become oneself that certain kind. To know is to be.

And here is the great paradox. The identity of being with itself will have each thing be what it is and nothing else. Despite the way we sometimes speak, bread can never be a rock (and remain bread), or an eel a serpent (and remain a fish). But we all know a lot of real rocks without ceasing to be human beings. Reading a patient's temperature does not raise the doctor's temperature. When an object of knowledge becomes actually such an object for me, it remains an object, *ob-jectum*, something that lies before me, is set before me, as something other than myself. Thus if we say that to know an object is to be that object, it is necessary to explain that the peculiarity of the cognitive relation consists precisely in this: that the knower can be the object only by respecting its character as ob-ject. The knower knows only by acknowledging the otherness of the object and preserving at the same time his own identity. He becomes *the other* without becoming *other*, without undergoing any alteration, precisely because the unique specifying function of the pure object of knowledge leaves intact the otherness of the subject who apprehends it. To know is to be the other as other.[15]

To safeguard the principle of identity, however, we must explain further that there are actually two distinct ways of being or existing. First, there is the order of existence in which what is is itself

---

[15] Thomas Aquinas, *Sum. th.* I, q. 14, a. 1: "Knowing beings are distinguished from non-knowing beings in that the latter possess only their own form, while the knowing being is naturally adapted to have also the form of some other thing; for the species of the thing known is in the knower." Similar ideas can also be found in ibid., q. 80, a. 1; *De ver.*, q. 2, a. 2, and many other places.

and nothing else. In this order, the principle of identity—which the fact of cognition brings into question—applies without exception, and nothing can receive the quality of another without losing its own, without becoming other than it was. But there is also another order of existence, in which what is and remains itself can also be the other. Only beings endowed with knowledge have access to this second order of existence, and it is this access that gives them that amplitude that we have recognized as their primary identifying characteristic. The striking difference between these two orders is stated with particular force in the text from Pascal quoted above. Immense extension, power to destroy, to dissolve, to kill—these belong to the *physical* order. But the glory of the knower, who embraces the universe in his thought and makes it exist in his skull, belongs to another order. It belongs to the order of *intentional* existence.

When one thing is united to another, the usual result is a third thing made up of the first two. When the soul is joined to a body, the result is man. When man is joined to virtue, the result is the virtuous man. When the wax is joined to the impression of the seal, the result is the stamped wax. But when an object of knowledge is joined to a knowing subject, no composite results from that union. We think of the union of a physical form with its matter, and we come up with a whole, composed of form and matter. But when we consider the union of an object of knowledge with a knowing subject, we come up with an entirely different kind of whole. Here there is no fusion of two realities into a third reality. If this whole possesses unity, it is because the subject has become the object, and this unity, in the famous phrase of Averroës, so often repeated by Latin Aristotelians, is the most intimate of all.[16]

---

[16] Averroës, *Major Commentary on Aristotle's On the Soul* III, 5 [the following translation is by Yves R. Simon from the Latin text established by F. Stuart Crawford (Cambridge: The Mediaeval Academy of America, 1953), pp. 501–508, the Arabic original being lost; it is taken from Simon's "An Essay on Sensation," *The Philosophy of Knowledge*, edd. Roland Houde and Joseph Mullally (Philadelphia: Lippincott, 1960), p. 68n16]: "'Thus, let us say that it is clear that man is not understanding in act except through the actual connection of the understood with him. It is also clear that matter and form unite with each other in such a way that what is made of them be one, and most of all the material intellect and the idea actually understood; for what is made of these

is not a third thing other than them, as in the case with the other composites of matter and form.'"

This great distinction between the two kinds of union, elaborated with such force and success by Arabic and Latin Aristotelians, seems to be derived primarily from reflection on the following text of Aristotle (*On the Soul* II, 12, 424A17): "By a sense is meant what has the power of receiving into itself the sensible forms of things without the matter. This must be conceived of as taking place in the way in which the piece of wax takes on the impression of the signet-ring without the iron or gold."

Aristotle's meaning, badly served by the inevitable deficiencies of the comparison he uses, is not easy to establish. Is not the reception of the form without the matter, writes Thomas Aquinas (*In De an.* II, lect. 24 (ed. Angelo Maria Pirotta [Turin: Marietti, 1928]—henceforth designated as P.—551ff.), what generally takes place in every kind of passion, understood predicamentally? For every agent acts in virtue of its form, impressing in the patient a form similar to its own and retaining its matter for itself. What distinguishes the reception on the part of sense from any other kind of reception, Aquinas goes on to say, is the peculiar relation that obtains, in the case of the sense, between the form that is received and the subject that receives it. In an ordinary reception, the relation between the form received and the subject receiving it is the same as that which obtains in the agent, with the matter of the agent considered as its subject. Thus it is that *the way of being* that this form has in the agent is also communicated with the form. But this way of being is precisely what is not communicated by the action of the sensible on the sense. In the sensible thing, the form has a physical and material being; in the sense, it has an intentional and spiritual being. With his usual precision, Cajetan (*In De an.* II, 11 [B. 161B]) points out that Aristotle's term "without the matter" can refer either to the "power of receiving" or to "sensible forms." The first interpretation is ambiguous; the second seems clearer, and should, therefore, be preferred. Thus the meaning of the text is that the sense receives *immaterial forms*, that is, forms stripped of the *material being* that they have in things. This difference in the relation of the sensible form to the subject that bears it— namely, either a thing or the sense faculty—reveals the existence of two kinds of unity. A form can be united to its subject in such a way that it constitutes with it a new whole, in which case the form is inevitably modified at the same time as it modifies the subject. But a form can also be united to its subject without creating a new whole. In this case, the form retains its purity as a form and acts merely to perfect the subject without undergoing any modification in return.

The notion of immaterial union plays a central role in the theology of Thomas Aquinas, allowing him to solve the problem of participation in the divine nature and to explain St. Peter's phrase "sharers of the divine nature") (*Cont. gent.* II, q. 1, a. 4). Cf. Jacques Maritain, *Distinguer pour unir; ou Les Degrés du savoir* (Paris: Desclée De Brouwer, 1932), p. 504: "the soul is thus rendered infinite in the order of its *relation to the object*. A formal participation in Deity, which would be impossible were it a question of having Deity for its essence . . . , is possible if it is a matter of having Deity as object" (*Distinguish to Unite, or The Degrees of Knowledge*, trans. Gerald B. Phelan [New York: Scribner's, 1959], p. 254). Thomas Aquinas, *Cont. gent.* II, q. 51 (The problem of the vision of God by His essence): "Nor can [the divine essence] be the form of another thing through its natural being. For it would follow that, once united to another being, it would constitute a third thing, which is impossible, since

The object of knowledge, then, which is the known aspect of the thing known, has a dual existence.[17] It exists, first, in nature, in the thing that has it as its own; and it exists, secondly, precisely as an object of cognition in the soul that knows it and, knowing it, possesses it as the other. The existence as well as the qualities possessed physically are limited to the dimensions of the natural thing itself; they cannot belong at the same time to anyone else. But the qualities and the existence that make up the known aspect of that thing, that constitute it an object of knowledge, are capable of being shared indefinitely and are eminently communicable to any number of potential possessor-knowers. This second existence, the existence of the object in the soul, is, of course, an *immaterial* existence.[18] But this term must be carefully explained.

When it is said that the form of what is known exists immaterially in the knower, this means first of all that the relation of this form to the knower is very different from that which ordinarily obtains between forms and matter. In fact, this difference presupposes a total liberation of this form from all the conditions that matter imposes on forms when they are joined to it to constitute with it a composite being. Nevertheless, one must take care to avoid either exaggerating or underestimating this liberation. For instance, we must always remember that an object of sense cognition, immaterial as it may be, does not fail to convey to the knower the formal conditions resulting from its materiality.[19] And we must also realize that even in the world of immaterial beings, it is still necessary to distinguish between the origi-

---

the divine essence is in itself perfect in its own nature. But an intelligible species [immaterial form], in its union with the intellect, does not constitute a third thing but perfects the intellect in understanding; and this is not inconsistent with the perfection of the divine essence."

[17] Thomas Aquinas, *In De an.* II, lect. 12 (P. 378): "That very nature that receives the intention of universality—e.g., the nature of man—has a twofold being: the one material insofar as it exists in natural matter, the other immaterial insofar as it exists in the intellect."

[18] John of St. Thomas, *Curs. th.* I, disp. 16, a. 1 (Vivès, II, 422B): "By 'immaterial' St. Thomas means here a purification from matter not just as that indicates with precision the negation or lack of matter, but also as it indicates an elevation above the mode of matter, allowing receptions of things other than itself."

[19] Thomas Aquinas, *In De an.* II, lect. 5 (P. 284).

nal existence of such a being and its existence as an object of cognition in the minds of those who know it.[20] In other words, *immaterial existence* in this context has a rather precisely defined meaning and, to guard against misunderstanding, we shall substitute for it the term *intentional existence*, coined in Latin Aristotelianism to express a notion found in Aristotle.

What I know exists in me, but the way in which it exists in me is different from the way in which it exists in itself. I am what I know, but the way in which I am the object known differs from the way in which I am myself and the way in which that object is itself. Nevertheless, the object introduced into the soul and the soul that has become that object are bound in the tightest of unions in a single act of existing. Note that this act of existing in no way affects the thing known. It is cold comfort for one who is dying to think that he will continue to live in the memory of his dear ones. If our only survival were such intentional survival, death would indeed be a pretty grim business. The entire benefit of knowing belongs to the knower, for it is he alone who is endowed by it with additional existence. But this additional, intentional existence remains fully dependent on that other, real existence. The object known, existing in the knowing subject, will always have only as much reality as the thing possesses in its extramental existence, so that if the relation between the object existing in the mind and the thing existing (or able to exist) in nature is severed, the object existing in the mind will retain not a trace of reality.[21]

---

[20] John of St. Thomas, *Curs. th.* I, disp. 16, a. 1 (Vivès, II, 423A) points out that there is material reception not only in the world of bodies, but also among spiritual beings, "since it is obvious that the substance of the soul receives powers, and the powers receive habits, in the same genus of material and receptive causes as that in which corporeal things receive their accidents and their forms." Thomas Aquinas, *Sum. th.* I, q. 56, a. 2, ad 3 (Whether one angel knows another): "One angel knows another by the species of such angel existing in his intellect, which differs from the angel whose likeness it is, not according to material and immaterial being, but according to natural and intentional being."

[21] This is not to say, of course, that there do not exist in the mind objects (beings of reason, mental fictions) to which nothing corresponds or can correspond in reality (except for a certain foundation), and which are formed by the mind in imitation of what is observed in reality. Thus a being of reason may be called intentional in the second degree. What is verified about the

The Thing and the Idea[22]

The notion of intentional being, then—and one cannot insist too much on this point—corresponds primarily to a problem of existence, not to any problem of essence or nature. Because what is known exists in the soul that knows it in a way different from its existence in extramental reality, the primary referent of *intentional existence* is precisely this different existential modality that the known assumes in the knower. In a derivative sense, such expressions as "intentional form" or "intentional being" (where the adjective "intentional" modifies a *quod*, i.e., "that which") may sometimes be used to refer to an essence, but only if we always remember that what is secondary is intelligible only in terms of what is primary. In other words, treating intelligible forms while ignoring the intentional mode of existing would be like trying to think of potency without relation to act. And yet, not a few historical misadventures of the theory of ideas have their source in initial misunderstandings as gross as attempts to explain the eye without consideration of sight would be, or the stomach without consideration of digestion. In the knowing subject, as was said before, either the thing known must be present in its own reality, or it must be re-presented there somehow. In

---

intentional in the first degree—about the real, actual or possible, existing in thought—immediately is verified about the intentional in the second degree only mediately. For instance, although *subjects* and *predicates* as such cannot exist in nature, they certainly exist in the mind. But they clearly could not exist in the mind if we had not previously thought, say, "Peter is a man." Cf. John of St. Thomas, *Log.* II, q. 2 (R, I, 284B42); Maritain, *Les Degrés du savoir*, pp. 257ff., 273ff.

[22] In this chapter, for lack of an unequivocal term, we shall use the word *idea* with the very general meaning of intentional form, presentative or representative, that the Greeks give to the word εἶδος and the Latins to the words *species* or *intentio*. In this sense, *ideas* are the forms, nameless in our language, that sensible objects impress on the external senses (*species sensibilis impressa*), the images, recollections, and instinctive representations, as well as the intelligible forms, both initial (*species intelligibilis impressa*) and terminal (*species intelligibilis expressa*).

Later on, however, we shall restrict the term "idea" to designate only the spiritual intentional forms, in contrast to the sensible, and when we shall have to distinguish such a form at the beginning of thought from one that is formed at its term, we shall call the first an idea and the second a concept. In all cases, the context should help to eliminate the possibility of confusion.

the latter case, clearly, that by which the thing is known must be a reality distinct from the thing itself, and we call that reality a likeness or an idea.[23]

---

[23] Aristotle, *On the Soul* III, 8, 431B29: "It is not the stone that is present in the soul but its form." Ibid., I, 2, 404B10. After he has outlined the theories that emphasize the soul as the principal mover of the animal, Aristotle turns to comment on various interpretations of the fact of knowledge. "All, on the other hand, who looked to the fact that what has soul in it knows or perceives what is, identify soul with the principle or principles of Nature. . . . Thus Empedocles declares that it is formed out of all his elements, each of them also being soul; his words are:
'For this by Earth we see Earth, by Water Water,
By Ether Ether Divine, by Fire destructive Fire
By Love Love, and Hate by cruel Hate.'"
St. Thomas' commentary on this passage (*In Phys.* I, lect. 4 [P. 43ff.]) pays a significant tribute to the efforts of the early philosophers. They were not completely mistaken; they saw very clearly that if the soul is to know the other, it must be the other; their mistake was only about the way in which the soul is the other. "The ancient philosophers were moved to affirm that the soul was made of principles [elements] because, compelled by truth itself, they had a vague knowledge of the truth. Clearly, knowledge takes place through a likeness of the thing known in the knower, and it is thus necessary that the thing known be in the knower in some way. But the ancient philosophers thought that the likeness of the thing known was in the knower in its natural being, i.e., with the same kind of being that it has by itself. Like must be known by like, they said, and so if the soul is to know all things, it must have within itself the likeness of all things in their natural being, as they said. They did not know how to make the distinction between the way in which the thing exists in the intellect, or the eye, or the imagination, and the way in which it exists by itself." Ibid., II, lect. 12 (P. 377). "All knowledge takes place because the known is in a certain way in the knower, namely, by way of a likeness." Ibid., III, lect. 13.
The very coarseness of Empedocles' theory clearly reveals the force with which this philosopher, just as Parmenides had done, perceived the need for an identity between the knower and the known. Parmenides: "One thing are thinking and being" (Diels, VIII, 34). With Democritus and Epicurus, the explanation of knowledge by the physical presence of the known in the knower tends to become a little less crude. In William James's scheme (*Pragmatism* [New York: Longmans, Green, 1908; repr. Cambridge: Harvard University Press, 1975], p. 13), Democritus would appear as one of the "tender-minded," whereas Empedocles would have to be one of the "tough-minded." The *atoms* of Democritus belong to a refined—I almost said civilized—physics, but it is still physics, and it is clear that the refinement does not abolish their material nature (Jacques Maritain, *Réflexions sur l'intelligence et sur sa vie propre* [Paris: Desclée De Brouwer, 1931], p. 61; *Les Degrés du savoir*, p. 233). "Realistically speaking," writes Octave Hamelin (*Essai sur les éléments principaux de la représentation* [Paris: Alcan, 1907], pp. 339–40), "it must be that things, in their own special way, enter into the soul and into consciousness. But how could it be that things themselves enter the soul, first the body and then the brain? Obvi-

But here one also confronts the great divide that separates different metaphysics of knowledge as well as epistemologies. If we lose sight of the fact that in knowledge, as elsewhere, existence is intelligibly prior to whatever supports it (as act is prior to potency), or if we concentrate on ideas, so to speak, and forget that their sole function is to make intelligible a certain kind of existence, we shall in all probability end by treating ideas as if they were things, with some other predictable consequences. The idea will become for us, then, the only object present to knowledge, the only object directly reached by it, and once we accept this view, we have three choices. We may conclude that there is nothing more to be explored, since the idea absorbs within itself the whole of reality. Or, assuming that beyond the idea there is a reality of which the idea is a copy, we may venture to speculate about this reality *by inference* from the idea. But if we suspect that the idea might not be a true copy, we shall have to renounce any reliable knowledge of what might lie beyond it. All other things being equal, the choice among these three outcomes of the initial error of all idealist philosophies seems to depend primarily on one's temperament and intellectual scruples.

But if we keep in mind that what we are trying to understand here is, above all, the kind of existence that the thing known assumes within the soul, we cannot fail to recognize that the difference between to be and to know—i.e., between physical existence and intentional existence—involves a corresponding difference between the thing and the idea, not in the mind but in the order of nature. The thing is what exists for itself, with an exis-

---

ously, an inkwell could not do it; but tiny images of it perhaps could. So there is no way of avoiding the Epicurean absurdity without undermining the ultimate basis of realism." But there is a way to avoid this Epicurean absurdity without abandoning realism, and that is to understand correctly the primordial existential function of the *idea*. When the difference and the relationship between the two modes of existence have been understood, we can safely abandon trying to explain the presence of a thing within the soul by infinitely miniaturizing it. For all that these miniatures could ever bring about would still remain a union of two things, which produces not an act of knowledge but a third thing. Between the stone and the subtle atoms that it sends forth in the system of Democritus, there is a difference in size only, not in kind. By contrast, between the stone and the *idea* that represents it in the soul in the Aristotelian system, there is a radical ontological diversity, involving a passage from one order of being to another.

tence that is physical, primary, complete, and independent. What permits the intentional existence of the thing in the mind; what allows the thing to exercise, above and beyond the existence it possesses for its own sake in nature, a second existence in the mind that considers it as an object; and what enables the mind to be that object, is the idea. Like everything real, the idea has its own being, which is united to the soul on the analogy of physical unions, producing a composite. But constituting such a whole is not the primary function of the idea. As a unique means of intentional existence, the idea is a reality that faces two ways. By its own natural being, it is distinguished from the thing that it represents, and it goes forth as such to rest in the soul as an accident in its subject, constituting a composite, like a form joined to matter. But it is by its intentional existence that the idea accomplishes its primary function, which is to become the object of knowledge. In fact, the idea is the object itself existing intentionally.[24]

---

[24] This twofold aspect, the natural and the intentional, of the idea as representative form is clearly perceived by Aristotle in the treatise *On Memory*. How is it possible, Aristotle asks, that under the influence of a present reminder our memory turns not to what is present but to what is absent? And his answer is that just as an animal painted in a picture can be considered either as an animal or as a shape, so the image existing in our soul is something on its own account and is also the image of something else. "A picture painted on a panel is at once a picture and a likeness: that is, while one and the same, it is both of these, although the 'being' of both is not the same, and one may contemplate it either as a picture or as a likeness. Just in the same way we have to conceive that the mnemonic presentation within us is something which by itself is merely an object of contemplation, while, in relation to something else, it is also a presentation of that other thing. In so far as it is regarded in itself, it is only an object of contemplation, or a presentation; but when considered as relative to something else, e.g., as its likeness, it is also a mnemonic token" (I, 450A25). Thomas Aquinas comments: "He gives the example of an animal that is painted in a picture; it is at the same time a painted animal and the likeness of a real animal. Now, although that to which these two characteristics belong is the same in subject, still they differ by a distinction of reason. Consequently, our consideration of it as a painted animal is one thing, and our consideration of it as the likeness of a real animal is another. Similarly, the image that is in us can be understood either as something in itself or as the likeness of something other. Thus, since the soul remembers by way of images, if the soul turns to the image as it is in itself, then there seems to be present to the soul either something intelligible that the intellect observes in the image or simply the image that the imaginative power apprehends. If, on the other hand, the soul turns to the image as the likeness of something other and considers it as the likeness of that other, previously sensed or understood, it is a different story. As was said about the painting, the man who is not looking at Coriscus but is

Ordinary language bears adequate witness to this dual reality of the intentional form we call the idea. When we say that we have lost the memory of an event, what we refer to is the natural or subjective being of the intentional form that is that memory. We are reporting that a quality, affection, disposition, an impression needed in order to have a past event made present to us, has slipped from our mind. But when we say that a particular event is our most beautiful memory, what we are referring to is precisely the intentional or objective being of that memory, which is identical with the event remembered. A frequent ploy of idealist philosophies is to confuse these two realities of the idea. Taking advantage of multiple meanings of words such as *idea*, *image*, and *representation*, and substituting at the opportune moment the intentional and objective meaning of these terms for their physical and subjective meaning, or vice versa, idealism often gives the impression of closeness to common sense and familiar experience. But do not ask a chemist what he thinks of the reality of barium sulfate; he will give you a bewildered look.[25]

What we thus need to recognize are two distinct universes, one of things and the other of ideas, the universe of nature and the universe of intentionality, whose qualitative diversity is derived exclusively from the diversity of their existential functions.[26] The thing is a being whose primary function is to exist for its own sake, although it may secondarily serve to make present to the mind a reality other than itself, as happens for instance

---

considering his image as the likeness of Coriscus is engaged in a very different sort of consideration, for this now pertains to the memory." *In De mem.*, lect. 3 (P. 340–41). See also John of St. Thomas, *Phil. nat.* IV, q. 6, a. 2 (R, III, 177B).

[25] George Urbain, "Essai de discipline scientifique," *La Grande Revue* (March 1920): "There is probably not a single chemist who confuses the reality of barium sulfate with his idea of it. I was curious enough to put the question to some of them. They all thought it extremely peculiar. From the bewildered look they gave me, I saw that they all thought I was crazy to ask such a question. This much is certain: the contemporary chemist takes *things* to be the actual substrate of their properties, and he does not worry about the hypothetical character of this conception."

[26] Cajetan, *In Ia*, q. 5, a. 5, ad 3: "The first thing to point out is that there are two kinds of beings. Some were primarily constituted in order to be, although they may in a secondary way represent other things, and we call them things. But there are also beings primarily constituted by their nature to represent other things, and we call these the intentions of things, the sensible or

when we take a footprint as the sign of a passer-by. By contrast, the primary function of the idea is to represent something other than itself. The idea always makes present to the mind something other that exists first of all for its own sake, and if the idea also has an existence of its own, this is only because it needs such an existence in order to exercise its representative, intentional function. Most instructive here is the case in which the thing known is present to the knowing subject not through representation by a reality other than itself but rather with its own reality as a thing. Clearly, in that case the need for the intentional reality proper to the idea disappears, and it is the thing itself in its natural being that plays the role of the idea as the object of knowledge.[27] That is what would happen in our knowledge of external things if Aristotle's stone and Hamelin's inkwell were able to enter the soul in their natural state. But this happens only in divine knowledge, in the knowledge an angel has of himself, and in the intuition by which the blessed see God as He is.[28]

Or consider the following contrast. We strive to acquire health

---

intelligible species. The need to posit these two kinds of beings arises from the necessity of the knower to be not only himself but other things as well. Indeed, a being with an intellect can be all things, as was shown in q. 14 and is known from the common conception of the soul held by philosophers, who agree that like is known by like. Clearly the natures of things as they are in themselves cannot exist in the knower, for there is no stone in the soul. Nor can the knower by his own finite substance be so great as to have within himself everything by which knowable natures, according to their proper principles, might be distinctly assimilated to him. And so we must conclude that since the natural being of the knower is not the principle by which knowable things are understood, and knowable things are not in the knower in their natural being, intentional being, by which the knower becomes the things known, had to be instituted by nature." Cf. also Cajetan, *In De an.* III, 4 (B. 237A); J. de Monléon, "L'Intelligence humaine," *Cahiers Thomistes* (March 25, 1932), 335–36.

[27] Bañez, *In Ia*, q. 85, a. 2 (Douai, 1614—hereafter designated as D—II, 392B): "The nature of the intelligible species is retained most properly in God, and in the angelic essence with respect to the Beatific Vision and the knowledge the angel has of himself."

[28] Thomas Aquinas, *De ver.*, q. 8, a. 6; *Sum. th.* I, q. 56, a 1; John of St. Thomas, *Curs. th.* I, disp. 21, a. 2 (Vivès, IV, 717Bff.). As far as the angel's knowledge of himself is concerned, the natural presence of the object (the substance of the angel) in the subject (the angelic intelligence) makes unnecessary any initial representative form (*species impressa*), but not the terminal representative form or concept (*species expressa*). The role of the initial representative form is to make the object present to the knower with the degree of

in order to be well, or to have health as something belonging to us. But we do not acquire ideas for the purpose of forming a physical union with them. Indeed, if we are truly after knowledge, we must treat ideas as nothing more than objective means that alone can lead us to it. The man who studies furiously and tries out many things, because he wants his peers to recognize him as a man with a lot of ideas, is just like the man who, in order to be noticed, strives after, say, sport records, or civic honors, or just money. Such a man does not love knowledge as it wishes to be loved;[29] his is a lusting after the idea rather than a friendship for the object of knowledge,[30] and true knowledge will be denied him. A leader at every conference, a member of every academy, he is nevertheless missing that true human greatness that knowledge confers only on those who love it for its own sake. His function was to serve the truth but, in reality, he cared only for himself. He cultivated ideas in their physical aspects, rather than in their intentional and objective being, and degraded his intellectual development to the level of the growth of a plant. While wishing to save it, he lost his soul.[31]

---

immateriality proportionate to his knowing power; but the substance of the angel is by its very nature present to the angelic intellect and by its very nature endowed with initial intelligibility. The union of the understanding and the object is far better assured here than it can be by any idea. (Thomas Aquinas, *Sum. th.* I, q. 56, a. 3: "There are three ways in which a thing may be known: first, by the presence of its essence in the knower [this is the case of the angel's knowing himself] . . . ; second, by the presence of its likeness in the power that knows it; and, third, when the likeness of the thing known is not drawn immediately from the thing known itself, but from something else in which it is made to appear, as when we behold a man in a mirror.") And yet a terminal representative form (*species expressa*) remains necessary because, as we shall see further on, our thinking has to have a concept for its term and because no created being enjoys by its own nature the immateriality of what is thought in act.

In the Beatific Vision, however, every idea disappears, the intelligence has its determination from the very being of God, and the act of thinking terminates directly in the absolute immateriality of the being of God. Thomas Aquinas, *Sum. th.* I, q. 12, a. 2.

[29] See the beautiful pages of Louis Lavelle on the humility of knowledge, in *La Conscience de soi* (Paris: Grasset, 1923), pp. 32ff.

[30] "Nathanaël, let what is important be in your look, not in the thing looked at." André Gide, *Les Nourritures terrestres* [Paris: Mercure, 1897], p. 17.

[31] "[He had but] a single concern: to follow his own speculative enterprise, cultivate 'his rational part'; and on every occasion these words flow from his

Indeed, between the laws of progress in knowledge and the supreme law of salvation there is a striking analogy. In both cases we are confronted with an interest that needs and desperately wishes to be preserved but can be preserved only by total disinterestedness. The drama of thought is like that of destiny. A nature that does not possess its supreme perfection by self-identity has necessarily an interest in its perfectibility, and in one sense only divine love is totally disinterested. Man cannot not desire happiness, the subjective beatitude of what is called the ego; but he will find happiness only when he turns away from himself and his happiness to lose himself in God. Similarly, our created intelligence cannot not desire the subjective qualification and enrichment that ideas bring to it, since it is by means of such qualification that the object of knowledge is delivered to it. But as soon as the mind goes after the ideas themselves, instead of the object, the ideas conceal the object by taking its place, and the thinker who wanted to know and conquer the world is left with but a system of thought of his own making. To grasp the object of knowledge, our thought must die to itself, just as love must die to reach the true good. In one case, we overcome selfishness; in the other, we transcend subjectivity. This ascetic requirement of our intelligence, bound by its own law that alone can lead us to objective knowledge, is just like the denial of oneself that leads to God. Happy, therefore, is he who seeks the truth in charity; his scientific asceticism will be mixed with his human righteousness, and he will move with undivided effort toward both intellectual and personal salvation.

Again, this requirement to transcend the subjectivity of thought in order to achieve its perfection becomes still clearer when we consider it precisely as a law proper to created human intelligence. Sense knowledge exists for the sake of life and for the sake of thought; where there is no thought, the objectivity of knowledge is subordinated to the subjectivity of need. The animal uses its senses for nourishment and reproduction; to the extent that man rises above animality, he puts his sense data at the service of thought. But if he puts thought itself in the service of the subjectivity of his intelligence, he will be like the beast even in his spiritual life. Nowadays many people, both in philosophy and in religion, seem to think that the main thing is to have a satisfied mind, rather than to possess the truth. What they do not seem to realize is that, far from providing intellectual and personal salvation, this sort of satisfaction is exactly like the pleasure that comes from a well-filled belly.[32]

THE SUPERABUNDANCE OF CREATION

The best chance we have to understand the true significance of the second existence of things in the intentional order is to recognize the world and all things in it as God's creation. Along the road that leads us to recognize God as the First Knower, we become aware of a converging movement of being and knowing culminating in the Sovereign Being in Whom they become one. Knowledge, as we have said, is amplitude, and the more perfect it is, the greater source of abundance it becomes. The heaven of understanding is infinitely vaster than the world of the senses; a keen intelligence takes in at a glance a range of connections that escape the ordinary man. In its absolute perfection, knowledge must be infinite. At the same time, limited only when mixed with real non-being or potentiality, being is by its very nature a plenitude. Indeed, as a universal principle of limitation and of want, potentiality is the common enemy of both being and knowing. By the same token, its total exclusion coincides with an abso-

---

adolescent pen: my thought, my culture, my autonomy, my cherished ideas, my ideal type, my intellectual superiority." Henri Massis, "Ernest Renan," *Jugements*, 1 (1924), 19.

[32] In addition to the texts previously quoted, let us add, as particularly important for the general theory of intentional forms, the following texts and works: John of St. Thomas, *Log.* II, qq. 21, 22, 23 (R, I, 646ff.); *Phil. nat.* IV, q. 6, a. 2 (R, III, 177b); *Curs. th.* I, disp. 12, a. 1 (Vivès, II, 182); Emile Peillaube, *Théorie des concepts* (Paris: Lethielleux, 1895); Maritain, *Réflexions sur l'intelligence*, chap. 2; *Le Songe de Descartes* (Paris: Corrêa, 1932), passim; *Les Degrés du savoir*, chap. 3 and Appendix I (several references); E. Pisters, *La Nature des formes intentionelles d'après saint Thomas d'Aquin* (Paris: Bossuet, 1933); P. Garin, *La Théorie de l'idée suivant l'école thomiste* (Paris: Desclée De Brouwer, 1932).

The theory of intentional forms as applied to the particular case of the *concept* has recently [1934] given rise to important discussions (cf. Maritain, *Les Degrés du savoir*, Appendix I). On this point we are following the teaching of John of St. Thomas in its entirety, and we agree with Maritain that it is impossible to deviate from it, no matter how slightly, without compromising the well-established principles of critical realism.

lutely unlimited amplitude in which being and knowing are no longer distinguishable.[33] Since every perfection realized or possible is present to the being of God by reason of the identity of His infinite being with itself—there is no more reality in God-plus-the-universe than there is in God alone—the divine knowledge occurs without the intervention of any idea distinct from the being of God. The divine knowledge does not involve an intentional existence added to a natural existence. It is by His very being that God knows Himself and all things since He is by Himself supereminently all things. In God, knowledge loses its intentional character because in Him existence has no trace of subjectivity. Objectivity reigns here in a sovereign way, the known being in no sense other, the knowing totally innocent of intentionality. Absolutely indistinguishable from the essence of God, the divine existence is in no respect possessed in a subjective manner. To say that in God essence and existence are really one is to say that His whole being is transsubjectivity—which is the same as saying that His being consists in an act of knowledge.[34]

Now, creation takes place only when a real possibility of being

---

[33] Thomas Aquinas, *Sum. th.* I, q. 14, a. 1 (On God's knowledge): "In God there exists the most perfect knowledge. To prove this, we must note that knowing beings are distinguished from non-knowing beings in that the latter possess only their own forms, whereas the knowing being is naturally adapted to have also the form of some other thing; for the species of the thing known is in the knower. Hence it is manifest that the nature of a non-knowing being is more contracted and limited, while the nature of knowing beings has a greater amplitude and extension. That is why the Philosopher says (*On the Soul* III, 7, 431B20) that 'the soul is in a certain way all things.' Now, the contraction of form comes from the matter. Hence, as we said above, forms as they are the more immaterial approach more nearly to a kind of infinity. Therefore, it is clear that the immateriality of a thing is the reason why it is cognitive, and the mode of knowledge is according to the mode of immateriality. Hence it is said (ibid., II, 12, 424B1) that plants do not know because of their materiality. But sense is cognitive because it can receive species without matter, and the intellect is still further cognitive because it is more 'separated from matter and unmixed,' as has been said (ibid., III, 4, 429A18). Since, therefore, God is in the highest degree of immateriality . . . it follows that He occupies the highest place in knowledge." Cajetan, *In De an,* III, 11 (B. 195A).

[34] John of St. Thomas, *Curs. th.* I, disp. 16, a. 2 (Vivès, II, 420Aff.); Réginald Garrigou-Lagrange, O.P., *Dieu, son existence et sa nature*, 5th ed. (Paris: Beauchesne, 1923), p. 399; Garin, *La Théorie de l'idée*, pp. 112ff.; Maritain, *Les Degrés du savoir*, pp. 219–20.
The broad modalities of knowledge in the hierarchy of intelligences may

is actualized in an act of existence, and this condition necessarily sets limits to the being of any creature. What arises from nothingness is limited by its nature, and even the divine generosity can do nothing about it. The so-called best of all possible worlds is a self-contradictory fiction, but we learn something from it. No matter how far we go imagining ever better possible worlds—and one can go up to infinity in that order—all that we shall ever find is limited being, separated from the divine perfection by an abyss as infinite as the one that separates the worst possible world from God.

But God does not do things by halves. He wanted to provide His creation with an image of His infinity. He wanted certain creatures at least, in very unequal degrees to be sure but always on an admirable scale, to be infinite in some way, as He is infinite in all ways.[35] But since every creature as it emerges from noth-

---

then be outlined as follows. (a) In man, whose intelligence, dependent upon the senses, is primarily turned to what is outside, knowing is an intentional existing added to a physical existing. This knowing has for its primary object the *other*—meaning that objectivity is achieved here under the form of otherness—and its indispensable means—apart from the supernatural case of the Beatific Vision—is an intentional form. Even when the soul knows itself, it does so by an intentional act, employing intentional forms referred to another. We know by reflecting on activities perceived as exercised by another. (b) The angelic intelligence [pure created intelligence] is primarily turned within, and its primary object is the substance of the angel. On this level objectivity does not initially imply otherness; angelic knowing will be the other only when the angelic intelligence contemplates God and the universe. But even with respect to his own substance, an angel's knowledge requires a separate intentional act. What must be considered here is that, since the natural being of every creature is an existence received in an essence, and thus present in it as in its subject, no natural being of any creature admits of a transsubjective existence by itself. By reason of his natural being, the angel himself exists only subjectively; and he can transcend this subjectivity only by a superadded intentional being. (c) In the knowledge that the angel has of himself, this intentional form intervenes not at the beginning but at the end of the act; in the Beatific Vision every intentional form disappears. (d) In God, natural being itself is transsubjective; here there is no more intentional existing, no more otherness, and no intentional forms. The transcendental essence of knowledge, we thus come to understand, is constituted by a transsubjective existence. In every intelligent creature, the transsubjective existence is an intentional existence, added to its natural being. Sometimes this intentional existence needs intentional forms; sometimes it does not. Moreover, though even in the first case it does not necessarily imply the otherness of the known, this is not necessarily excluded even in the second case.

[35] Thomas Aquinas, *De ver.*, q. 2, a. 2: "A thing is perfect in two ways. First, it

ingness is reduced to the measure of its nature, and essentially limited to it, what was left to do was to endow the universe with a certain superabundance that allows privileged natures to overcome their natural limitations—and even approach a kind of relative infinity—by being able to become in a sense all things.[36] It is this superabundance of creation that makes things spill over into or, better, radiate, ideas. The universe of nature so generously created is at the same time the universe of intentionality, and that is how we are able to know it, and in knowing it imitate the divine infinity.

It is not by accident that those whose thought is full of God have the deepest awareness of the quasi-divinity of man. One must have contemplated the greatness of the true God, as far as that is possible in this life, to understand what it means to say

---

is perfect with respect to the perfection of its act of existence, which belongs to it according to its own species. But since the specific act of existence of one thing is distinct from the specific act of existence of another, in every created thing of this kind, the perfection falls short of absolute perfection to the extent that perfection is found in other species. Consequently, the perfection of each individual thing considered in itself is imperfect, being a part of the perfection of the entire universe, which arises from the sum total of the perfections of all individual things. And so, *in order that there might be some remedy for this imperfection*, another kind of perfection is to be found in created things. It consists in this, that the perfection belonging to one thing is found in another. This is the perfection of a knower insofar as he knows; for something is known by a knower by reason of the fact that the thing known is in some fashion in the possession of the knower. Hence, it is said in *On the Soul* III that the soul is in a certain way all things since its nature is such that it can know all things. In this way it is possible for the perfection of the entire universe to exist in one thing. The ultimate perfection achievable by the soul, then, according to the philosophers, is to have inscribed in it the entire order and causes of the universe. And they also held this to be the ultimate end of man. [We, however, hold that it consists in the vision of God; for, as Gregory says, 'What is there that they do not see, who see Him Who sees all things?']"

How packed with emotion are these simple lines, so free from pathos. We think of Michelangelo's fresco in which the newly created man touches the hand of God, Who does not abandon him. St. Thomas uses the word *remedy*, something given only to the sick, and for good reason. Every created being is a poor thing if we consider how seriously any kind of limitation violates the very nature of being. A limited being carries, in what is most intimate to it, its own worst enemy, non-being, just as Princess Urania carried her fever. But let us also make it clear that we speak here metaphorically, and that none of this implies the presence of Leibnizian *metaphysical evil*.

[36] Thomas Aquinas, *Sum. th.* I, q. 54, a. 2.

that there is something divine in every intelligent creature. Such contemplation confirms that the true greatness of intelligent beings consists in participation in the greatness of God. Those who think that this greatness is their own are bound to forfeit it, for they truly do not understand even themselves. It is impossible to conceive a more horrifying suicide than the pride of Lucifer.

The intentional being of knowledge appears thus as manifestation of a superabundance by which the divine generosity permits some creatures to be more than they are. Yet the intentional existence of the known in the knower is only the most striking aspect of this superabundance. In the order of formal causality, the superabundance of being is shown in the ability of the knower to become the known in intentional existence. But superabundance is found as well in the order both of efficient and of final causality. In the order of efficient causality, the superabundance of being manifests itself in the existence of the active power of the principal agent in the instruments he uses;[37] in the order of final causality, in the presence of the end in the means

---

[37] Thomas Aquinas, *De ver.*, q. 26, a. 1, ad 8; q. 27, a. 4, ad 4. In q. 27, a. 7 St. Thomas writes: "Grace is in the sacraments not as an accident in a subject but as an effect in a cause—in the matter in which the sacraments can be the cause of grace. Now, an effect can be said to be in its cause in two ways. In one way it is in the cause inasmuch as the cause has control over the effect, as our acts are said to be in us. In this sense no effect is in an instrumental cause, which does not move except when moved. Consequently neither is grace in the sacraments in this way. In another way, the effect is in the cause by means of its likeness, inasmuch as the cause produces an effect like itself. This happens in four ways. (*a*) When the likeness of the effect is in the cause as regards its natural existence, and in the same manner as it is in univocal effects. In this way one can say that the heat of the air is in the fire that heats it. (*b*) When the likeness of the effect is in the cause as regards its natural existence but not in the same manner, as is the case with equivocal effects. In this way the heat of the air is in the sun. (*c*) When the likeness of the effect is in the cause not as regards its natural existence but as regards its spiritual existence, and yet statically, as the likenesses of works of art are in the mind of the artist; for the form of a house in the builder is not a real being, like the heating power in the sun or heat in a fire, but an intellectual intention at rest in the soul. (*d*) When the likeness of the effect is in the cause not in the same manner, not as a real being, not statically, but as a dynamic influence, as the likenesses of effects are in instruments, by means of which the forms flow from the principal causes into the effects. It is in this way that grace is in the sacraments." *De pot.*, q. 3, a. 7, ad 7; a. 11, ad 14; q. 6, a. 4; "The capability of cooperating with God that

that is ordered to it. In fact, superabundance is lacking only in the order of material causality, or potentiality—and with good reason.[38]

A painter's brush is a poor thing: a wooden stick with a tuft of hair at one end, held in place by a metal ring. And yet there is nothing of the deep thought, love, and spirituality that we experience, say, in the *Museum of the Hôpital Saint-Jean* that has not gone through Memling's brush, that has not been caused by this wooden stick and this tuft of hair, the true cause, albeit an instrumental one, of everything this painter's art, as the principal cause, has brought into being. We see here the humble brush raised to a level infinitely transcending its own nature by the transitory, flowing, intentional existence put into it by the painter's art. But we become truly aware of this miraculous superelevation of the humblest things when we contemplate their supernatural effect when they are used by divine causality. The rebirth of a soul through grace is a far greater wonder than the creation of the whole natural universe. And yet, its true cause is the plain water of baptism.

Likewise, we know that food is good only for maintaining the

---

the saints have in the working of miracles can be understood as so many imperfect forms, called intentions, which are there only by reason of the presence of the principal agent; this is the case of light in the air and of motion in an instrument." *De malo*, q. 4, a. 1, ad 16; a. 3; *Sum. th.* III, q. 62, a. 4, ad 1. John of St. Thomas, *Phil. nat.* I, q. 26 (R, II, 513A45ff.); *Curs. th.*, III, disp. 24, a. 1 (Vivès, IX, 203Aff.); Maritain, *Réflexions sur l'intelligence*, p. 60; *Les Degrés du savoir*, p. 222; H. D. Simonin, "La notion d'*intentio* dans l'oeuvre de saint Thomas d'Aquin," *Revue des Sciences Philosophiques et Théologiques* (1930), 445.

[38] It goes without saying that this scheme of the system of superabundance is far from complete. We have deliberately restricted ourselves to those cases in which the existence arising from the effect of superabundance involves no appropriation on the part of the thing in which it is realized. For it is only then that the existence can be called intentional.

The fact of superabundance is present in every act of causality; any effect has its reality only from the superabundance of its cause, but it possesses it as a perfection that, at the term of the causal activity, belongs to it as its own. Every created formal cause gets its reality from the superabundance of the uncreated exemplar, but its reality belongs to it. Every principal efficient cause has its efficiency from the first cause, yet its efficiency belongs to it. Every intermediate end gets its goodness from the ultimate end, but its goodness belongs to it. The goodness of a means, however, does not belong to the means, the instrumental efficiency does not belong to the instrument, and the object known does not belong to the (created) knower.

life of the body, and that an evening at the circus is good only as a diversion. But whether eating or drinking, working or suffering, or simply taking his ease, the man who has made up his mind to do everything he has to do for the love of God acquires an increase of divine life in all his activities. A saint cannot make the slightest move without approaching closer to God; he lives in the divine household. The familiar things that surround the man of God are all worthy of respect and admiration, because they all can be made God's instruments and means offered to human freedom to arrive at its end in the sovereign good.

We are thus led to realize that in addition to the intentional being of knowledge, there is an intentional being of sheer instrumentality as well as an intentional being of transcendent goodness in things used as means. Our understanding of the concept of intentional being will, therefore, include analogically these three distinct cases: the presence of the object in the soul that knows it, the efficiency of the principal agent present in his instrument, and the goodness that bestows dignity upon even the humblest of means. Investigating this analogical concept of intentional being seems to us to hold great promise of progress in metaphysics. What we are more aware of are things in their primary, natural existence; the range of their secondary, intentional existence is a magical territory. Little explored, it is bound to hold some marvelous surprises for us. We are convinced that showing the unity, tenuous as it may be, of this transcendental concept of intentional being will, far from reducing the dignity of knowledge, actually throw new light on it.

The Veracity of Our Cognitions

"For Who is God, except Yahweh? Who is a rock, save our God" (Ps 18:31)? As created images of the divine stability, the necessary relations implied in the least of God's creatures are, in the order of objective possibility, just as indestructible as the divine being itself, and God can no more annihilate the possibility of a blade of grass than He can annihilate Himself. But the necessary structure of what is possible in no way determines its position in existence, and the progress of the created essence in the real world, in the course of physical events, is never free from contingency. The curve that a projectile will follow in fact can never be calculated as rigorously as the curve of a mathematical function. But what about the argument that contingency in nature must necessarily destroy our power to know things?[39] How do we explain why the reality of contingency by no means invalidates our inductions and deductions about the things of nature?

Even if absolute necessity is confined, for creatures, to the order of essential possibilities, it does not follow that nature in its existential reality must be abandoned to a lawless doctrine of contingency, for an authentic notion of necessity is quite capable of confronting contingency without abolishing it. As far as the creative act is concerned, the essential necessities of things possible play but a *formal*, specifying role; they do not affect the creative act as such. Yet once brought into existence, the essential necessities of a created nature assume more than just a formal, specifying role; in the actual existence of a thing of nature, they play also an *efficient* role, however conditional and limited. The possible will be what it is if it is. The kind of thing it is has no influence at all on its actually being brought into existence. But the created nature is not only formally predetermined to act in a particular way if it acts; combined with its actual existence, its essential necessities will also push it to act *effectively* in that way, unless of course it is impeded.[40] Thus if we do not want a metal rod to expand in contact with fire, we must find ways to cool it. But since such introductions of impediments do not arise out of any necessity, it follows that the essential necessities of things will simply be translated, so to speak, into frequencies. In other words, every nature, by reason of self-identity, possesses a tendency to develop in the order of actual existence in conformity with the laws of its constitution. And most of the time this tendency will prevail over contingency.

---

[39] E. Goblot, *Traité de logique*, 2nd ed. (Paris: Colin, 1920), p. 314. This same author (*Essai sur la classification des sciences* [Paris: Alcan, 1898], p. 196) seems to think that determinism (at least as he conceives it, i.e., as excluding chance, miracle, and free will) is the object of an act of faith—a curious example of the humiliations this type of rationalism must submit to.

[40] We are referring here to natural functioning of all creatures. In certain privileged beings, this is supplemented by an ability to take deliberate action. But this in no way destroys—and the point cannot be made too strongly—their natural functioning as indispensable support.

Applied to the particular case of natures possessed of knowledge, these considerations lead us to the following critical evaluation of the truthfulness of our knowledge. Where there is a real distinction between to be and to know, as in any knower who knows not because he is but because he becomes the object known in an additional, intentional existence, there will also be a real distinction between the faculty and the act of knowing. Either the knower is the other by his very nature, or he possesses by nature only an aptitude to be the other. But every created nature is, of itself, only itself and nothing else; to be the other by identity with oneself is the exclusive privilege of the divine nature. Here is a telling analogy between to be and to know. To be identified with the very act of being, a subject must possess the fullness of being by nature; but that turns his faculty of being into a necessity of being or, more accurately, makes the subject a self-subsistent being. It is the same with knowledge. To be identified with the very act of knowing, a subject must be by nature everything knowable; and that turns his faculty of knowing into subsistent knowing that is identical with his being. What we have here is complete equivalence. As far as the ontological distinction between the act and the faculty is concerned, it makes little difference whether the faculty of knowing is sometimes in potency and sometimes in act, or always in act, whether it originally lacks union with its object or is united to it as soon as it arises out of nothingness. The only thing that the notion of a faculty of knowing inevitably implies, over and above the ontological distinction between to be and to know, is a relation of potentiality between the knower and his act of knowing, regardless of when this potentiality is actualized.

The faculty of knowing belongs to the order of nature and is rooted firmly in physical reality. But this faculty is a power to exist intentionally. By its very nature, it is urged toward the other existing intentionally, and by its act enters that order of intentionality. By that act, our faculty of knowing makes the leap from the universe of physical existence to the universe of intentional existence. Imperfect as it is, the classical analogy between human intelligence and prime matter is helpful here. Human intelligence, it has been suggested, originally lacks any form in the order of intentionality, just as prime matter lacks any form in the order of nature. But what we need to recognize is that, whereas for the physically indeterminate prime matter, the absence of any form means the absence of any nature, since no determination can be prior to its physical constitution in a specific nature, the original indetermination of the human intelligence, which obtains only in the universe of intentionality, not merely is compatible with a determination in the physical order but absolutely demands that this intelligence possess a determined physical nature.[41] Thus although before it becomes one with its object in intentional existence the faculty of knowing may well be without specification, it is still not a nature closed upon itself and definable by reason of its intrinsic reality alone. Even by its physical nature, the faculty of knowing is pre-eminently something open to things other than itself. An intelligible account of its proper reality, therefore, requires that we concentrate on its relation with the term toward which its whole

---

[41] Cajetan, *In De an.* III, 1 (B. 195A). Commenting on the passage in which Aristotle says that "[the mind] too, like the sensitive part, can have no nature of its own, other than that of having a certain capacity" (*On the Soul* III, 4, 429A21), Cajetan explains that the formula is equivocal and has been responsible for many misunderstandings. "For it can have either of two meanings. First, the phrase 'whatever is thinkable' may specify the order or genus of things in which the mind is contained, and then the meaning is that the intellect is a pure potency contained within the order or genus of immaterial things in the sense in which we would say that prime matter is a pure potency in the genus of sensible things, i.e., that prime matter is contained within the order of sensible things. Secondly, we can understand the phrase 'whatever is thinkable' to be a condition that somehow weakens the character of pure potency, and then it means that our intellect has only incomplete potency in a particular genus, that of the intelligibles, as we say that the eye has potency in the genus of colors, but not completely, for it is actually diaphanous. Now, even though both interpretations make sense, it is totally impossible and contrary to the teaching of Aristotle to think of the intellect as a pure potency in the first sense. It is impossible, for it would follow that the same thing at the same time would be in act and not in act, or that prime matter were forever to be without any forms. Indeed, it is not easy to imagine a *substantial* form for the *possible* intellect through which it would exist, and there are other similar impossibilities. And it is also contrary to Aristotle, both because he located the mind in the order of act, and because he says that it is something, i.e., a part, belonging to the soul. It follows from this that the intellect is part of an act, since every soul is active in some way. . . . But a part of an act is either the same as the act or an accident of it. If it is identical with the act, it obviously cannot be a pure potency; if it is an accident of the act, its presence requires that it be a certain sort of act. And so, with Aristotle, we must say that our intellect by which we understand and form opinions is a special kind of intellectual form that is potentially whatever is thinkable."

nature propels it. For the faculty of knowing has its nature from its object.[42]

But is that not the same as saying that our knowledge is in some sense fundamentally indefectible, at the very least with respect to its object? If our analysis so far is correct, the object of knowledge, in the exercise of its objectivity, has two modes of existence, the effect of the second of which is to make the knowing subject conform to it. The conformity between the knower and the known is the essence and perfection of knowledge. The non-conformity between the knower and the known is a defect of knowledge, distortion, falsity. The latter may be said to affect our knowing in a way analogous to that in which evil as privation bores into being. A nature evil in itself is a contradiction, for it implies a being that by identity with its reality would combine being and non-being. A power to know not made to become its object as this object is itself would be like a nature evil in itself, i.e., self-contradictory. Besides, it is its object that confers upon our faculty of knowing its identity. As a superabundant form, intentional as well as natural, this object is made to render the knowing subject that confronts it conform to it. Specified by its object and constituted in its identity by the relation it has with its object, our cognitive faculty is made for truth.

In the order of being, the divine stability expresses itself in supreme necessity; in the order of knowing, in supreme truth. The truthfulness of our knowledge thus imitates the divine stability in the latter order, just as the rest of creation, possible as well as actual, imitates it in the former. The symmetry is nearly perfect. Just as the divine truth owes its absolute indefectibility to its real identity with the totally necessary being of God, so the essential veracity of our faculty of knowing is indefectible because of its identity with its own necessary nature.

Now, it is true that just as the intrinsic necessity present in any created nature does not necessarily determine its existential destiny, so the intrinsic veracity of our faculty of knowing by no means excludes every possibility of accidental error, even with

---

[42] Aristotle, *On the Soul* II, 4, 415A18ff.; Thomas Aquinas, *In De an.* II, lect. 6 (P. 305–308); *Q. De an.*, a. 13; *Sum. th.* I, q. 77, a. 3; John of St. Thomas, *Log.* II, q. 21, a. 4 (R, I, 670B21); *Phil. nat.* IV, q. 2, a. 3 (R, III, 74ff.).

respect to the object that specifies it. Still, we need not despair of ever knowing the truth. For just as its intrinsic necessity determines any created essence to act and be acted upon effectively according to its constitution in the order of physical existence, so its essential veracity makes sure that our power to know conforms with its object in intentional existence. Contingency is not excluded in either case. But neither is the ability of the faculty of knowing to prevail over accidental error, just as other natures triumph over the contingencies they encounter in their existence.[43]

This, then, is how we necessarily begin the critique of knowledge on realistic grounds, without the slightest trace of question-

---

[43] Thomas Aquinas, *Sum. th.* I, q. 17, a. 3 (Whether falsity is found in the intellect): "I answer that, just as a thing has being by its proper form, so the knowing power has knowledge by the likeness of the thing known. Hence, as natural things cannot fall short of the being that belongs to them by their form, but may fall short of accidental or consequent qualities, even as a man may fail to possess two feet but not fail to be a man, so the knowing power cannot fail in the knowledge of the thing with the likeness of which it is informed, but may fail with regard to something consequent upon that form, or accidental to it. For it has been said that sight is not deceived in its proper sensible, but only about common sensibles that are consequent to that object, or about accidental objects of sense. Now, as the sense is directly informed by the likeness of its proper sensible, so the intellect is by the likeness of the essence of a thing. Hence, the intellect is not deceived about the essence of a thing, nor the sense about its proper sensible. . . . But because the falsity of the intellect is concerned *per se* only with the composition that the intellect performs, falsity can occur also accidentally in that operation of the intellect whereby it knows the essence of a thing, inasmuch as the composition of the intellect is involved in it." Aristotle, *On the Soul* III, 3, 427A11; 418B18. "Perception of the special objects of sense is always free from error." Ibid., 6, 430B26. "Assertion is the saying of something concerning something, e.g., affirmation, and is in every case either true or false; this is not always the case with mind. When the mind has an essence for its object, it is always true; but not when it also affirms an attribute of that subject." Aristotle, *Meta.* V, 29, 1024B26; IX, 10, 1051B17; Thomas Aquinas, *In De an.* II, lect. 13 (P. 384); III, lect. 4 (P. 630), lect. 5 (P. 645), lect. 6 (P. 661), lect. 11 (P. 761, 762, 763); *In Meta.* IX, lect. 11 (in the Cathala edition—hereafter identified as C.—1904ff.); *De ver.*, q. 1, a. 12; *Cont. gent.* III, 108; *Sum. th.* I, q. 17, aa. 2, 3; q. 85, a. 6; John of St. Thomas, *Phil. nat.* III, q. 4, a. 4 (R, III, 126 ff.); Joseph Gredt, *Unsere Aussenwelt* (Innsbruck: Verlagsanstatt, 1921), pp. 159ff.; J. de Tonquédec, *La Critique de la connaissance* (Paris: Beauchesne, 1929), p. 144. It should be noted that sometimes Aristotle and St. Thomas state simply that sense and intellect are infallible with respect to their proper objects, and sometimes they state that even then an accidental error remains possible. The formulae of the first kind are concise formulae referring to an essential indefectibility.

begging, and by a simple analysis of the terms involved in any judgment about the validity of our power of knowing. Clearly, before claiming to evaluate the power of knowing, one has to explain what knowledge is, and what the faculty is of which knowledge is the act. But there is no way of expressing the nature of the faculty of knowing without declaring at the same time that it is made for truth. Still, the very principle at the basis of realism imposes certain limits on it. The reason for the essential veracity of our faculty of knowing lies in its natural relation with its object, and here error can enter only by accident. But outside this relation truth in knowledge is not guaranteed by nature and depends on our ability to produce a second nature, as it were, made in the image of the first. Thus science is perfected when our scientific intelligence reaches the point where it is able to judge scientific matters with a certitude equal to that by which our natural intelligence brings forth its first principles. To arrive at that point, however, the faculty of knowing must be developed, refined, indeed, superelevated. For scientific knowledge is no more identical with the light of natural understanding than rational moral knowledge is.[44]

But how is one to recognize this object that makes the faculty of knowing conform to it? Clearly, rather than through some previously known intermediary, this object must be directly accessible to us. And since it definitely is not the thing itself, this specifying object must consist of some attribute, some characteristic of the thing known, that enters into intentional existence alone and brings the rest of the thing along only indirectly and virtually. The object of our faculty of knowing shares this property of the object in act, yet the two objects do not coincide; the first includes the second and goes beyond it. For instance, the

---

[44] On the theory of the habitus, and on the intellectual habitus in particular, see Aristotle, *Categ.*, 8, 8B26; *Phys.* VII, 3, 246A10; *Meta.* V, 20, 1022B4; *Ethics* II, 5, 1106A14; VI, 3, 1139B14; Thomas Aquinas, *Sum. th.* I–II, qq. 49–57; Maritain, *Réflexions sur l'intelligence*, pp. 112ff., and *Le Songe de Descartes*. With Descartes the notion of intellectual habitus is totally lost. The great concern is no longer, as with the ancients, to emphasize the natural affinity of the mind for truth but to recover some "natural light of reason," which Descartes believed to be encumbered in its operation by the prejudices acquired in childhood and in the schools. See his *Discourse on Method*; *Principles of Philosophy* I, 1, 47, 50, 66, 75; and *Rules for the Direction of the Mind* I.

act of seeing red is specifically different from the act of seeing blue, and yet there is no hesitation about referring these two acts to one and the same faculty. Likewise, the act of knowing what is speculatively true is specifically different from the act of knowing what is morally good, but theoretical and practical knowledge are not attributed to two different minds. Thus although an objective diversity can be formal and specifying with regard to an entire habitus as well as a simple act of cognition, as far as the faculty itself is concerned, this diversity remains merely material. But do we not have to stop somewhere? What is the relevant criterion, the point beyond which objective diversity breaks up the unity not only of specific acts of cognition and particular habitus but also of the knowing faculty itself? We clearly cannot refer all our acts of knowledge to a single faculty, any more that we can do so with our other kinds of acts.

The unity of a faculty is clearly dissolved when the acts under consideration are so diverse that we are obliged to endow the faculty with a contradictory essence. For example, it is impossible for the power of knowing the sensible and the power of knowing the intelligible to be one and the same power. For if we were to attribute both sensible knowledge and intellectual knowledge to a single faculty, we would be endowing it simultaneously both with an intrinsic materiality, required by sensible knowledge, and with an intrinsic immateriality, required by intellectual knowledge. Thus any objective diversity incompatible with the self-identity of a faculty is, of necessity, a diversity that specifies not only acts of cognition and habitus but faculties of knowledge. Still, one might wonder if this criterion, sufficing to establish the minimum number of faculties that have to be distinguished, allows one to define their actual number as well. In other words, just because doing so is not contradictory, are we thereby constrained to assign any plurality of acts to a single power? Assigning both theoretical and practical knowledge to a single faculty makes sense. But are we thereby justified in concluding that they are the same kind of knowledge?

In nature, forms and activities exist in luxurious profusion. But there can be no such luxury among natures whose entire essence is constituted by a power. Two powers one of which is superfluous are readily reduced to a single power which, if the other is superfluous, *can* do the job. Consequently, devising a

35

system of faculties is subject to a rigorous law of economy. Confronted with two kinds of objects, we ask whether referring acts determined by these objects to a single faculty is contradictory. If the answer is "Yes," we must conclude that specifically distinct faculties are required; if the answer is "No," we are satisfied that the faculty retains its unity.

But if we are to proceed in this manner and to decide by a simple application of the principle of non-contradiction whether or not to assign a particular plurality of objects to a single faculty, it is clear that we have to have an ontological knowledge of the objects involved. Now, we do have sufficient such knowledge of several kinds of objects, including the true and the good, the sensible and the intelligible, of the external sense and the object of each of the internal senses, the object of the external sense, to know that identifying the faculty of the true with the faculty of the good, for example, or the faculty of the sensible with the faculty of the intelligible, would be contradictory. But when it is a question of defining each of the external senses in its specificity, we cannot be so sure. Is it totally wrong to refer the sense, or rather the cognition, of taste and that of smell to the same faculty? To know for sure, we would have to know very specifically what taste is and what smell is, but we do not have that kind of knowledge. What we know of physical species or things is what we know of the object of sense cognition, and that does not go very far. Thus although we certainly can tell them apart, we are unable to tell whether the cherry tree and the apple tree represent ontologically distinct species, or whether they are simply varieties of a single species, as the black man and the white man are simply varieties of the human species. We are aware that taste and smell are material in their being, and that they belong in the category of quality; but we do not know how to distinguish one from the other ontologically.

Must the philosopher, then, give up dealing with the details of the external senses, just as he abstains from dealing with the details of physical species? Is he, then, not to speak of sight, hearing, touch, except by way of examples? To accept such a renunciation would be, in my opinion, to underestimate what our empirical knowledge can contribute to our ontological knowledge when the latter can no longer advance by its own appropriate methods. Clearly, we cannot tell whether flavor and odor are so different as objects that no single faculty can include them as its proper objects without contradiction. But even though ontological analysis of the object may be lacking here, we do have enough anatomical and functional data that allow us, in most cases, to determine fairly the limits of our sense faculties.[45] One may be deaf without being blind and blind without being deaf. The organs of sight and the organ of hearing are easily identifiable, and we are plainly justified in affirming a real distinction between the faculty of hearing and the faculty of sight. Since color is the only object immediately present to the sense of sight, as sound is to the sense of hearing, we have the certitude that color is the proper object of the faculty of sight, as sound is of the faculty of hearing. Moreover, we are also sure these senses are as indefectible with regard to their own proper objects as any faculty

---

[45] Thomas Aquinas attempts to base the division of the external senses on an ontological analysis of the relation between the sense and its object (*In De an.* II, lect. 14 [P. 418], and *Sum. th.* I, q. 78, a. 3). In this attempt we see a characteristic example of what Maritain has called the philosophical imperialism of the ancients, the rash claim to be able to settle by philosophy problems that pertain to another level of knowledge. For us, such an enterprise is doomed to failure (see chap. 3, note 17). Aquinas rejects, in so many words, as illogical the very method we think one must use here. To distinguish the senses and their objects, we must first of all distinguish among sense organs. "Powers are not for the sake of the organs, but organs are for the sake of the powers" (*Sum. th.* I, q. 78, a. 3). While all this is true, however, what makes necessary an experimental science over and above the philosophy of nature is the fact that the details of nature are so obscure as to be penetrable only with the help of a highly specialized system of inquiry. It is worth noting that a few lines after the formula just quoted, Aquinas himself comes to an implicit recognition of the need to take the organs seriously in order to distinguish the sense faculties. The objection is raised that touch is not a single faculty, and so there would be more than five external senses. Aquinas replies: "As the Philosopher seems to say (*On the Soul* II, 11, 423B34), the sense of touch is generically one but is divided into several specific senses, and for this reason it extends to various contrarieties (e.g., hot and cold, moist and dry, etc.). These senses, however, are not separate from one another in their organ, but are spread throughout the whole body, so that their distinction is not evident. But taste, which perceives the sweet and the bitter, accompanies touch only in the tongue, not throughout the whole body, so it is easily distinguished from touch. We might also say that all contrarieties agree, each in some proximate genus, and all in a common genus, which is the object of touch according to its common notion" (*Sum. th.* I, q. 78, a. 3, ad 3). *Seems to say, we might say*—such phrases keep us in the conditional, which is inevitable in the absence of the empirical physiological data that alone can decide such questions.

of knowledge can ever be. But where such clear anatomical and functional differentiation is lacking, the question of the proper object and unity of a faculty, and consequently the problem of its veracity, may be much more difficult to solve. Aristotle wondered whether touch is a single faculty or a genus including specifically diverse faculties, and his question still awaits a philosophically certain answer.[46] Indeed, the mystery surrounding things most familiar to us may well be the main and probably permanent source of imperfection in all our philosophical speculations.

The purpose of the present work, however, is not so much to define degrees of validity in different types of knowledge as to inquire what knowledge is. What the preceding critical comments are intended to establish, then, is simply that an inquiry into the essence of knowing can never be completely separated from judgment about its validity, as if knowing were not about *truth*, and *truthfulness* were not the essence of cognition. It is granted that a complete *critique* of knowledge presupposes a fully developed *theory* of knowledge. But without an initial critique, however summary and sketchy its statement of the value of knowledge may be, any theoretical treatment of knowledge is bound to be incoherent, making a sound critique in turn forever impossible. The most subtle psychology of the senses relying on the most elaborate data is still not capable of demonstrating the objective value of sensible knowledge—unless this value has previously been established by *a priori* reasoning. Furthermore, if we were to put aside all questions concerning the value of knowledge until we have completed a full-fledged theory of knowledge, would we know what we are talking about when we use words such as "sense" and "intelligence"? Those who refuse to make a preliminary judgment that the faculty of knowing has a certain indefectibility, while readily proclaiming that it can be deprived of it, are starting in the wrong direction. They want to proceed without telling anyone the conditions on which their interpretation of knowledge will avoid being contradictory.

---

[46] On the problem of the unity of the sense of touch, see Aristotle, *On the Soul* II, 11, 423B34; Thomas Aquinas, *In De an.* II, lect. 22 (P. 521ff.); *Q. De an.*, a. 13, ad 17; *Sum. th.* I, q. 78, a. 3, ad 3; Cajetan, *In De an.* II, 10 (B. 153Bff.); John of St. Thomas, *Phil. nat.* III, q. 5, a. 6 (R. III, 163 ff.); Gredt, *Unsere Aussenwelt*, pp. 46ff.

2

Cognition and Activity

OBJECTIVITY AND ACTIVITY

BECAUSE IN CREATED BEINGS to know is not the same as to be, and because creaturely knowledge is thus but a special faculty of its subject, every act of such knowledge appears necessarily to be the work of an efficient cause, the result of an activity. Nevertheless, before we turn to examine the active factors in human cognition, at its different levels, moments, and particular modalities, we need to consider briefly the general question of whether each and every kind of cognition requires activity on the part of the knower. For it is not inconceivable that in at least a few cases, knowledge may be caused in the knower, completely and in every respect, by an efficient *external* principle. This could be what we have called the object of knowledge, or it could be a teacher, an angel, or even God. What we want to know is whether the knower can be a pure recipient of the cognitive act. Can any kind of knowledge result from pure passivity on the part of the knowing subject?

Passivity is derived from potentiality, and in pure passivity potentiality rules supreme. But have we not established that potency is the negation of knowing just as it is of being? In the order of nature, all created things are subject to the law of potentiality: they are only what they can be. Beings endowed with knowledge who can become, literally, what they cannot be are the exception. It is knowledge as superexistence that triumphs over the potentiality of being and provides certain creatures with an opening upon the infinite not available to the rest of nature. Thus between the limitless scope of knowledge and the limiting function of potentiality, there is an absolute antinomy. Any form received by way of pure passivity is thereby limited to the possibilities of the receiver, subjectively trapped, as it were, and the result of pure passivity can never be more than a material union, in which the receiver becomes other than it was, but only such as it itself could ever be. But cognition is not like that. We have already established that to know means to become the other and as one could not be. The objectivity of knowledge thus clearly presupposes activity on the part of the knower. A subject can be united objectively—not subjectively—to a form only if he actively participates in that union. This absolute exclusion of potentiality, which in God is the root of His omniscience, is imitated in the created knower by what is his most characteristic and vital activity. A knowledge resulting from pure passivity would be an absolute contradiction, a fictitious potentiality that denies itself. Cognition is action as well as existence.[1]

But precisely because knowledge appears not only as a unique

---

[1] The interpretations of the ideas of Thomism concerning the activity implied in cognitive acts have had a curious history. I have heard Professor Bréhier, in a course given at the Sorbonne, contend that it was from Thomism that Descartes borrowed his own passivist conception of our cognitions. This is, indeed, possible, but only in the sense that Descartes with his poor understanding of St. Thomas oversimplified the latter's proposition *intelligere est quoddam pati*. This adage settles the question for many of our contemporaries, as the reading that victimized Descartes still has gullible adherents. But anyone who has read Aquinas carefully knows that the texts where he speaks of that which is passive in created knowledge are admirably completed by many passages in which he defines knowledge as immanent action and indeed the highest form of activity. To be sure, Aquinas regularly identifies cognitive faculties as *passive powers*, but we must understand what this expression means; it refers only to the object of the faculty, not to its act. A power is called active when it produces its object or imposes a form on it. Thus digestion is an active power since it imposes on the food the form by which what is ingested becomes a part of the living substance. By contrast, a power is called passive when it receives its form from the object. Thus to say that the human intelligence is a passive faculty means no more than that it is measured by its object and required to *receive* its ideas. It does not mean that knowledge consists in nothing but passive reception. And that is why Aquinas himself calls the faculty of knowing also an *active power* (*De ver.*, q. 14, a. 3).

Nevertheless, it does not appear that Aquinas has anywhere expressly demonstrated that all knowledge implies activity on the part of the knower, and the reason for it seems fairly clear. Even though he said it a thousand times, Aquinas never bothered to prove that all knowing involves activity on the part of the knower simply because for him this was never in doubt. And though his successors had more occasion to discuss the purely passivist conception of knowledge maintained by some Scholastic thinkers, they too pass over it lightly, even with a touch of contempt, as if it were an absurdity that offends the common sense of philosophers. Consequently, they also feel no need to *demonstrate* the contrary. For instance, Capreolus (*Defensiones theologiae divi Thomae Aquinatis*, Sent. 14, dist. 49, q. 4 [edd. Ceslau Paban and Thomas

Pègues, 7 vols. (Turin: Cattier, 1900–1908), 7 208B]) answers his own question "Is the intellect completely passive in the Beatific Vision?" as follows: "We must say 'No' because understanding is an immanent action where the same reality serves as subject and efficient cause. Consequently, the created intellect can have no understanding unless it be the cause of it, along with the object or the intelligible species of the object." In the pages that follow, Capreolus shows that the arguments of the adversary (Peter Aureole) are not conclusive, but he produces no defense of his own thesis. The same attitude is found in Bañez, in a discussion of considerable doctrinal and historical interest (*In Sum. th.* I, q. 79, a. 2., *Dubitatur secundo* (D, II, 289B). The question is set forth with perfect clarity: *Whether understanding is always produced effectively by the intellect itself or comes about by its being passive, at least where the absolute power of God is involved.* For some authors, the answer to the second part of the question is "Yes" because for them the intellect plays a completely passive role even in ordinary understanding. Among these authors are Godfrey [of Fontaines], Adam [of Anglia], John of Jandun, Paul of Venice, and Giles of Rome, and Aquinas is often lumped together with them. For other authors, e.g., Marsilio [of Padua] and Gabriel [Biel], though the intellect under natural conditions produces thought actively, in the Beatific Vision it remains completely passive. For Sonzinas, the intellect is *de facto* always active, but it is up to God to let it know without its active participation. For still others, however, though God can by His absolute power produce an act of intellection in a man's understanding, the quality so produced does not qualify the man as a genuine knower. This is the position taken by Capreolus, Cajetan, Sylvester of Ferrara, Soto, and some others, and Bañez sides with them. "The Beatific Vision," Bañez writes (ibid., 290B), "is a vital operation, like walking and eating, but a man is not said to be walking or eating unless he is the effective producer of these acts; likewise, therefore, the created intellect is not said to be seeing God unless it is effectively producing the vision." But just like the others, Bañez makes no effort to demonstrate his major premiss. Because vision is an operation of the understanding, he declares it to be evident. John of St. Thomas, likewise, in rejecting the hypothesis that identifies sensation with mere reception of the sensible form, states simply that sensation is life and, hence, activity (*Phil. nat.* IV, 4, 1 [R, III, 107A36]). In another place (*Curs. th.* I, disp. 25, a. 1 [Vivès, IV, 1036A]), where the question is how angelic communication takes place, he says the same thing. Arguing against Scotus, who maintains that the angel who "speaks" produces the understanding in the angel who "listens," John of St. Thomas grandly proclaims this opinion "totally unacceptable since *it is contrary to the whole of philosophy,* which teaches that knowledge or understanding is a vital and immanent act and consequently requires, by everything that is essential to it, that it not be impressed from outside but have its origin from an intrinsic principle."

The reasoning implicit in these statements seems to be the one we have presented: cognition cannot be totally passive because a pure reception can end only in a material union. This is the reasoning used by Gredt (*Elementa philosophiae* I [Freiburg: Herder, 1921], p. 363) and Maritain (*Réflexions sur l'intelligence,* pp. 324–25). Hamelin also adverts to it (*Essai sur les éléments principaux de la représentation,* p. 341) when he challenges what he perceives to be the absurdities of realism. "No one seems to be asking," he writes, "how an image introduced into a receiver of whatever sort—dark room, brain, soul—can become an object for a subject rather than remain a thing within a

sort of existence but also as a particular activity totally without parallel in the physical world, our next step must be a thorough review of the general theory of activity.

THE FACT OF CHANGE: FIRST DEFINITION OF ACTION

The starting point of any theory of action must be the fact of change. For instance, "immobile" and "inert" mean about the same in ordinary language, and when we wish to express the activity of the most immutable of realities, the power of our images and words is such that we tend to express ourselves in a way that seems to deny God's immutability. "In God there is no immobility, only an eternal movement."[2] We are well aware, of course, that we are speaking metaphorically here. Addressing a completely motionless activity, we call upon the idea of mobility to make ourselves understood, even though we run the risk of being badly misunderstood. But what the awkwardness of our expressions in this case clearly shows is how closely linked the notions of activity and change are in the basic conceptions of our mind, which determine the primary meaning of our words. There is no doubt about it. Of all the different kinds of action, the one we recognize first and retain as clearest is the action experienced through change.[3] Starting with change, then, in order to arrive at the understanding of activity free from all becoming, we follow the correct procedure of empirical inquiry.

Change comes in many forms. Revelation, for instance, presents us with the fact of a total change that has no subject and

---

thing." If Octave Hamelin had not died in profound ignorance of medieval philosophy (see his *Le Système de Descartes* [Paris: Alcan, 1921], chap. 1), he might have observed that reputable realistic thinkers had solved this problem almost without trying when they accepted as self-evident the proposition that an image could become an object of understanding for a thinking subject *only* by that subject's own efficient causality.

[2] M. V. Bernadot, *De L'Eucharistie à la Trinité* (Paris: Les Editions du Cerf, 1919), p. 55.

[3] Aristotle, *Meta.* IX, 3, 1047A30: "The word 'actuality,' which we connect with 'complete reality,' has, in the main, been extended from movements to other things; for actuality in the strict sense is thought to be identical with movement."

that affects the term of the change in the whole of its being.[4] By contrast, the philosophical explanation of the course of physical events demands, at whatever cost to our desire for clarity, that we affirm the existence of changes so profound that their subject is reduced to nothing more than a pure real possibility. In our immediate experience, however, change often presents itself as a superficial sort of event, bearing only on the position, qualities, or dimensions of a subject, but leaving it fundamentally intact. Thus only the Sophists would claim that Coriscos at the Lyceum is not the same man as Coriscos in the Agora.[5] Indeed, considering these familiar kinds of change suffices to make us recognize one of the primary conditions of the intelligibility of change: namely, that *what changes depends for its change upon a reality distinct from itself, from which the change originates.* Here we have the basic statement of the principle of efficient causality, which cannot be denied without compromising the principle of non-contradiction.[6] A particular subject that we observe changing may indeed possess that particular determination by identity with itself, and in that case the law of non-contradiction is not violated. But if there is no such identity between the subject and its determination, and it is not of itself that the determination is joined to the subject, the change must be attributed to another cause. There is no other way.[7]

Now, the facts of change attest that there are subjects with determinations that they do not possess by pure identity. What

---

[4] *Sum. th.* III, q. 75, a. 4 (Eucharistic transubstantiation).

[5] Aristotle, *Phys.* IV, 11, 219B18: "This is an identical *substratum* (whether a point or a stone or something else of the kind), but it has different *attributes*— as the sophists assume that Coriscus' being in the Lyceum is a different thing from Coriscus' being in the market-place."

[6] Ibid., VII, 1, 241B24: "Everything that is in motion must be moved by something." If there are beings that move themselves, it must be conceded that they have heterogeneous parts; otherwise the diversity between the mover and the movable would not hold. Ibid., VIII, 4, 254B30: "It would seem that in animals, just as in ships and things not naturally organized, that which causes motion is separate from that which suffers motion." Thomas Aquinas, *Cont. gent.* I, 97: "Those beings that move themselves, such as animals, are composed of a mover and a moved." John of St. Thomas, *Phil. nat.* I, q. 22, a. 1, ad 4 (R, II, 450B16).

[7] Cf. Réginald Garrigou-Lagrange, o.p., *Le Sens commun* (Paris: Beauchesne, 1909), pp. 168ff., and *Dieu, son existence et sa nature*, pp. 170ff.

one has by identity is not acquired and cannot be lost without the annihilation of oneself. The seed is not the same as the fruit; we observe it become fruit. And that is how the efficient cause appears to us first of all as the *source of change*.[8] Within the limits of movable being, then, action, *the actual exercise of efficient causality*,[9] is nothing other than change in relation to its origin, the counterpart of passion, which is change in relation to the receiver.[10] Still, between action and passion, there is more than just a logical distinction. The gift one gives is identical to the gift the other receives, but to give a gift is not the same as to receive one. And so, in complete agreement with common sense, we are brought to the following conclusions. Action and passion, identical with change, and with each other, on the analogy of a thing's remaining itself under different modalities, are really distinct from change as well as from each other precisely as a thing under one modality is really distinct from the same thing under another modality. Although the finger extended is the same finger as when bent, there is a real distinction between the finger bent and that finger extended.[11]

---

[8] Aristotle's standard definition of the efficient cause is "the primary cause of change." *Phys.* II, 3, 194B29.

[9] John of St. Thomas, *Phil. nat.* I, q. 12, a. 4 (R, II, 263A34): "It is commonly held that action consists in the causality of the agent as mediating its influence in producing the effect. For that the cause does not cause by its own mere entity, and that the effect does not proceed from its own entity, are inferred from the difference between efficient and formal causality. The effect of formal causality is nothing other than the cause itself as communicated to and united with another; given the application or union, there is no need of any medium to produce the effect. The efficient cause, on the other hand, does involve an effect distinct from itself, with which it is in contact or which it alters as its term, which passes from non-being to being. Hence, besides its application to action, it needs something in addition to its own reality by reason of which it may be said to be actually moved. The entity alone of the cause is not enough for actual causality. There are times when it is not actually causing, and the entity of the cause is there. Nor is the cause one with the altered entity of the effect, for it is still there after it produces the effect."

[10] Aristotle, *Phys.* III, 3, 202A13: "The solution of the difficulty that is raised about the motion—whether it is in the *movable*—is plain. It is the fulfilment of this potentiality, and by the action of that which has the power of causing motion."

[11] Ibid., 202B10: "Nor is it necessary that the teacher should learn, even if to act and to be acted on are one and the same, provided they are not the same in *definition* (as 'raiment' and 'dress'), but are the same merely in the sense in

Moreover, since the subject of change, *that which changes*, is the movable, the recipient of the change, and not its source, we also realize that wherever action consists in a change, the proper subject of that action is not the agent but the patient. Basically identical with the change, this action affects primarily the patient. Substantially a determination of the patient, it belongs to the agent only in a modal sense.[12]

The object first reached by human intelligence in conjunction with the senses is the being of sensible natures making itself known by their action on the sense organs. But although joined to the sense, our intelligence succeeds by dint of an heroic effort, as it were, surmounting its natural bent, in grasping from that sensible being also certain characteristics of being as being. We may say that the true life of the spirit, in which we imitate however imperfectly the spirits who have no bodies, begins at that

---

which the road from Thebes to Athens and the road from Athens to Thebes are the same. . . . For it is not things which are in a way the same that have all their attributes the same, but only such as have the same definition." Thomas Aquinas, *Sum. th.* II–II, q. 90, a. 3: "The action of that which is acted upon and moved is the same as that of the agent and the mover; thus the movement of the arrow is a certain operation of the archer." John of St. Thomas, *Log.* II, q. 19, a. 2 (R, I, 627B19): "For motion is called the act of a being in potency, a form of act in flux, as it were, because it changes in becoming, from one thing to another. Necessarily, then, a twofold formality is to be observed, viz., from something and in something, for every motion is from an agent and is in a patient or receiver. And so motion cannot be understood without that twofold formality of action as from something and passion as in something." *Phil. nat.* I, q. 14, a. 2 (R, II, 300A33): "Action and passion are distinguished not simply by a distinction of reason, but by a modal, a real formal distinction, both from each other and from motion."

[12] Aristotle, *Phys.* III, 3; *Meta.* IX, 8, 1050A30; *On the Soul* III, 2, 426A9; John of St. Thomas, *Phil. nat.* I, q. 14, a. 4 (R, II, 312A11): "By its proper nature, action is not seeking a subject to inhere in but one to emanate from. In fact, however, the emanating action implies a twofold formality, one of which originates and inheres in the agent, while the other is related to the term of the action and thus resides in the patient. . . . In created agents . . . action is in the agent in an inchoate way and is fully realized only in the effect. . . . Inasmuch as action, the causality emanating from the agent, puts the activated agent in second act and changes it from inactive to active, it leaves its formality in the agent initiating the effect. But as it puts the effect caused and proceeding from a cause into a subject, it also places this formality into the effect, by which the action is rendered complete, and from which we get the name *acting*. For nothing is said to be acting prior to an effect, and for this reason action is in the term simply."

point. As befits metaphysical thought, the meaning of causal notions is thence deepened and purified, as they are stripped of everything that the characteristics proper to sensible natures add to their essence. We still have to talk about change, but what the fact of change will teach us at this level are the laws of being as being, which are indifferent to mobility and its sensorial manifestations. Here, we learn that being a source of change is only one particular form of the idea of efficient cause. Able to grasp this cause in the intimacy of its being, and consequently in its universality, we come to understand it precisely as *the source of actuality*, not only of change but also of the perfection of being. The requirements of the laws of causality remain in full force also at this level. As long as the being under consideration is not identical with its act, a source distinct from it is required, regardless of whether we are dealing with the imperfect actuality of change or with the actuality of perfection in being. And since existence itself is the one act that no finite being possesses or can possess by identity with itself, we recognize that this law of efficient causality, understood as applying precisely to being as being, extends to every finite being, regardless of whether the subject is in act by way of change or in any other way. Moreover, if action is nothing more than the actual exercise of efficient causality, then we must understand that its essence does not require us to identify it with change. There is not a trace of change in the purely conserving action by which God keeps the creature in existence, the just soul in the state of grace, and generally maintains realities united to one another that are not one by identity.[13] What happens at the beginning of things, at the very instant when the nature that does not possess existence

---

[13] Thomas Aquinas, *Quodl.*, q. 4, a. 9 (Whether God is continually producing new grace): "We have to say that action is of two kinds. One of these takes place with motion and is always accompanied by some innovation, for something always comes to be and something ceases to be as it approaches or departs from a term. . . . The other kind of action, however, is without motion and takes place by a simple communication of form, inasmuch as the agent impresses its likeness on a suitably disposed recipient. This action is initially accompanied by some innovation, since a form is newly acquired in the subject; but the continuation of that action has no innovation, since it has no motion connected with it, only a simple influx or communication. It is in this way that grace is caused in the soul by God."

by itself arises out of nothingness? Well, here not only is action unaccompanied by any change, which clearly presupposes an existent that would change, but it is also unaccompanied by any kind of reception, there being nothing to receive it. And that is how we learn that the idea of efficient action is expressed most excellently in the act of creation. No longer involving either change or reception, action here becomes pure production, that is, efficiency elevated to unconditional freedom.[14]

THE NOTION OF IMMANENT ACTIVITY

But does the concept of action, as we have just defined it, cover every kind of action? Or are there realities consisting specifically in something other than the exercise of efficient causality to which the name of action can be applied without resorting to metaphor? If we find that such an extension of the idea of action is necessary, we shall have to investigate what it does to the univocity of the concept. But we do not want to prejudge the matter.

A famous passage from Aristotle gives an answer to the question just asked. In Book IX of the *Metaphysics*, after showing that act is logically prior to potency, and that in one sense it is prior to it in time, the philosopher wonders about its priority in nature. Now, priority in nature is priority of perfection, and since every being owes its perfection to its form and its end, Aristotle concludes that by the twofold title of formal and final cause act is prior to potency also from the point of view of nature. The adult man who lacks none of his specific qualities enjoys a priority of nature over the baby boy who has them only in potency. In fact, does not everybody agree that act is the end goal of potency? It is not in order to have the power to see that animals see; it is in

---

[14] The divine efficiency, really identical with the being of God (and more generally every *metaphysical* efficiency exercised by a pure spirit), is first and foremost something quite different from what we ordinarily understand by efficiency, because although it does *produce* a term distinct from itself, it does so only secondarily and *virtually*. Thus creation is not formally the production of the world; it is formally God. Still, this is the purest type of efficiency: productivity, arriving at its perfection, is reabsorbed into immanence.

order to see that they have the power of seeing. Likewise, it is in order to build that one becomes an architect, and one acquires theoretical science in order to be able to contemplate truth.

At this point, however, a doubt arises: Do we have to say that the end of every agent is some kind of product? Or are there not also agents that go about their business without producing any effect? In response to this doubt and in order to show that the act is the end of potency in every kind of activity, Aristotle, without using these very terms, is led here to distinguish between two kinds of activity, immanent and transitive.

And while in some cases the exercise is the ultimate thing (e.g. in sight the ultimate thing is seeing, and no other product besides this results from sight), but from some things a product follows (e.g. from the art of building there results a house as well as the act of building), yet none the less the act is in the former case the end and in the latter more of an end than the potency is. For the act of building is realized in the thing that is being built, and comes to be, and is, at the same time as the house.

Where, then, the result is something apart from the exercise, the actuality is in the thing that is being made, e.g. the act of building is in the thing that is being built and that of weaving in the thing that is being woven, and similarly in all other cases, and in general movement is in the thing that is being moved; but where there is no product apart from the actuality, the actuality is present in the agents, e.g. the act of seeing is in the seeing subject and that of theorizing in the theorizing subject and the life is in the soul (and therefore well-being also; for it is a certain kind of life).[15]

---

[15] Aristotle, *Meta.* IX, 8, 1050A23. This passage in the Greek original has been interpreted in a variety of ways. According to the commentary of Alexander [of Aphrodisias], the sense is that while in transitive action the act is obviously the end, in immanent action it is less so, but still more than potency. This law, then, that action has the character of an end would be verified especially in transitive action and only indirectly in immanent action. But there is also the opposite interpretation. The meaning conveyed by the Latin text used by Aquinas is that in both cases the act is the end of the potency ("Tamen non minus quidem his finis hic autem magis finis potentiae est," and in his *Commentary* he repeats the phrase "finis potentiae" [*In Meta.* IX, lect. 8]). The reading by Julius H. Kirchmann (*Die Metaphysik des Aristoteles* [Berlin: Heimann, 1871]) agrees with this interpretation: "Nevertheless, the act is the end of potency no less in one than in the other case." We go along with Ross's

But is it enough to say simply that immanent activity is an activity whose entire product remains totally within the acting subject? It is certainly true that from the action of seeing or thinking nothing passes onto the thing seen or the thing thought, and the whole business is completed within the soul. But there is more to it, since both sensation and thought are essentially averse to leaving the subject and resist assuming any aspect of a passage or a flux. The distinctive feature of immanent action, defined in a wholly negative but perfectly clear way by Aristotle, is precisely never to consist in the production of anything, never to be a way leading to a term distinct from itself. Thus immanent action is not and can never be an exercise of efficient causality, and our first definition of action given above does not cover it. To see or to contemplate is not to produce anything.

---

interpretation (*Aristotle's Metaphysics* II [Oxford: Clarendon, 1910], p. 259): "In some cases the exercise is the ultimate thing (e.g., sight), while in others there is a separate result (e.g., a house as well as the act of building results from the building art); the actuality is in the first case the end, in the second at any rate more of an end than the potency." See also Octave Hamelin, *Aristote, Physique II: Traduction et commentaire* (Paris: Vrin, 1931), p. 80.

In the passages in which he draws the distinction between the action *quae manet in agente* and the action *in exteriorem materiam transiens*—the terms "immanent action" and "transient action" do not appear until much later, in the commentators on St. Thomas, as has been shown by F. A. Blanche, "Sur la langue de s. Thomas," *Revue de Philosophie* [January–February 1930], 15— Aquinas constantly refers to this text from the *Metaphysics*. Other texts of Aristotle on the distinction between these two kinds of activity are to be found in *Ethics* VI, 4, 1140A1: "In the variable are included both things made and things done; making and acting are different." Ibid., I, 1, 1094A3: "But a certain difference is found among ends; some are activities, others are products apart from the activities that produce them. Where there are ends apart from the actions, it is the nature of the products to be better than the activities." See also ibid., VI, 5, 1140B4 (where Aristotle defines prudence). But let us also point out that the distinction between making and doing, between *poiesis* and *praxis*, does not coincide, as some writers maintain, with the distinction between transitive activity and immanent activity. For not every immanent act is *praxis* but only the free act of the will. Aristotle, *Meta.* VI, 1, 1025B24: "In the case of things done the principle is in the doer, viz., the will, for that which is done and that which is willed are the same."

Among the more important texts in which Aquinas explains the distinction between what are now called transitive and immanent actions, we may cite the following: *In I Sent.*, dist. 40, q. 1, a. 1, ad 2; *In II Sent.*, dist. 12, a. 4; *De ver.*, q. 8, a. 1, ad 14; q. 8, a. 6; q. 14, a. 3; *De pot.*, q. 2, a. 2; q. 3, a. 15; q. 5, a. 5; ibid., ad 14; *Cont. gent.* I, 53; II, 1, 22, 23; *Sum. th.* I, q. 14, a. 5, ad 1; q. 54, a. 1, ad 3; ibid., a. 2; q. 85, a. 2; q. 87, a. 3.

But do we have to say, then, that seeing and contemplating are not really acting? Ordinary language says that they are, but reluctantly. Though we speak spontaneously of acts of seeing and thought, and of minds ever on the alert, we also tend to set the contemplative and the active in opposition to each other, as if only what manifests itself in external effects deserves the name of real action. These hesitations of language give us a warning. If realities as remote from each other as transitive and immanent action are to be brought together under some general, transcendental definition of action, it will have to be by way of analogy.

A SECOND (TRANSCENDENTAL) DEFINITION OF ACTION

When in the notion of being and its simplicity under innumerable valencies the metaphysician recognizes the intelligible source of the whole of reality, he knows at once what he has to do. Although all these objects of thought provided by experience must be derived from the unique source of being, he can ultimately explain them only by recognizing the way in which being, developing its valencies by combining with itself, produces—in all its complexity—the intelligible inhering in the object of sensation. And so, the metaphysician proceeds both by way of analysis and by way of synthesis. He works from complexes perceived confusedly in sense experience toward the abstract simplicity of the notion of being; but he also utilizes the notion of being in order to illuminate the complexes given in experience.[16]

Now, the last step but one in the analytic regression of the metaphysician and the first step in his synthetic progress is the division of being into act and potency, which expresses its primary valencies, and beyond which there is nothing to be said

---

[16] We function feebly as metaphysicians because we are frequently unable to trace an unbroken line from a particular existing thing perceived in experience to the idea of being. Consider, for instance, the following statement by Hans André: "The plant is the quiddity of the daisy" ("La différence de nature entre les plantes et les animaux," *Cahiers de Philosophie de la Nature*, 4 [1930], 15). The remark is as enlightening as it is incorrect. The quiddity of the daisy includes features in no way expressed by the generic concept of the plant, which applies to the mushroom and the oak as well. We simply lack terms by which to specify such ontological differences. Thus if I want to proceed from

except "Yes" or "No." To arrive at the idea of act by way of analysis, then, we obviously have to start with the fact of action. As with the contrast between the body and the soul, or between essence and existence, we approach here the distinction between potency and act best by analogy with the contrast between sleeping and being awake, between inertia and activity.[17] But if at the same time we start from the notion of being and try to get back to the notion of activity, we recognize instantly that all action belongs strictly to the order of being in act. Indeed, at this first step, we do not yet feel any need for distinguishing between transitive and immanent action. For although they may not be exactly equal, they both represent without doubt being in act.

Let us nevertheless acknowledge that among the realities belonging to the transcendental order of being in act, transitive activity stands out not only because it is so familiar to us but also because the notion of act is realized in it with special force. The soul is to the body what act is to potency. The spiritual qualities from which the activities of the soul proceed, such as the understanding and the will, art and science, are to the soul what act is to potency. But it is transitive actions, such as the workman's hammering, the scientist's conclusion, the lover's delight in the possession of the beloved object, that convey to us far better the transcendental notion of being in act. These actions appear to us as more concrete, more precisely determined actualities compared to the soul and its faculties and virtues. Yet the fact is that from its beginning in pure potency to its fulfillment in act, being reveals a line of successive determinations and perfections each of which adds to the preceding one. Thus while the soul gives the body its perfection, intelligence and will give perfections to the soul. Art and science perfect the intelligence in a similar fashion: the execution of the work is the perfection of art; the possession of truth, the perfection of science. Whether the activ-

---

the daisy to the idea of being, I have to make a leap from the *daisy* to the generic complex *plant*, abandoning along the way the specific characteristics of the daisy. And conversely, in the order of return, even if I manage an ontological definition of the genus *plant*, I cannot go any further with the notion of being and must give up getting back to the concept of the *daisy* in its specificity. The metaphysician in the meadow treads a melancholy path.

[17] Aristotle, *Meta.* IX, 6, 1048A35.

ity be immanent or transitive, then, the end of the line is always its *terminal act.*

But though thus united in the notion of terminal act, immanent and transitive actions cannot be said to exhaust its meaning and scope. For in its own way existence itself also has the character of a terminal act. Without existence there are only dreams. Even activity itself, though ultimate perfection in a certain sense, has to be completed by existence; Roland's mare cannot drag a cart. Existence is the supreme good.[18]

---

[18] The distinction between initial act (*actus primus*) and terminal act (*actus secundus*) plays an extremely important role in the development of the Aristotelian metaphysics of act and potency. *Phys.* VIII, 4, 255A33: "One who is learning a science potentially knows it in a different sense from one who while already possessing the knowledge is not actually exercising it. . . . for one who possesses knowledge of a science but is not actually exercising it knows the science potentially in a sense, though not in the same sense as he knew it potentially before he learned it." *On the Soul* II, 1, 412A9: "Now matter is potentiality, form actuality; of the latter there are two grades related to one another as e.g., knowledge to the exercise of knowledge." Ibid., II, 5, 417A22: "We can speak of something as a 'knower' either (*a*) as when we say that man is a knower, meaning that man falls within the class of beings that know or have knowledge [pure potency], or (*b*) as when we are speaking of a man who possesses a knowledge of grammar [initial act]; each of these is so called as having in him a certain potentiality, but there is a difference between their respective potentialities, the one (*a*) being a potential knower, because his kind or matter is such and such, the other (*b*), because he can . . . realize his knowledge in actual knowing at will. This implies a third meaning of 'a knower' (*c*), one who is already realizing his knowledge—he is a knower in actuality and in the most proper sense is knowing, for example, this A." See also Cajetan's important commentary on this passage, *In De an.* II, 5 (B. 110A).

Following Aristotle, Aquinas defines the terminal act by its most conspicuous case and often seems to treat its notion and that of operation as equivalent, as if every terminal act were no more than an operation. *De pot.*, q. 1, a. 1: "But act is twofold: the first act, which is form, and the second, which is operation." The same formula is to be found in *De malo*, q. 1, a. 5: "But there are two kinds of act, first and second. The first act is the form and integrity of the things, the second act is operation." Some readers, taking these texts quite literally, have concluded that for Aquinas existence is but an initial act (see Etienne Gilson, *L'Esprit de la philosophie médiévale* [Paris: Vrin, 1932], pp. 93, 136). But we also have passages in which Aquinas presents existence as the ultimate act and supreme perfection. For instance, in *De pot.*, q. 7, a. 2, ad 9, he writes: "To be is the act of acts, the perfection of all perfections, and nothing is more formal than to be" (see also *Sum. th.* I, q. 3, a. 4; q. 4, a. 1, ad 3; q. 7, a. 1). In support of Gilson's interpretation one might quote this text from the *Commentary on the Sentences I*, dist. 7, q. 1, ad 2: "For it is the essence itself that gives the act of existing (*esse*) to that which possesses it; and this is, so to speak

But does not experience bear witness that this being before us, whatever it may be, posited in existence but reduced to its bare substance, has as yet only an initial perfection, and that it is hurrying on, by means of its activity, to new achievements? To exist is obviously not enough; *il faut agir*. But since any activity has its reality from its being put in existence, we have to sort these two out and establish precisely when and where existence asserts its pre-eminence over activity, and vice versa.

Here, it seems, we have to go back to the primary data of metaphysical thought. At the peak of that intensive abstraction that provides the intelligence not with ever more inclusive genera but with an ever-increasing plenitude of actuality approaching infinity,[19] the metaphysician has before him the treasury of every perfection.[20] Imperfection of any kind arises from a defect of being. But a thing may be defective with regard to its own

---

(*quasi*), the first act. But there issues from the essence another act, which is also the act of that which possesses the essence as an agent and the act of the essence as the principle of action; this is the second act and is called operation." Nevertheless, that *so to speak* is there for a purpose, and it modifies significantly the scope of that *first act*. For so qualified, the meaning this statement conveys is that even after the gift of existence has been granted to *the possible*, the last word has not been said; the essence remains in potency in relation to another act, even as it enjoys actual existence. The matter is thoroughly clarified by John of St. Thomas (*Phil. nat.* I, q. 4, a. 1 [R, II, 83B22]): "The second act is called the ultimate act, because it is to it that the form is ordered. But there are two kinds of second act, one in the order of being, the other in the order of operation. By its actuality, the form is the principle of both being and operating, but existence is its ultimate act. It is called ultimate both because every action and motion is in it and terminates in it. For once existence has come upon the form, there is no further motion in the order of being, because existence presupposes something already constituted in its essence. In the order of operation, however, the operation itself is called the second act simply because it activates this essence, whose existence is called the first act." *Curs. th.* I, disp. 4, a. 3 (S, I, 456B); a. 4 (S, I, 469B); disp. 8, a. 2 (Vivès, II, 17A).

[19] For the theory of intensive abstraction (*abstractio formalis*) and extensive abstraction (*abstractio totalis*), see Thomas Aquinas, *Sum. th.* I, q. 40, a. 3; *Super Boethium de Trinitate*, q. 5, a. 1; Cajetan, *In De ente et essentia*, prol.; John of St. Thomas, *Log.* II, q. 27, a. 1 (R, I, 822B4); *Curs. th.* I, disp. 5, a. 1 (S, I, 501A).

[20] Thomas Aquinas, *Sum. th.* I, q. 3, a. 1, ad 3; a. 4, ad 1; I–II, q. 2, a. 5, ad 2; Cajetan, *In Ia*, q. 8, a. 1; Louis Lavelle, *Dialectique du monde sensible* (Strasbourg: Publications de la Faculté des Lettres, 1921), p. xliv: "We have set down at the foundation of our whole analysis the notion of being, not only because all other notions presuppose it, but also because it is a principle of

perfection (i.e., in relation to the requirements of its nature), or with regard to absolute perfection. In the first case, there is privation; in the second, simple limitation. Privation is an encroachment of non-being upon what belongs to a thing according to its nature; limitation is the circumscribing of being as such by an area of non-being. Fill in the privation, the gap that makes a thing poor, with being, and the thing becomes good, i.e., perfect according to its nature. Fill with being the area of non-being that circumscribes every limited thing, and there is absolute perfection. In other words, being as such is perfection.

The primary object of metaphysics, this being *qua* being, actually neither implies nor excludes any imperfection; it excludes only contradiction, which would annihilate it. One can see here how this idea of being as such leads to the idea of God. For if, of itself, being implies no restriction or limitation, when we exclude all limitation from its concept, we posit a being that exists by pure identity with being, a self-subsistent being. And if we turn the perspective around, that is, posit a self-subsistent being, a being that exists by pure identity with being, without admixture of anything distinct from itself, we arrive at the idea of being without limits, the absolutely infinite being. Here every perfection is given all at once, the problem of completion does not arise, the distinction between initial act and terminal act has no meaning, and only the name, Pure Act, suggests what we are unable to put in words.

But how, then, are we to conceive *limited being*? If being admits of limitation, it does not limit itself. Nor can it be limited by some absolute non-being, for what is nothing has no role to play. What purely and simply does not exist cannot affect the existent. Therefore, any limitation of being has to be the work of a relative non-being, of a non-being that consists, so to speak, of a potency or a real possibility of being.

Consequently, though unlimited being is simplicity itself, being everything that it is by identity with itself, limited being neces-

---

infinite fecundity. Many think of being as an abstract and inert genus (i.e., as if it were the term of an extensive abstraction from all particulars). But the notion of being actually expresses a single act that is tirelessly renewed as it begets an ordered diversity. It is like a voice which, while uttering an inexhaustible variety of sounds, heard by a multitude of individuals, still remains forever one."

sarily implies a duality of principles. In it there is both being and some non-being; it includes both being in act and being in potency, as well as a real distinction between essence and existence. And this is why in considering limited being there is always the problem of fulfillment. Any subject lacking being by identity has reality only by virtue of its participation in existence; but in the created essences the gift of existence always leaves a residue of potentiality.

Before they are brought into existence, created natures pre-exist in the divine intellect. As yet, they are not, but already they are *this* or *that*. They do not yet exist, but they are already completely determined in their possible existence, because the divine art proceeding from an infinite wisdom leaves nothing unforeseen. Except for being in the divine intellect, these natures, which do not have existence by identity with themselves, have not yet been brought into existence, and have not yet emerged from nothingness, are indeed non-beings. But the wisdom of the divine art has already determined their *capacity to be*, as well as the extent of the limitations that will govern their existence. The angel who is not yet *will be*, if it pleases God to make him be, *greater than man*, and so also will man *be* something more than plants, and plants something more than atoms. From the highest of the Seraphim to the least of the atomic particles, not yet existing but able to exist, all creatable natures are there, present to the divine mind as possible objects of the divine art, carefully measured with regard to the non-being that will be mixed with their existence. The angel and the man who are not yet are already angel and man. In the divine thought, their relative proportions of non-being have already been determined, and with the gift of existence they will infallibly turn out to be angel or man, and not something else.

When we understand that created natures prior to creation are completely determined in their ability to be, we can easily understand what kind of perfection they receive when the creative act brings them into existence. *Such as they were able to be, so they are.* Their *quality* is in no way modified. Their capacity is neither increased nor diminished; it is simply fulfilled. The limitations on their being are there but in strict proportions to their capacities. There is more reality in a hundred existing thalers than in a hundred possible thalers, but when a hundred thalers pass from possibility to existence they do not become a hundred and one thalers. An existent man has greater ontological value than a possible man, but he is no more than a man; his nature as a human being is no better simply because he exists. Activity does improve existence by relating it to its ends. But this very activity that improves active natures is itself subject to the law of all creation; the activity brought into existence will in no way change its own nature. Thus although there is infinitely more reality in an actual act of justice than in one merely contemplated, the deed done does not thereby become an act of charity.[21]

---

[21] In the case of immanent activity, it is evident that action is the perfection of the one acting. This is also clear in the case of vital activities, whose effects remain within the acting subject (see below, pp. 74). But in the case of action that passes into an external effect, this is not so clear. To be sure, the primary beneficiary of the physician's treatment is the patient, not the physician. And yet, there is more actuality and consequently more perfection in the physician working than in the physician on vacation. (If the vacation lasts too long, the man of action feels diminished.) As a matter of fact, if it is true that transitive action, identical substantially with change, is found principally in the patient and in the being that is moved, this action can belong to the agent—and be its perfection—only in a way that distinguishes it from change. Still, the reason why we cannot assign any such additional effect to transitive action, and must not think of it even as a modest perfection of oneself by oneself, is the fact that the way in which it intrinsically affects the agent arises not from any efficiency proper to the agent but as a consequence of divine premotion. As we shall see shortly, no created agent is the cause of its union with its action. The whole of the intrinsic perfection of the being that acts *ad extra* consists in that union and nothing else. Thus the transitive action may be said to be caused by the agent only to the extent that another receives it and is perfected by it. See John of St. Thomas, *Phil. nat.* I, q. 14, a. 4 (R, II, 315A7; 275B); *Curs. th.* I, disp. 4, ad 6 (Vivès, III, 290): "The power that issues in action *ad extra* perfects the effect rather than being perfected in itself. And so, when it breaks off its action, it just breaks off the communication of itself to others, which rather than to its own perfection belongs to the perfection of the other. Although being able to communicate oneself is indeed a perfection, actually communicating perfects the other. Nevertheless, and strictly in contrast to its abstaining from all transitive action, actually communicating its power may be said to contribute also to the perfection of the agent." Ibid., disp. 11, a. 2 (Vivès, III, 916). Against Vasquez, the author shows that in action *ad extra* the relation between the agent and the effect presupposes additional determination of the agent (except in the case of the pure act and on the highest level of actuality by identity): "The power to act cannot be the source of this relation since, of itself, this power is indifferent to acting or not acting and, besides, it does not always have a relation to an effect. And so, when there is established a relation between agent and effect, the action must have for its basis something beyond sheer indifference. There must be some determined way by which this power passes

And so we come to understand how activity and existence are to be distinguished within the notion of the terminal act. Existence is not *this* or *that*, a particular kind of thing; it is what causes things to be set outside of nothingness. This does not mean, of course, that the existence of one particular species is the same as that of any other. They all *are* different. But we must realize that these differences, even as they affect it, come not from the act of existence itself but rather from the *things* that are.[22] Of itself, existence is indifferent to the kind of nature that it causes to be, provided any intrinsic repugnance to being, namely self-contradiction, is excluded. But given this condition, the only potency that existence fulfills in its subject is this potency

---

from potency to act, from inertia to operation. But this determination of the power in act is not entirely for the sake of action performed or completed; it is also a determination of the agent beginning the action, the very actuality in acting."

Still, if the action *ad extra*, even just as a simple initial modality, is the perfection of the agent, does it not follow that here the mover is moved precisely as a mover, which is in violation of the principle of causality? John of St. Thomas replies: "We say that it does not follow that the agent is being moved inasmuch as it acts, but only that, inasmuch as it acts, it moves. To the extent that the agent is in potency and indifferent to acting, it needs to be moved to pass from inactivity to action; and the novelty causes some motion in the agent, not as agent but as going from inactivity to act. Indeed, the agent is hardly affected by transitive action, because this action terminates in the patient, not in the agent. To the extent, therefore, that the agent is changed by that action to pass from idleness to action, from potentiality to actuality, *this must be due to another agent*, namely God, who ultimately controls all created agents and moves them not inasmuch as they act but inasmuch as they are in potency to act."

[22] John of St. Thomas, *Curs. th.* I, disp. 4, a. 4 (S, I, 469A): "The actuality of the form and the actuality of being or existence are quite different. The form is the act that constitutes something in a determined genus and species, and so by its very nature sets the limits of its perfection. *Esse* or existence, on the other hand, in its proper and formal concept, is not a form that establishes something in a determinate genus and species. Existence sets the thing already determined outside its causes, and perfects it thus by its actuality. True, we take and measure the perfection of existence by the natures or essences to which it is linked. For example, we consider the existence of a man more perfect than the existence of a rock. But the formal concept of existence bespeaks an actuality that removes the potentiality by which something is kept within its causes, and so it places it outside its causes. The concept of existence does not imply any composition of the genus and the specific difference of a thing, its quiddity. It is an actuality outside of the quiddity, because it does not bespeak an essential connection with any creature but is present exclusively by divine participation."

to be, common to all things that do not imply contradiction. This point cannot be made too strongly: the potency stemming from the internal relations of their specific characteristics is a property common to all things possible and in no sense involves what is original in each species. If existence completes essence, it does so *in the universal order of being*, not on the level of specific constitutions. This is why an affirmative answer to the question of whether a thing exists (*an sit res*) tells us nothing about its nature. The certainty that a particular object of thought really exists assures us only that we are dealing with a real object of thought, i.e., with a possible thing; it does not give us even a hint about what kind of thing it is (*quid sit res*).

In order to know what a thing is, we look at its activity. For minds that do not grasp essences directly and intuitively, that is the only way. But is it is also a perfectly safe way, because if it is true that activity (at least in created beings) is a terminal act really distinct from existence, a thing's action fulfills it precisely on the plane of the specific nature, the essence, or the quiddity. Thus from the characteristics of the action observed, our mind spontaneously infers the characteristics of the acting nature, and metaphysical deduction establishes the legitimacy of this inference. This entire procedure may be summarized as follows. Proceeding analytically, first we recognize two kinds of apparently irreducible realities that reveal the characteristics of the terminal act—existence and action. Then, proceeding synthetically from the primary object of metaphysical thought, namely, being as being, we also recognize that every finite being, because of the duality of the principles that it includes, has two possibilities of fulfillment: one of them opens on the act of being; the other is deployed on the level of essences. The first is accomplished in existence; the second, in activity, which we are now able to define more precisely as *the terminal act that fulfills the active nature in accordance with its specific constitution.*[23]

---

[23] John of St. Thomas, *Curs. th.* I, disp. 4, a. 4 (S, I, 471B). In reply to objections against the Thomistic thesis on the absolute primacy of existence with respect to essence, the author writes: "The answer is that the perfection and worthiness of things can be looked at in two ways. It can be looked at in terms of their generic and specific differences, and in this respect created natures have their hierarchy, some being better and more perfect than others.

THIRD (TRANSCENDENTAL) DEFINITION OF ACTION

But there is more to be said. The above formula, rather than clarifying its proper nature, gives us no more than a basis for constructing a comprehensive notion of action. To arrive at a truly general definition of action, we need to return once again to the analysis of ordinary thought as it arises spontaneously from experience.

As already pointed out, of all the realities that may be called actions, common sense and ordinary language are most willing to consider as unquestionably such the transitive actions identified with change. We call the political leader who is introducing many important reforms a man of action; if he then becomes satisfied just to keep the system going, we say that he is now preserving rather than acting. Yet to preserve is also to exercise efficient causality, to engage in transitive action. How are we to account for this difference in interpretation?

Well, one reason for it is that we do not pay much attention to the actions of a head of state unless they bear the mark of his personality, unless we can see clearly that the observed effects

---

But the perfection and worthiness of things can also be looked at not in terms of degrees of difference between genera and species, but with respect to the contrast between actuality and potentiality, which is a difference in status rather than a difference in degree. In the first case, worthiness and perfection refer to the intrinsic, essential form that constitutes a thing. But in the second case, any thing is deemed worthy and perfect not insofar as it has a given form but rather insofar as it has actuality in being. Thus even though their entire essential and constitutive perfection lies there in their potencies, all things are perfected by the actuality of existence, because it is existence that sets them outside their causes, and because without existence they remain literally nothing." Now, as far as action is concerned we understand that it plays its role as an ultimate act within the hierarchical order of natures and essences. Ibid., 472B: "The worthiness and perfection of action as of nature are understood in terms of essential perfections, because operation follows upon the specific degree of perfection of the agent. But it is existence that gives value and perfection *in the formal order of being*, since it sets the entire perfection of any essence and nature (regardless of degree) outside of nothingness and outside its causes." Ibid., disp. 4, a. 1 (Vivès, III, 219A): "The inclinations of things are not consequences of existence, as existence, but of the forms that constitute their nature. Thus different natures specify inclinations to different ends. But upon this specific and essential being given to things by their forms there descends the being of existence, which rather than supplying them with their constitutions draws things outside their causes."

have their origin in him. The life of a state in which there are few noteworthy changes seems to proceed less from the leader than from the nation. The term *active* is attributed par excellence to the agent who draws from his depths an effect that no other can produce. Those are called active who take initiatives, preferably of the kind that others would not have taken.

Ordinary language reveals a similar perspective, the relevant differences being kept in mind, with regard to immanent activities. Just think of the common distinction of psychological facts under the headings of knowledge, affection, and activity. Though it would be wrong to insist that this represents an ontological division of the powers of the soul, this classification rests on sound observations, which make it quite useful in contexts other than the ontological. For instance, willing is an immanent activity, and if it looks more like action than either knowing or desiring does, it is not only because willing is closer to transitive activity, commanding as it does the most important of our external acts. Willing is for us the same as acting, because in free volition the self is in a special way the principle from which its determination issues. When our intellect confronts its object, it is not up to us to recognize or not to recognize that object; nor is it up to us to cause or withhold attraction in our sense appetite in the presence of things desirable. But in free volition, the person is the master of his determination, and in it we all experience a uniquely intense feeling of *activity*.

But let us also note that even though there is no freedom of choice in cognitive processes, we can and do speak of them as being active or passive. For instance, when a student is satisfied simply to accept what his teacher or textbooks tell him, we call him passive. But when a student makes an effort to review the evidence of the demonstrations on his own, so that the judgment in which his intellectual labor terminates issues truly and profoundly from himself, we honor and praise him for his "active mind."

Thus whether in transitive or in immanent activities, the idea of activity is intimately linked to the recognition of the origin, of the derivation, emanation, or processing, of something. The notion of activity becomes clearer and is accompanied by more intense emotional certainty as that activity is recognized more clearly as an emanation. Therefore, born in the womb of the acting nature, action may be said to be an *emanating terminal act*, standing in an "AB" (from) relation to the potency which it fulfills.[24]

By contrast, existence does not proceed in any way from the nature that it brings into being. The non-existent nature is but a shadow of reality in nothingness, and of itself it can do nothing to become incarnate.[25] Being, the spouse of nature, so to speak, always comes to their encounter from the outside. Therefore, received from without, existence may be said to be the terminal act that fulfills any nature through a special "IN" (in) relation.

---

[24] Thomas Aquinas, *De pot.*, q. 1, a. 1, ad 1; q. 7, a. 9, ad 7; q. 8, a. 2; *De ver.*, q. 8, a. 6; q. 4, a. 2: "In speaking of divine persons, we find certain expressions that imply origin, not in reality, but only according to our manner of thinking. For while *operation* certainly implies *something proceeding from an operant*, [in God] this procession is only according to our manner of thinking." John of St. Thomas, *Phil. nat.* IV, q. 1, a. 1 (R, III, 138B2) (referring to the Aristotelian definition of the soul as the first act of an organized body): "And so the second act, which is operation, is excluded [from the definition], not only because it is in the nature of accident, but also because it is an emanation from some agent, who must be prior to it." Ibid., IV, q. 2, a. 2 (R, III, 70B20) (commenting on the real distinction between substance and its operative powers): "It is impossible that the substance itself be the proximate operative power if we posit that operation is an accident, as we must do for creatures, since *it is an emanation from them, which sometimes takes place and sometimes does not.*" *Curs. th.* I, disp. 16, a. 2 (Vivès, II, 438ff.). In creatures, operation is the terminal act of an initial act, and it is an emanation from the one acting (*egressio ab operante*). In God, there is no distinction between initial and terminal act, but the idea of emanation is preserved in divine activity *virtually and eminently* rather than *formally.*" Ibid., disp. 4, a. 2 (Vivès, III, 232A): "We have said that the nature of operation and of its principle in His understanding is present in God in an eminent way, and we say this not on the basis of a distinction between the first and the second act but by distinguishing between the principle and the emanation of the operation from Him. The distinction between first and second act is contrary to the concept of pure act that has to be retained in all our concepts of God's attributes. Even the distinction between principle and emanation would be contrary to the simplicity and unity of God if we held it to be real. But its eminent and virtual presence is not repugnant to Him because His supereminent perfection realizes in one single essence whatever we find multiplied through the distinction of creatures." Ibid., I–II, disp. 1, a. 3 (Vivès, V, 47A): "Action is essentially an emanation from its principle."

[25] This is to speak metaphorically, for in reality the non-existent nature possesses not even a shadow of reality; except as prefigured in the divine understanding, it is nothing.

FOURTH (TRANSCENDENTAL) DEFINITION OF ACTION

What we have to do now, however, is to examine more carefully the nature of the emanation implied in all activity to decide whether this emanation is realized in the same way in immanent and in transitive activity.

In some purely logical emanations, there is no distinction among the emanating effect, that from which it emanates, and the emanation itself. But except for God, activity in all things is an accident really distinct both from the nature acting and from its existence.

Moreover, there are also real emanations that do not imply ontological dependence of the term emanation on its principle. Faith teaches us that the person of the Son proceeds really from the person of the Father, and the Holy Spirit from the Father and the Son, without there being any relation of dependence or subordination among the divine persons. With that exception, a relation of efficient causality seems implicated in every activity.[26] And the best way to understand what that means is to examine the problem of the efficient cause of action itself.

The two realities that emanate or can emanate from the terminal act of the efficient cause are effect and action. The effect proceeds from its cause *by means of* a transitive action, which is the intermediary through which the effect flows from its source to its term. The transitive action itself, however, proceeds immediately from its cause, for if the subject acting produced its action

---

[26] That is why activity, in whatever its notion adds to the notion of actuality, is attributed to God only *virtualiter et eminenter*. Divine activity, identical with the being of God—and in the language of Trinitarian speculation not a notional but an essential predicate—excludes any real emanation, for such would destroy the formality of His concept. John of St. Thomas, *Curs. th.* I, disp. 16, a. 2 (Vivès, II, 438B). (Let us note that considered as the terminal act of an initial act activity cannot be attributed to God in any way, not even virtually.) "Moreover, if one takes into consideration not what belongs to the second and final act but what belongs to the emanation from an operating principle, what is found in God is not any formal principle from which an operation issues, but rather eminently and virtually whatever perfections created things have from the operations issuing from their principles." Ibid., 440A. "But if in that understanding we do not consider what belongs to the ultimate actuality in the intelligible order, but rather what belongs to an operation issuing from its principle, then we say that this is not to be found formally in God, but is there virtually and eminently." Ibid., 444–45.

by another distinct action, we would have an infinite regression of intermediary actions between the cause and its action. Moreover, action by any created efficient cause cannot be attributed in its entirety to the created efficient cause from which it so proceeds without any intermediary. As a reality distinct from the subject acting, to which it does not belong by identity, action can be joined to it only by a separate cause. Therefore, to explain the union of any created cause with its action, we have to call upon a higher cause whose causality is exercised unconditionally and whose action belongs to it by pure identity. This is how we establish the theory of physical premotion and recognize its connection with the theory of creation. For just as the thing distinguishable from its actual existence cannot, of itself, place itself in existence or preserve itself there, so the being that does not have its action by identity cannot, by itself, join itself to its action. It is just as impossible to claim that an agent really distinct from its action can act without the divine concurrence as it is to claim that a contingent being can exist without having been created.

In the purity of its conception, immanent action implies no term distinct from itself. Here there is only a single emanating reality, namely, action, and the efficient cause of this reality can be none other than the acting subject. Immanent action proceeds really from its subject, on which it depends and to which it is bound by what we have called an "AB" relation. But what that dependence, direct emanation, and "AB" relation amount to is precisely a case of efficient causality.[27] The efficient act by which the agent produces its immanent action is incorporated in the latter without constituting it in its specificity. Thus what acts of thought or of volition may be said to "produce" is something that is basically indistinguishable from those acts themselves.

In view of all this, then, activity may finally be defined as *a terminal act emanating by way of an efficiency with which it is identified without being necessarily absorbed in it*. It is a definition that nicely confirms the insights of common-sense thought revealed in the ordinary use of language. We reserve the term *active* for those

---

[27] Cajetan, *In De an.* II, 6 (B. 114B); John of St. Thomas, *Phil. nat.* I, q. 13, a. 2 (R, II, 282B24); q. 14, a. 3 (R, II, 309A34); Gredt, *Unsere Aussenwelt*, pp. 125–26; *Xenia thomistica* I, p. 315.

whose life is spent in producing external effects precisely because transitive action alone qualifies as efficiency formally considered. But we also speak of *acts* of thought and of will because these immanent activities, too, are produced by efficient causality. Moreover, we attribute the character of activity more readily to making decisions than to acquiring knowledge or having desires precisely because in the act of free choice the soul is the efficient cause of its determination not once but twice: first by nature, and a second time by reason of its freedom. Finally, we can see how even in matters of cognition we distinguish between active behavior and passive behavior as a kind of shorthand for distinguishing degrees of involvement. For there is no doubt that the soul is the efficient cause of its cognitive determination in proportion to the alertness of its faculties and the functioning of the will that moves the intellect.

Though the idea of efficient causality is thus common to both these kinds of action, their unity is imperfect and analogical. For there is no generic unity between an efficient act whose entire essence consists in efficiency and another efficient act whose specific character consists rather in immanent perfection. It is true that both transitive and immanent actions emanate from the subject that performs them as terminal acts of an efficient cause; that is what they have in common. But this common element is, in the two cases, affected by irreducible differences. In the case of transitive action, the terminal act of the efficient cause does what efficiency is supposed to do: lead to a term distinct from itself. In immanent action, that does not happen. Hence, it is *in* itself and in *its essential idea* that this common element is modified, and this intrinsic differentiation between these two kinds of action absolutely rules out the formation of a univocal concept. Transitive action is efficiency. But even though it includes efficiency, immanent action is not efficiency; it belongs in the category of quality.

ACTION AND QUALITY

If prime matter could exist without form, it would appear to an observer, if it could be observed, as an ocean of indetermination that is indefinitely the same. Diversity is the result of determination. What causes a thing to be such and such also makes it different from everything else.

The two elements that constitute the corporeal substance, form and prime matter, show their characteristics in its internal attributes, namely, its quantity and quality. Quantity is uniformity, homogeneity; when we move from one part of the quantitative whole to another part, remaining strictly within the order of quantity, we pass from the same to the same. The reason for this is that quantity is related to a substance not on account of its particular form but on account of its matter, which, despite all its determinations, shares in the uniform clay of which all lower things are made. By contrast, the parts of a qualitative whole are all different from each other. The powers of the soul form a whole, but the will does not resemble the sense of touch; courage does not resemble mercy. Just as the specific form is what, in the order of substance, causes a being to be this or that, so quality proceeding from the primary form is what, in the order of accident, causes a being to be precisely such and such.[28] The broader use of the term quality, which is often applied to whole species, confirms this analogy.

Immanent activity has all the characteristics of quality. It is a

---

[28] Aristotle, *Categ.*, 8, 8b25: "By 'quality' I mean that in virtue of which people are said to be such and such." In his famous logical deduction of the categories (*In Meta.* V, lect. 9 [C. 891ff.), Aquinas states that an attribute belongs to the category of quality when it is related to the subject in such a way as to express a reality inhering in it, absolute, and derived from its form: "For it should be noted that a predicate can be referred to a subject in three ways. This occurs in one way when the predicate states what the subject is, as when I say that Socrates is an animal. A predicate is referred to a subject in a second way when the predicate is taken as being in the subject, and this predicate is in the subject either essentially and absolutely as something consequent on its matter and then it is quantity; or as something consequent on its form, and then it is quality; or it is not present in the subject absolutely but with reference to something else, and then it is relation." There is a similar analysis in *In Phys.* III, lect. 5, and in *Sum. th.* I–II, q. 49, a. 2: "For quality properly speaking implies a certain mode of substance. Now, a mode, as Augustine says, is that which a measure determines; hence it implies a certain determination according to a certain measure. Therefore, just as that in accordance with which the potency of matter is determined to its substantial being is called quality, which is a difference affecting substance, so that in accordance with which the potency of the subject is determined to its accidental being is called an accidental quality, which is also a kind of difference." *Sum. th.* I, q. 28, a. 2; III, q. 90, a. 2; John of St. Thomas, *Log.* II, q. 18, a. 1 (R, I, 609Aff.).

reality that is completely within the acting subject and well suited to introduce into it many different modalities, which cannot be reduced to any sort of uniform pattern. Immanent activity is what by intrinsic determination of the terminal act makes one be a particular kind of person, actually good or bad, sad or happy, intentionally possessing this or that object. Indeed, though this qualitative nature of immanent action is nicely revealed in desire, it shows up even better in the case of cognition where all that matters is to exist as qualified by the object.[29]

The category of quality, however, includes several very different kinds of realities that need to be distinguished from one another.[30] As far as immanent activity is concerned, two things are certain. Because of its spiritual character, immanent activity differs from all those qualities that for whatever reason require

---

[29] I know of no text in which Aristotle or Aquinas addresses specifically the question of whether immanent action belongs to the category of action or to the category of quality. (The text quoted by John of St. Thomas, Op. 48, *Summa totius logicae Aristotelis* is not authentic.) No importance should be attached to this, however, because Aquinas never tires of saying that immanent action lacks the characteristics that the whole Aristotelian school considers to be the essential properties of the category of action: to exist with motion, to produce a passion, to be the perfection of the patient. Indeed, one would have to be rather obtuse to assume that anything could be preserved of the Thomistic theory of knowledge if immanent action were to be placed in the category of action. All major Thomists are unanimous in affirming that immanent action is a quality. The contrary is held by some minor Thomists and para-Thomists, which makes for an interesting distinction.

Cajetan, *In De an.* II, 5 (B. 114B): "It is only grammatically that immanent actions are called actions; in reality they are operations that are truly kinds of qualities." Sylvester of Ferrara, *In Cont. gent.* II, 9: "Immanent action does not belong to the genus of action but to the genus of quality." Javellus, *Compendium logicae, De praedicamentis*; Bañez, *In Sum. th.* I, q. 79, a. 2 (D, II, 290A): "The act of intellection is not an action but a quality, though it may have the mode of an action." The subject receives magisterial treatment in breadth and in depth by John of St. Thomas. See, in particular, *Phil. nat.* IV, q. 6, a. 4 (R, III, 195B41) (the text is quoted below, in note 46), and q. 11, a. 1 (R, III, 344B) (see below, chap. 3, n. 54); also *Log.* II, q. 18, a. 2 (R, I, 613B16); q. 19, aa. 1, 2 (R, I, 622B19, 626B25); *Phil. nat.* I, q. 12, a. 4 (R, II, 265B21); q. 14, a. 3 (R, II, 308A24).

[30] Aristotle, *Categ.*, 8, 8B26: "Quality is a term that is used in many senses." There follows the well-known division of quality into four genera: habitus and disposition, capability and incapability, affective quality and affection, and figure and shape. For a discussion of the principles and value of this division, see Thomas Aquinas, *Sum. th.* I–II, q. 49, a. 2; John of St. Thomas, *Log.* II, q. 18, a. 2 (R, I, 610B46).

material support. And because its nature is that of a terminal act, immanent activity also differs from all those qualities that in any way imply potentiality. These exclusions suggest that as a quality immanent activity may be a special kind of disposition.

The term "disposition," or "arrangement" (*diathesis*), brings to mind first of all the idea of several things in definite spatial relations with one another. The fruit vendor begins the day by arranging her fruit not haphazardly but rather by kind, apples with apples, cherries with cherries, etc. She is concerned with producing the handsomest arrangement, even though she might not know a great deal about relations of volume and color. If she succeeds in making an attractive display, we shall say that her stall is well arranged. If, by negligence, damaged fruit end up in front and on top, we shall say that the display is badly arranged. And if it were possible for a vendor to be so clumsy as to pile up different kinds of fruit at random, we would have to say that she never bothered to arrange her display.

Going beyond spatial imagination, we understand by disposition any order, systematization, arrangement, or organization of the parts of a whole.[31] It is not just any sort of distribution, as might result from some kind of casual gesture; it is a purposeful distribution, set out with a view to an end. We judge the arrangement of the fruit at the fruit stand with regard to whether the display is more or less likely to attract buyers. Thus every disposition of the parts of a whole is either good or bad precisely because disposition is relative to an end, whether the parts involved are fruits displayed in a stall or divisions of an army deployed in battle.

---

[31] Aristotle, *Meta.* V, 19, 1022B1; Thomas Aquinas, *In Meta.* V, lect. 20 (C. 1058ff.): "Aristotle gives the common meaning of this term, saying that a disposition is nothing else than the order of parts in a thing that has parts. He also gives the three senses in which the term disposition is used. The first designates the order of parts in place, and in this sense disposition or posture is a special category. Disposition is used in a second sense as the order of parts is considered in reference to power or virtue, and then disposition is placed in the first species of quality. For a thing is said to be disposed in this sense, for example, as healthy or sick, by reason of the fact that its parts have an order in its active or passive power. Disposition is used in a third sense according as the order of parts is considered in reference to the form and figure of the whole; and then disposition or position is held to be a difference in the genus of quantity."

These exemplary characteristics of disposition arrived at inductively are confirmed also by metaphysical analysis. The sheer fact that a thing is composed of parts and that it is possible to distinguish within it a real plurality of essences (incomplete and accidental essences, to be sure, whose real distinction leaves the substantial unity of the whole untouched) tells us that it contains an obstacle to its perfection. This plurality of parts is like an inner enemy that must be overcome before any other; it is like a weight laden with indifference or potentiality that must be lifted before that thing can attain its end. Surely, the perfection of a whole has to be, in one way or another, single or unique: if the whole is one, so also must its act be. But the whole includes a plurality of parts and, precisely to the extent that they are several, the parts remain indifferent to the perfection of the whole. The function of disposition is to establish an order among them that will overcome this indifference. By disposition harmony is introduced into the plurality of parts which will enable them to cooperate for the good of the whole. Victory is promised to the army that marches as one man. But to make an army act as it must to be victorious is not easy. The thousands of men who make up an army are more than likely inclined to follow each his own whim, which may have nothing to do with the end pursued by the army. Consequently, the first task of a commander is to overcome this obstacle for the good of the army, which arises from the sheer fact that an army includes a multitude, and he does that by assigning each man his proper task.

To make it easier to talk about it, we have been using examples in which the unity of the whole is accidental, each of the parts retaining is substantial integrity. But the metaphysical notion of disposition applies to all kinds of wholes with parts. It is relevant to the understanding of a whole that is substantially one, such as the living body, and it is relevant to the understanding of a dynamic whole, in which the plurality of parts does not imply the location of the parts outside each other. For instance, considered in its natural state, so to speak, before any acquisition of knowledge or moral qualities, a particular faculty of the human mind presents a plurality of possibilities or dynamic parts which, because they are not yet reduced to unity by a disposition, constitute an interior obstacle to the perfection of the faculty. Thus the will may prefer either material goods or spiritual goods, may make either lust or friendship prevail within itself. The intellect, likewise, may consider things either in their true light or in a false light, may attach itself either to more fruitful or less fruitful aspects of reality. Each of these possibilities, the dynamic parts of these faculties, does exactly what soldiers in a disorganized army do: it pushes and pulls in its own direction, without any concern for the good of the whole. And so, for the good of the faculty, a disposition must intervene to put these dynamic parts in order, just as the commander-in-chief organizes and deploys his divisions with a view to winning the battle. The possibilities inherent in the intellect having to do with theoretical knowledge, with moral activity, and with material production are put in order through the stable dispositions we call science, prudence, and art. By overcoming the initial plurality of possibilities that blocked from the inside the pursuit of its ends, these dispositions enable the intellect to perform its acts with ease and joy. The moral virtues of temperance, courage, and justice do the same for the will.[32]

---

[32] Aristotle, *Meta.* V, 20, 1022B4; Thomas Aquinas, *Sum. th.* I–II, q. 49, a. 2. John of St. Thomas, *Curs. th.* I–II, disp. 13, a. 1 (Vivès, VI, 242B) shows that habitus is essentially defined with reference to something in the acting subjects, rather than with reference to some act or effect. He establishes this thesis from an analysis of the idea of disposition, since habitus is but an essentially stable qualitative disposition. "This proof is derived *a priori* from the very function of a disposition, which is to determine or order something toward a particular form, or to obtain some end, or not lose it. And so Aristotle says in the fifth book of *Metaphysics*, chap. 19, that *disposition* is the arrangement of that which has parts. And this is to be understood not only of quantitative or material parts, but also of the parts that make for quality. So wherever a certain multiplicity has to be arranged in some order, or reduced in some way, there is need for a disposition. . . . If, therefore, the proper function of a disposition is to arrange for and provide a determination to some end, it is necessary to consider how this function is located in the subject, i.e., well or poorly; for any ordering to some form or end clearly implies appropriateness or inappropriateness. . . . Consequently, disposition is called an order among parts, that is, their fitting or correct positioning. Thus even among the powers of the soul, as with regard to any other kind of things which have to be set down, located, or determined, there is need for a disposition. Because a faculty may chose indifferently among several things, acts, or forms, some further determination must be added to it. . . . But to be so determined and ordered is to be disposed, namely, to have parts positioned and arranged with a view to how their order would fit a form or an end. Here the question of correct, i.e., good, or incorrect, i.e., bad, measurement cannot be avoided."

These habitual dispositions of the active faculties are not, however, ultimate determinations. The scientist not actually thinking about what he knows, or the just man not at the moment rendering someone his due, remain, in relation to the act of scientific thought, or in relation to the just act of the will, in a state of potency. Thus, although its dynamic parts have been perfectly disposed and reduced to unity as far as is possible without going beyond the limits of potency, a particular faculty falls short of being a fully united whole until it executes its terminal act. The scientist who relaxes his mind by playing bridge has the potency to think of an infinity of objects; his intellect, disposed for theorizing, remains open to a multitude of possibilities; and this multitude of dynamic parts will be reduced to unity only by his turning his mind to a particular scientific object. And if it is true that this act is a quality, we have to think of it as a disposition, as *the supreme ordering of the dynamic parts of a vital faculty in relation to its end actually possessed.*[33]

The conclusion to which we are driven by this analysis is that the immanent activity of knowing combines in a wondrous union two antinomic characteristics. On the one hand, it is a qualitative perfection consisting simply in a disposition. To know modifies the knowing faculty only by an arrangement of its possibilities; beyond this disposition there is present in cognition only the intentional object, which neither alters nor is altered by the faculty. One cannot conceive anything more delicate or more intimate than the modification of the subject in the act of knowing. While nothing could be farther from alteration by way of a contrary, there is yet no contact more radical and penetrating than that of a knowing mind with its object. Because its delicacy and depth are so perfect, the quality of knowing is a masterpiece of interiority. On the other hand, does not cognition imply more than just efficiency, or active causality, which we usually

---

[33] John of St. Thomas, *Log.* II, q. 18, a. 2 (R, I, 613B16, 613B32). "From what has been said, it is clear that this division (i.e., of quality) is adequate and complete. Besides habitus and dispositions, which manifestly are what these terms mean, all immanent acts and concepts, as well as impressed ideas, are reduced to the first species; they are good or bad dispositions of powers according as they represent their object successfully or not." Ibid., q. 19, a. 2 (R, I, 627A18); *Phil. nat.* IV, q. 11, a. 1 (R, III, 346A); Javellus, *Compendium logicae, De praedicamentis.*

associate with things exterior? The answer is that "to know" includes this efficiency, not as a reality presupposed and distinct from itself, but in the supremely intimate bond of absence of real distinction. The importance of the insight opened by this notion of an activity that resembles both efficiency and quality, so clearly separated in the rest of the world, cannot be over-emphasized. The one who knows moves himself in his inner-most depths in order to give himself over to the object and attain thereby his final perfection, which is identical with that activity that he exercises on himself.

MOTIONLESS ACTIVITY

The theory of immanent activity allows us to understand better the problem of the relations between activity and change. First of all, we note that although efficiency does not necessarily imply mobility, change appears by contrast to be an essential property of transitive action. The subject of transitive action, as the receiver of its effect rather than its producer, is an imperfect being that has to wait for its completion until the transitive action exercised upon it is ended. And when this happens, the action belongs in the past.[34] Work is done only upon what is incom-plete, considered precisely in its incompleteness and to the extent that it demands further perfection. Thus transitive action appears necessarily related to imperfect being to the extent that it is imperfect—which is the very definition of change.[35]

Immanent action, on the other hand, is essentially resistant to any kind of mobility. Once a truth has been discovered, the intel-lect does not cease knowing it, as the workman must stop work-ing when a particular job is done; nor does the heart, in posses-

---

[34] For grammar, perfect means past; the reason is that language knows tran-sitive action best.

[35] Thomas Aquinas, *Cont. gent.* III, 22: "In one kind of operation a thing moves another, as for example in heating or cutting. It is another kind of operation when a thing is moved by another, e.g., when it is being heated or cut. But there is still a third kind of operation, which is not passivity, not motion, not alteration of external matter, but consists rather in the perfection of the agent himself already in act. Understanding, sensing, and willing are operations of this sort."

71

sion of its object, stop loving it.[36] Contemplation and joy are above time, because they are above change.[37] Of course, it is true that human intelligence proceeds by way of *discourse* and that human desire involves *effort*. But the discourse of our reason and the striving of our will—spiritual images, as it were, of mobility—share in the nature of becoming not as immanent activities but rather because of the imperfection of our spiritual faculties. We reason only because our knowledge is insufficient; we desire the good only because we do not fully possess it. Stripped of these accidental imperfections, knowing is the act of a perfect subject and so also is loving.

The main reason why people have trouble grasping the notion of motionless activity is that the primary object of our intelligence, after all, is material reality. And yet this notion of an

---

[36] The concept of motionless (immanent) activity plays a primary role in the metaphysics and ethics of Aristotle. *On the Soul* I, 3, 407A32; III, 7, 431A4: "In the case of sense, clearly the sensitive faculty already was potentially what the object makes it to be actually; the faculty is not affected or altered. This must therefore be different from movement, for movement is, as we saw, an activity of what is imperfect, [but] activity in the unqualified sense, i.e., of what has been perfected, is different from movement." *On Sense and Sensible Objects*, 6, 446B2; *Ethics* VII, 14, 1154B26: "There is not only an activity of movement but an activity of immobility." *Meta.* IX, 6, 1048B28: "For every movement is incomplete—reducing, learning, walking, building; these are movements, and incomplete at that. For it is not true that at the same time a thing is walking and has walked, or is building and has built, or is coming to be and has come to be, or is being moved and has been moved, but what is being moved is different from what has been moved, and what is moving from what has moved. But it is the same thing that at the same time has seen and is seeing, or is thinking and has thought. The latter sort of process, then, I call an actuality, and the former movement." See also Léon Brunschvicg, *L'Expérience humaine et la causalité physique* (Paris: Alcan, 1922), p. 153. Thomas Aquinas, *In De an.* I, lect. 6 (P. 82); lect. 8 (P. 125–26); III, lect. 12 (P. 765); *Sum. th.* I, q. 14, a. 2, ad 2; q. 18, a. 1; *Cont. gent.* I, 13; Cajetan, *In De an.* III, 3 (B. 235A); John of St. Thomas, *Phil. nat.* I, q. 14, a. 1 (R, II, 296A24). We must point out, however, that sometimes Aquinas uses the term *motion*, which in its strict sense designates the act of an imperfect subject, to designate any kind of operation, even the immanent act of a perfect subject. *Sum. th.* I, q. 9, a. 1; ibid., ad 3; q. 50, a. 1, ad 2; q. 53, a. 1, ad 2; ibid., ad 3; q. 58, a. 1, ad 1; q. 59, a. 1, ad 3; q. 73, a. 2; I–II, q. 31, a. 2, ad 1; II–II, q. 180, a. 6; III, q. 21, a. 1, ad 3. But Aquinas also explains that the analogy that allows us to call the acts of the intellect motions is only a metaphor. *In De an.* I, lect. 10 (P. 160).

[37] Thomas Aquinas, *Sum. th.* I–II, q. 31, a. 2: "And so we must say that of its very nature, joy is not in time; for it concerns good already gained, which is, as it were, the term of the movement."

activity that coincides with rest refers to nothing other than what emanates continuously from a perfected being. This being is fully at rest, and rather than satisfying some momentary need, its activity represents its own fulfillment. Because most people's minds are not trained to go beyond mental images, their idea of activity is so bound to the idea of change that even when considering the active life of the spirit they spontaneously prefer whatever most closely resembles the dance of atoms or the surging surf. Or to put it in another way: they imagine all activity to be like work, and they confuse rest with idleness. They thus recognize only the imperfect joy of effort, dreading the repose either of contemplation or of true love, which to them appears as emptiness, ennui, and death of desire. To truth without research they prefer research without truth; to Abraham's bosom they prefer the allure of earthly glory.

Finally, concerning production unaccompanied by change, such as God's creative and conserving activity, we need to understand that what it involves has nothing to do with transitive action but represents rather efficiency wrapped up in wholly immanent activity. Every divine action is identical with the being of God and is consequently immanent in the highest degree. The universe is thus simply the result of divine superabundance and adds nothing to the creative action that is God. His activity in the first six days is identical in God with His rest on the seventh.

VITALITY

Art imitates Creation, and we think that is succeeds when the work it brings into existence is characterized by plenitude, originality, and boldness, all of which are marks of the divine art. Then we say that this work is *alive*. Surely, a painter of a *still life* would be insulted if we intimated that his painting lacked vitality. For if is is not alive, the work of any artist is a failure.

Thus, to indicate that something is very real, well made, and true to the idea that gave it birth, there is no term more expressive than life. The reason is that, since every natural being is endowed with some sort of activity, any work of art that leaves the impression of inertness is judged an abortive production in which the image of Creation cannot be recognized. Better to convey this feeling of activity, which has been spontaneously adopted as the criterion of successful creation, of true being, we use all sorts of words that refer to the highest kind of activity, life. And that is how—because beauty endows being with splendor, and there is no more splendid kind of activity than life—in the poetic contemplation of the world whatever is active is imagined to be alive.

Of course, we know better than to take literally the language of the poets meant to express beauty when we have to address seriously questions of being and truth. For while all things are indeed active, not every activity is life. A datum of common sense, this distinction between animate and inanimate is verified by both science and philosophy, each of which elaborates on it in its own way.

Significantly, our speech manages to enlarge as well as to restrict the application of the idea of life. We say that plants live and die, and we thus distinguish them from inanimate things. But we also restrict the application of the name *animal* to beings that we conceive and treat very differently from plants. And yet there is nothing in the original sense of "animal" that is not present in the term, "animate being." ζῷον has no other root than ζωή, life. Thus if there are several kinds of life, animal life is the one we recognize most easily, and all we have to do to identify the primary intelligible aspect of the idea of life in our mind is to designate that by which we distinguish an animal from a stone or a plant.[38]

Any movement alerts the man who is tracking animals in the

---

[38] Aristotle, *On the Soul* I, 2, 403B25: "Two characteristic marks have above all others been recognized as distinguishing that which has soul in it from that which has not—movement and sensation." Thomas Aquinas, *Sum. th.* I, q. 18. a. 1: "We can gather to what things life belongs and to what it does not from such things as manifestly possess life. Now, life manifestly belongs to animals. . . . and so we must distinguish living from the non-living things by comparing them to that by reason of which animals are said to be live." Albert the Great, *De veg.* I, i, 4: "For in the Greek *living* has the same meaning as *animal*: for ζῷον means animal and ζῶν is the same as alive, and so the term living seems convertible with animal and non-living with non-animal. Moreover, since there is no intermediate state between living and non-living, it seems plausible to hold that every living thing is an animal, and what is not animal is not living. That is why many Greek and Latin writers said that because it is not an animal, a plant is not alive."

forest, but sometimes what the hunter thinks is game is only a branch rustling in the creek. The difference expressed in daily speech is that an animal moves *when it wants to*, whereas a branch moves only when a current of water or a gust of wind makes it move. Anthropomorphism aside, it is evident that animals move themselves. The source of their motion is in themselves, in contrast to other things that are moved by impulses from without.

This, then, appears to be the first intelligible object on which our idea of life is based: a local movement originating in the being that moves, combining the mover and the movable in a single individual. But local movement, albeit clearest to us, is only one kind of change. For even though they are apparently stationary, unless some external force intervenes, plants have a life of their own, which consists of movement the source of which is within them. The change from a grain of wheat to a plant is an internal development brought about primarily by that grain of wheat itself. This is one of the reasons why in agriculture, in contrast with industry, one does not expect miracles.

Thus the notion of life, which arises first of all at the sight of a local movement by a being that moves itself, extends generally also to all changes completed within the subject from which they are understood to proceed. But when, on the metaphysical level, we replace the notion of change with that of *actuality*—change being only one kind of actuality—we arrive at a more comprehensive understanding of life as being the power to confer upon oneself some kind of actuality, to act upon oneself, or to give oneself one's appropriate perfection.[39]

---

[39] Plato, *Phaedrus*, 245E: "A body deriving its motion from a source within itself is animate or besouled" (trans. R. Hackforth). Aristotle, *Phys.* VIII, 4, 255A5: "It is impossible to say that their motion [light things rising, heavy things falling] is derived from themselves: this is a characteristic of life and peculiar to living things." *On the Soul* II, 1, 412A14: "By life we mean self-nutrition and growth." Ibid., 413A25: "Hence we think of plants also as living, for they are observed to possess in themselves an originative power through which they increase or decrease in all spatial directions." *On the Movement of Animals*, 4, 700A16: "All things without life are moved by another, and the origin of all things so moved are things which move themselves." Let us note that although he recognizes in animal life the kind that, being the clearest to us, is foremost in the formation of our ideas, Aristotle is far from holding, as so many modern as well as ancient writers do, that the properties common to life and the privileges, so to speak, of animality (i.e., knowledge and desire)

The indispensable metaphysical minimum that permits us to speak of life is, then, the non-fortuitous coincidence of the efficient and of the material or receptive causality in the same individual subject. But if the efficient causality of a particular living subject produces not only the effects that remain within it but also the *predeterminations of its actions*, then what we have is not just life but the realization of a superior degree of vitality.

Every efficient cause that is not identical with its action has to be predetermined with reference to that action. It is impossible to do anything at all unless one knows beforehand what one wants to do. The workman who does not have in his mind a precise idea, a definite exemplar, of what he is going to make, will only botch the job. At the very least, he has to have some idea of what he wants to make so that he can chose appropriate materials and tools. The image of any emerging reality must be inscribed somehow in the source from which that reality emanates; otherwise there is no intelligible reason why this reality rather than some other should emerge. If not preinscribed in its source by some image of itself, the emanation would have to be "nothing in particular." But "nothing in particular" can have no reality, for only what is determined is capable of existence. And that is why before any action can be performed, not only must it have an object but the form of that object must be present in the agent. In the case of transitive action, the object is pursued as an effect; in the case of immanent action, it is something to be contemplated or loved; in either case, for the object to be specified properly, its form must in some way pre-exist in the agent. What this requirement for an objective determina-

---

must necessarily go together. He has a very clear notion of vegetative life, which he distinguishes from other modes of action common to corporeal things. For him, vegetative life represents indeed a *psychic* activity, but only in the sense of being superior to mere material processes, and for this reason he attributes it not to a form but to *the soul*. We must not let this usage confuse us. If the term "psychic" is restricted to designate only what belongs to knowledge and desire (born of knowledge), Aristotle would gladly concede that vegetative activity is completely physical and apsychic. Eduard Zeller, in *Die Philosophie der Griechen* II (Leipzig: Reisland, 1920), p. 498, after quoting several texts on the distinction between plants and animals, comments: "Most of these texts make a special point of the distinction between ζών (the living) and ζώον (animal)."

tion, which covers every kind of action, expresses, then, is precisely the need for any agent to be predetermined formally with
regard to its action, the need for an idea to direct the activity.[40]

---

[40] Aristotle, *On the Soul* II, 4, 415A18: "we must go farther back and first
give an account of thinking or perceiving, for in the order of investigation the
question of what an agent does precedes the question, what enables it to do
what it does. If this is correct, we must on the same ground go yet another step
farther back and have some clear view of the objects of each; thus we must *start*
with these objects, e.g. with food, with what is perceptible, or with what is
intelligible." The specification of an action (and, by way of the action, of the
faculty and the habitus) by its object is a principle found commonly in the
philosophy of Aristotle and Thomas Aquinas. Occasionally, however, Aquinas
also holds that action is specified by the form that initiates it. Thus although in
De ver., q. 20, a. 1, ad 2, he writes: "An activity does not receive its specification
from the agent but from the source of the activity," in *De virt.*, a. 2, ad 3, he
seems to reverse himself when he writes: "Actions are determined by the form
of the agent, as shown, for instance, in the cases of heating and cooling." But
there is really no opposition between these statements if one keeps in mind
that the form or the idea that produces an action is itself dependent, in the
order of formal causality, on the object that it must resemble. *Sum. th.* I, q. 14,
a. 5, ad 3: "For the intellectual act is specified by its object insofar as the intelligible form is the principle of the intellectual operation, since every operation
is specified by the form which is its principle of operation, as heating by heat."
Ibid., q. 85, a. 2: "And as the form from which an act tending to something
external is the likeness of the object of the action, as the heat in the heater is a
likeness of the thing heated, so the form from which an action remaining in
the agent proceeds is the likeness of the object." Sylvester of Ferrara, *In Cont.
gent.* I, 55: "It should be pointed out that just as science assumes a relation to
the knowable, so any action, whether transitive or immanent, assumes a relation to an object. For everything that operates operates by some sort of form,
which is in some manner a likeness of the object in which the operation terminates. In other words, the principle of any operation is a likeness of its object.
This is how St. Thomas explains the act of understanding: the very form by
which the intellect understands is the likeness of what is understood. The act
of understanding the stone has its term in the stone and is elicited by the
likeness of the stone." These comments on the specifying role of the object
and of the active idea as a resemblance of the object permit us to develop an
exact notion of the nature of the proper efficient cause and of the logical
character of explanation by efficient causality. The proper efficient cause of
an effect is that active cause in which is inscribed the idea or the resemblance
of the effect and which operates on the principle of that idea. Here is a crude
example. A man eats salty meat for supper, and as he goes to the well at night
to get a drink, he is killed by an enemy. One could argue that if he had not
eaten the salty food, he would still be alive, but clearly his death cannot be
explained by saying that he ate salty food. The effect, the outcome, the killing
is in no way inscribed in the cause, salty meat. It is inscribed only in the thought
of his enemy, and it is the murderer, not the butcher, who will be charged.
Explanation by efficient causality can also be considered as consisting in

But there is more to it, because one may have plenty of good ideas about what one would like to do without doing anything· about them if one does not like to work. The lazy artist could produce a fine painting—if only he would make up his mind to go to work. If he should decide to paint, this artist would paint one thing rather than another, and he would produce either a good or a bad painting. He could do a landscape rather than a portrait, and he could do a cubist rather than an academic piece. But if he does not have the desire to paint, he will not do anything. And the reason for it is that the possession of artistic talent is in the nature of a simple formal determination, which is not enough to cause action. Over and above the idea of the object that provides its *formal predetermination*, the efficient cause that is really distinct from its action and that brings about the action also needs an *existential predetermination* provided by the desire for an end. An action without a formal object could never appear in existence because of the lack of any kind of form; but without a final cause, an action would still not make it into existence, because there would be no reason for it to appear rather than not to appear.[41] At the term of every action, there is an object and an end; at its beginning, an idea and a tendency.

As pointed out in the previous chapter, it is knowledge alone that can guarantee this preordination of the present with respect

---

identification. By the active idea (whether this be a natural form or a product of cognition) the agent resembles what it produces. The intelligible features of an effect cannot be different from the intelligible features of its proper cause. And here we discover that relation of homogeneity that makes sense of the notion of becoming. It does not matter that becoming must remain somewhat obscure, because a radical explanation of the relation of cause and effect by way of identification forces one to deny all change and leads directly to the conflict between *identity* and *reality.* Following the ways of causal explanation, reason always seeks to show an identification of the diverse (since only what is identical is fully intelligible, all diversity implying potentiality). But in this case, we can easily give up the need for identification pure and simple, and for a very good reason. In this created world, which will never be fully intelligible to us, the difference between cause and effect is a real difference.

[41] The causalities of object and end, very often confused, are nicely distinguished by John of St. Thomas in *Phil. nat.* I, q. 13, a. 1 (R, II, 273в16). The question is about the distinction, *in the good itself,* between the character of the object—*formalis ratio objecti*—and the character of the end. "The answer is that the object and the end are not the same in nature . . . for they differ in both their functions and their relations. The function of the object is to deter-

to the future, of the possible with respect to the actual, without which there can be no effective action of any sort. Of course, we do not attribute thought or will to our machines. But we know that the designers and the engineers, having thought and willed, have built in, so to speak, particular ideas and tendencies into these soulless things. After all, nature itself is an idea and a tendency realized by the divine art in the basic constitution of all created things, as machines are ideas and tendencies built by human art in a secondary disposition of things already basically constituted.[42]

In natural, apsychic, activity the idea that directs the agent and the tendency that moves it are given with the nature of the agent and are in no way attributable to the agent's own causality. The secretion of glucose by one of our organs, and of adrenaline by another, is the result of a law inscribed in these organs, not of something we have prescribed for ourselves. Such activities belong properly to vegetative life. They are natural, they turn back upon themselves, and they have for their goal the perfection of the agent.

---

mine the action as an extrinsic principle on which all actions depend for their specification. Consequently, the object is to be found both in what serves as end and in what does not, that is, in relation to desire as well as in relation to cognition. This is so because all actions receive specification from their object. On the other hand, rather than to specify or determine the constitution of anything, the function of the end is to serve as a term or final goal for those things that require a specific effort or performance to be done. For no one is ever moved to do anything unless he has before him an end of the operation as well as a motive." Ibid., IV, q. 2, a. 3 (R, III, 75B6): "It is evident that every dependence upon an efficient cause is a dependence solely in terms of existence. The efficient cause, as such, is related to the thing solely in terms of existence, for all it does is to set that thing 'outside its causes.' Similarly, all that the final cause does is to move the efficient cause to action, which means that its relation to the effect is in the same order, the order of existence. Indeed, no relation either to an efficient cause or to an end, as such, specifies anything; these relations pertain not to the nature of things but to their existence." Ibid., a. 3 (R, III, 76A33): "To the extent that the end may be said to specify the human act, it does not do so by its causality as an end, but rather by assuming the character of an object. . . . And so the causality or movement arising from the final and efficient causes is one thing, the formalizing and specifying causality of the object is quite another." See also John of St. Thomas, Curs. th. (Vivès, I, 514A).

[42] Thomas Aquinas, In Phys. II, lect. 14, at the end: "Nature is nothing other than the principle of a certain art, i.e., the divine art, inscribed in things, by which those things are moved to a determined end."

What needs to be recognized at this point is that the two pre-determinations of the agent, the need for which we have just established, can also be separated in such a way that one of them springs from the initiative of the agent while the other is decided by nature. Take, for instance, an automatic reflex action in response to some sense stimulus. What the agent will do, the form of that reaction, has been knowingly predetermined by the agent himself; but when the occasion arises, it is nature alone that triggers it by joining to the idea of the object the further note of suitability or goodness. But both predeterminations can also belong to the agent himself, and what we have then is a free agent. The power of deciding that a particular object knowingly proposed by the agent himself is good or bad, the power of joining or separating the formal and the existential predetermination of one's actions, of giving one's self a goal to be reached by one's own power—that is what we call liberty. Thus the mind alone, we learn, is the cause of its perfection in every order of causality, and only beings who have minds can be said to be fully alive.[43]

---

[43] Thomas Aquinas, *Sum. th.* I, q. 18, a. 3: "Accordingly, there are things that move themselves not in respect of any form or end naturally inherent in them, but only in respect of the executing of the movement, the form by which they act and the end of the action alike being determined for them by their nature. Plants are of this kind, for they move themselves according to the form given to them by nature, with regard to growth and decay. Other things have self-movement in a higher degree, that is, not only with regard to executing the movement, but even as regards the form which is the principle of movement, and which form they acquire of themselves. Of this kind are animals, in which the principle of movement is not a naturally implanted form, but one received through sense. Hence the more perfect is their sense, the more perfect is their power of self-movement. Such as have only the sense of touch, e.g., shellfish, move only with the motion of expansion and contraction; and thus their movement hardly exceeds that of plants. But such as have the sensitive power in perfection, so as to recognize not only what is joined to and touches them, but also objects apart from them, can move themselves to a distance by a progressive movement. Yet although animals of the latter kind receive through sense the form that is the principle of their movement, nevertheless they cannot of themselves propose to themselves the end of their operation, or movement; for this has been implanted in them by nature, and by natural instinct they are moved to any action through the form apprehended by sense. Hence such animals as move themselves in respect to an end they themselves propose are superior to these. This can only be done by reason and intellect, whose province is to know the proportion between the end and

Still, no created minds can realize the notion of life in its fullness, since no creature is the sufficient or ultimate cause of what it causes, except in the order of material causality, that is, in the order of passivity. Thus even though all natural beings are characterized by spontaneity that is lacking in our machines—and the living things show more spontaneity than the non-living, the animal more than the plant, man more than the animal, and the angel more than man—still, no created being enjoys an absolute spontaneity.[44] Thus whatever the role played by the created efficient cause in making ready its action, the performance of that action requires divine premotion. The created mind may be the knowing cause of its formal determination, but it is never the ultimate cause of it. The birth of thought in the human intellect is not entirely free, for it presupposes an influence exercised on our senses by external objects. And as for pure spirits, if it is true that their ideas in no way depend on things, it is also true that they do not possess them by identity but have received them from God. Similarly, the created intelligent being cannot be the ultimate cause of his own actual development, for it is the weight of his nature, received by the grace of Him Who created him, that inclines him toward his final end. If he is free to choose among particular ends, it is only within the limits of the general end to which he is inclined by his nature.

Thus the idea of life, originally derived from the observation of material nature, appears to leave behind the whole created world to acquire a unique meaning in God. Actually, however, what we learn when we thus reach the summit of the hierarchy

---

the means to that end, and to order the one to the other. Hence a more perfect degree of life is that of intelligent beings, for their power of self-movement is more perfect."

[44] When during the last century the scientific study of irritability showed that even the actions of the living are (always?) reactions to external stimuli, partisans of mechanistic reductionism anticipated that, vital activities being so compromised, the very notion of life, as a specific kind of activity, would not long survive. A clear understanding that in any created being the power of self-movement is always limited puts us at ease in this respect. Why should living organisms not need to be externally stimulated to produce a secretion, movement, heat, electricity? With due respect for the differences separating them, this dependence on external stimuli finds its analogue even in the highest activity of the angels.

of life is that our idea of life, already turned metaphysical and analogical, must undergo a further purification based on an even more profound analogy. The first of living beings offers no grip to the notion of a causality that turns back upon itself. God is not the cause of His perfections, since His perfections are not really distinct from His being. To give expression to its first and supreme analogate, then, we need to rework our idea of life. If to live means to bring about change in oneself, or to confer upon oneself some kind of actuality, then, we come to realize, it is He Who possesses every actuality by identity with His own being, activity, and goodness Who is Life itself, and everything else is by comparison as if it were dead.[45]

Every immanent activity, since it remains as well as originates in the agent himself, deserves the name of vital activity. But the converse is not necessarily true, and we should be aware of the harmful equivocations to which such a view may lead.[46] In the

---

[45] Thomas Aquinas, *Sum. th.* I, q. 18, a. 3: "That being whose act of understanding is its very nature, and which, in what it naturally possesses, is not determined by another, must have life in the most perfect degree. Such is God; and hence in Him principally is life." John of St. Thomas, *Curs. th.* I, disp. 16, a. 2 (Vivès, II, 242a): "And so God is said to move Himself in the sense that His life and His activity are one and the same, in contrast to living creatures for whom they are separated into first and second acts."

[46] Following Aristotle, the Scholastics regularly define life as the power of self-movement or, better still, of conferring upon oneself one's own perfection. For as Aquinas warns us, having in mind the life of the spirit, the expression "self-movement" needs here to be taken in the broadest sense in which it designates any kind of activity at all (*Sum. th.* I, q. 18, a. 1). We note that many contemporary biologists, including those totally unacquainted with Aristotle, seem to accept a notion of life in full agreement with his definition. L. Vialleton, "Types d'organization et types formels," *Archives de Philosophie*, 6, No. 1 (1928), 92; Hans André (a good Aristotelian), "La Typologie des plantes," *Cahiers de Philosophie de la Nature*, 2 (1928), 40; H. Ebbinghaus, *Précis de psychologie* (Paris: Alcan, 1912), p. 64; C. B. Grassi, *La Vita: Ciò che sembra a un biologo*, p. 4: "Anyone who thinks about the way in which a chick is hatched from an egg feels a deep astonishment. While the biologist is familiar with even the slightest details of this evolutionary process, his knowledge cannot quite dispel the feeling of awe, since what he is observing is a miracle not unlike that of a great palace rising spontaneously out of a heap of mortar and bricks without the help of any workmen, with doors and windows opening bit by bit, and window panes, shutters, balconies and furniture all coming into being and fitting in place." Or as Plate (a mechanist, quoted by Rémy Collin, "Réflexions sur le psychisme," *Cahiers de Philosophie de la Nature*, 3 [1929], 33) puts it: "'A living being resembles a machine in motion, which, however, has

vegetative life, what is immanent is only the effect of the activity, which makes this activity not immanence but production. The term of the nourishment is distinct from the activity of nourishing oneself, for nourishment is but a way of maintaining organic integrity. In other words, as an efficiency rather than a quality, vegetative activity consists in change aimed at the improvement of an imperfect subject; and we recognize it as an efficiency

---

the special quality of being able to maintain itself in motion; *it is like a clock that rewinds itself.*"

It should be pointed out that, contrary to an opinion widely accepted these days (cf. Joseph Kleutgen, s. J., *Die Philosophie der Vorzeit verteidigt* I [Innsbruck: Rausch, 1878], pp. 1, 3, and Hans André, loc. cit), neither Aristotle nor the Scholastics ever, to the best of our knowledge, identified the self-movement characteristic of life with immanent activity, and as a result they never defined life as immanent activity. John of St. Thomas provides all the needed clarifications on this subject. Within the category of action, vegetative activity, like the action of the *intellectus agens* (*Phil. nat.* III, q. 10, a. 1 [R, III, 303B27]), is a transitive activity, because it is essentially a production of a term; thus this activity does not really differ from the activity of inanimate things, and we call it vital only because the term it produces remains within the agent and constitutes its perfection. To call it for that reason also an *immanent* action betrays a totally materialist outlook. *Phil. nat.* III, q. 1, a. 4 (R, III, 40A28ff). Now, the objection is also made that vegetative life could not really be life since all the vegetative operations are transitive actions: alteration, increase, attraction, repulsion, all of which are also found in inanimate bodies (nowadays the objection would be that the scientific study of the so-called vital activities reveals nothing more than physico–chemical forces). John of St. Thomas replies: "Even though vegetative life is a transitive rather than an immanent activity, it still deserves to be called life because it in fact operates of itself; this is shown in particular in the vital action of generating life, even though this, too, is a transient action and one that depends on alteration. . . . And so even the mode in which they are performed pertains to the species of these operations." Ibid., q. 6, a. 4 (R, III, 195B41): "Immanent action is not formally physical action, in the category of action, but a metaphysical action, in the category of quality. Immanent activity may be virtually transitive and productive [e.g., knowledge produces concepts], but as immanent, it is formally a quality. Otherwise it would be immanent not *per se* and of its own nature but by reason of a term inhering in the agent itself, which means immanent not by virtue of action *inasmuch as it is action* but owing to a term not as achieved by action but as passively received. Such immanence or inherence of a term, whether in the agent itself or in another subject, is wholly accidental with respect to action *in its character as action*, because such action itself does not perfect the agent immanently nor actuate the agent. It is the coming to be of the term, and it is the term that actuates and inheres in the agent not as agent but as a subject of inherence. What does it matter for the essential distinction of an action whether its term which inheres in a subject has for subject the agent itself or some subject outside?"

rather than a quality, because when its term is reached, the activity cannot continue. It is only in animal life, or more precisely in knowledge and desire, that there appears genuine immanent activity that completes itself within itself, is not related essentially to any effect, and, involving no change, represents the act of fulfillment of a perfect subject.

Are we to conclude, then, that there is a greater distance between animal life and vegetative life than there is between this latter and the externally directed activity of things inanimate? This is a question that must be considered from several points of view. If we compare the different kinds of activities simply with regard to the idea of action and their participation in the transcendental notion of the emanating terminal act, it is quite clear that there is less distance between the activity of inanimate things brought about by external forces and the efficiency-type vegetative action than there is between this latter and immanent action. The first two belong to the genus of efficiency, whereas the last belongs in the category of quality; for whether the term produced remains within the agent or is outside of it is merely accidental to any action producing an effect. On the other hand, if we consider the entire complex constituted by the active being, its activity, and its fulfillment, it seems that there is less distance between immanent activity and vegetative activity than there is between this latter and the activity of inanimate things. The reason for this is that all living things share in the higher perfection of being able to satisfy their various needs by themselves and to determine their own potentialities according to their natures. Finally, if we consider the mode of being that the different kinds of activity demand on the part of the one that acts, and the measure of ontological independence that these kinds of activity presuppose, we have to say that the superiority of cognitive life over vegetative life is actually incomparably greater than that of vegetative life over inanimate nature. Vegetative activity, like the activity of inanimate things, takes place completely within the order of physical existence and, as a direct function of nature, is limited by that nature. By contrast, cognition presupposes that the being endowed with it has access to an order of existence transcending the limits set to its existential capacity by its constitutive idea. And this access gives birth, with the appearance of understanding, to something marvelously resembling divine infinity.

3

Experience and Thought

Experimental Knowledge[1]

Since the object of knowledge is strictly a qualifying principle, it is in no way essential for it to have real existence. The change from the possibility of existence to actual existence introduces no qualitative change in the thing that comes to be. It is like an awakening that leaves the thing awakened essentially the same as it was asleep. We best imagine the act of creation as light revealing things that just an instant before were hidden in darkness. Because knowing is a pure function of becoming a particular object in the absolute immanence of intentional existence, the *state* of that object makes no difference to it. Knowing an object does not depend on anything external to its quality; its nature, awake or asleep, remains unchanged.[2]

---

[1] We use this term because it seems the least confusing. In the language of the Scholastics what we here call *experimental knowledge* is called *notitia intuitiva*, i.e., a knowledge whose object is reached as it actually exists outside the mind; *notitia experimentalis* properly denotes only a special kind of intuitive knowledge, viz., sense intuition (cf. Thomas Aquinas, *Sum. th.* I, q. 54, a. 5; Gredt, *Elementa philosophiae* I, no. 16). In contemporary usage the word intuition has taken on a great many meanings (cf. Maritain, *La philosophie bergsonienne*, pp. 152ff.), while the word experience has become so flexible that we do not find it shocking to speak of angelic experience.

On experimental knowledge so defined, see Thomas Aquinas, *De ver.*, q. 3, a. 3, ad 8; *Sum. th.* I, q. 14, a. 9; I–II, q. 15, a. 1; q. 17, a. 7, ad 3; Cajetan, *In Ia*, q. 57, a. 2; John of St. Thomas, *Log.* II, q. 23, a. 1 (R, I, 722Bff.).

[2] Thomas Aquinas, *De ver.*, q. 3, a. 3, ad 8: "The science of vision adds to simple knowledge something beyond the order of knowledge, viz., the existence of things." John of St. Thomas, *Log.* II, q. 23, a. 1 (R, I, 724B3). It does not follow, however, that every knowledge that reaches existence in some way is an experimental knowledge. John of St. Thomas, *Curs. th.* I, disp. 22, a. 1 (Vivès, IV, 788A): "Consequently the knowledge that bears on existence is an intuitive vision if it is a knowledge of that existence in itself; but if it is from an effect or some other extrinsic source, it is an abstractive and confused knowledge, depending on whether the thing exists."

Consider theoretical science. To the extent that it achieves its ideal, it moves beyond the existential data to concern itself with general types and intelligible laws, or, in other words, with formulae of possibility, with essential necessities. Unsupported by rational analysis, empirical hypotheses derived from factual observations represent an incomplete kind of knowing, indeed, a partial defeat of science.[3] The perfection of theoretical knowledge depends above all on the necessity of its object. Thus every time we manage to abstract from existence to reach a necessary object,[4] our understanding, though bearing now on an object separated from existence, is more perfect than our experimental knowledge, which bears on physical existence alone.[5]

Having made that point, we find that the whole problem of the need for an experimental knowledge is still with us. Even though abstractive knowledge is a true knowledge, and under certain conditions realizes the idea of knowledge much better than most kinds of empirical knowledge, we have to wonder whether a being endowed with knowledge can get along without any reference to experience. If we were completely cut off from every opening on actual physical existence, would it be possible for us to know anything?

---

[3] Cf. Goblot, *Essai sur la classification des sciences*, pp. 22ff., 283ff. A comparative study of the relationship of knowledge to existence in theoretical and practical thought will be found in Yves Simon, *Critique de la connaissance morale* (Paris: Desclée De Brouwer, 1934).

[4] The effort to incorporate history into science, made today by so many thinkers in the most varied fields, is, perhaps, after pragmatism, the greatest menace ever to threaten theoretical thought. The continuity, within a single system of reference, between the intelligible necessities, which are the object of science, and the contingencies of existence, which are the object of history, can be established only by granting to the actual unrolling of events the same kind of intelligibility that is expected from the ideal development of the essential properties of things. At that point either contingency will give way and the universe will be conceived in the manner of an axiom that, for some unknown reason, feels the need to spread itself through space and unroll itself in time, and science will rest on a fundamental lie; or necessity will yield, and science will rest on nothing at all.

[5] Abstractive knowledge here means knowledge derived by abstraction from the actual extramental existence of the thing known. It is sometime said that even the external sense performs an abstraction, meaning simply that the sense does not receive within itself the entire reality of the thing known. It is not that kind of abstraction we have in mind here.

The answer to this question is to be found in the ontological hierarchy implied in the definition of knowledge as intentional existence. Physical existence comes first here. In a significant paradox, nothing is more revealing of the dependence of the intentional on the physical than the existence of the *beings of reason* in the mind.[6] Intentional in the second degree, with nothing in the natural world that corresponds or can correspond to them, these beings of reason exist in the mind only as a function of the intentionals in the first degree, to which there corresponds in nature at least a possibility of existence. The science of logic is constructed in the image of the science of the real; privation is conceived as the lack of a perfection, and the imaginary numbers are modeled on real numbers. What can have nothing but an intentional existence can have this existence only by analogy with what can have physical existence. If every proposition putting together real objects were to disappear from my mind, the beings of reason, *subject* and *predicate*, would not last there an instant. Against the claim that every *esse* can be reduced to a *percipi*, perhaps the best argument is to point out that whatever consistency there is in a *percipi* is derived from a distinct and prior existence. Thus even within the intentional, the physical affirms its supremacy. There is no intentional existence that does not have a basis, directly or indirectly, in a physical existence, actual or possible. This, we think, is the first law of the intentional.

How could we claim that the mind was in communication with the possible real if it had no way of communicating with the actual real? The possible real does not exist in nature and can have objectivity in the mind only in relation to an existing real. Thus just as all possibility would disappear from the universe of nature if all actuality vanished, so all representation of the possible would have to disappear from a universe of knowledge in which actual existence ceased to be represented. We could almost say, then, that empirical knowledge in the intentional order plays a role analogous to that played in nature by the divine being. As the *actuality of physical existence existing intentionally*, empirical knowledge supports in intentional existence everything that can exist intentionally, just as *He Who Is* maintains in physical exis-

---

[6] See above, chap. 1, note 21.

tence, actual or possible, every contingent being that does or can exist. Philosophies that are worlds apart in their principles and conclusions strive equally to find a source of experimental knowledge by giving the mind some opening on what exists, and the history of the metaphysics of knowing reveals many instances of nostalgic yearning for experience that is exactly like the attitude that the metaphysicians of being, even in the most unexpected ways, show for aseity. This is not surprising, because the investigation of the absolute in experimental knowledge is the exact counterpart of the investigation of the ontological absolute.

For the fundamental veracity of our cognitions to be preserved, however, actual existence must have a definite role to play in the proper *object* of the faculty whose function it is to put the whole system of human knowledge in touch with actual physical existence. Unless there is some opening on that actual physical existence, there is no knowledge. If there is no certitude in experience, all certitude disappears from our knowledge. But if there is no power of knowing that is essentially empirical, there is also no certainty in experience. Consequently, it is not enough just to recognize one of our faculties as the experimental source of our knowledge; we have to establish that this faculty is essentially *made to be experimental*, that with its first act and by virtue of its very constitution it puts us in touch with existent reality. We are obviously capable of experimental knowledge.[7] We represent to ourselves in our mind the singular existent in its existentiality, and we make judgments about it. But what we still have to decide is whether the *object* toward which the mind tends naturally and directly implies, in its character as object, existence in act.

One of the primary meanings of the *cogito* identifies our mind as the pre-eminent source of empirical knowledge, and we can

---

[7] John of St. Thomas, *Log.* II, q. 23, a. 1 (R, I, 723B25) (The writer wants to prove that an intuitive knowledge can be mediate and take place *per species alienas*): "It is St. Thomas' opinion that the intellect has no direct idea of individual things and yet is able to know corporeal individuals intuitively when they are present in virtue of the senses." Ibid., a. 2 (R, I, 738A16): "Although our intellect does not have a direct idea of individual things, it may derive from its image a concept that properly represents it . . . and this is enough to enable us to say that we have an intuitive knowledge of the thing present."

safely say that anyone who talks about intellectual experience as an original, underived, direct, non-reflexive experience is an unreconstructed Cartesian. But if, as many familiar arguments indicate, we accept that the real object of the human intelligence is nothing other than the universal essence of sensible things, then we must also recognize that our thought in its first movement does not reach physical existence. There is an intellectual experience of the sensible singular, but it is an indirect experience; there is also an experience of the thinking self, but this is a reflexive experience.[8] Thus although the minds of pure spirits may indeed be a source of their experimental knowledge, this is not so for the minds joined to matter.

As for our imagination and memory, it is only too clear that their acts presuppose a prior exercise of the external senses and that they are connected to the actual existent exclusively through the activity of the external senses. Thus it is only by being incorporated in a synthesis of which sensation is the organic center that the memories involved in perception reach the actual existent. Indeed, there is little doubt about it; the whole of human experience has its source in sensation. Neither scientists nor many philosophers care to object to this conclusion of common sense. But we wonder how many fully appreciate the far-reaching consequences of this familiar truth.

If it is true that the senses are basically indefectible with respect to their proper objects, and if every object of sensation, as an object of experiential knowledge, envelops actual physical existence, then it follows that *the act of sensing has to be made such as to reach the actual existent without error.*[9] Any theory of sensation,

---

[8] On the intellectual knowledge of the singular, cf. Thomas Aquinas, *In De an.* III, lect. 1; *Sum. th.* I, q. 86, a. 1; John of St. Thomas, *Phil. nat.* IV, q. 10, a. 4; on the soul's knowledge of itself, Thomas Aquinas, *De ver.*, q. 10, a. 8; *Sum. th.* I, q. 87, aa. 1, 2, 3, 4; John of St. Thomas, *Log.* II, q. 23, a. 3 (R, I, 741B); Gredt, *Elementa philosophiae* I, nos. 482ff.; H. D. Gardeil, *La Structure de l'âme et l'expérience mystique* II (Paris: Gabalda, 1927), pp. 95ff.; Emile Peillaube, "Avons-nous l'expérience du spirituel?" *Revue de Philosophie* (November–December 1929), 66off.

[9] The experimental character of the knowledge of the external senses is insisted on throughout the whole of Aristotelianism. Cf., in particular, *On the Soul* II, 5, 417B19, and Thomas Aquinas, *In De an.* II, lect. 12. After noting a resemblance between sense and understanding, Aristotle writes: "But between the two there is a difference; the objects that excite the sensory

therefore, that does not preserve before all else the notion of a knowledge made to reach external reality *as it is* will be at fault, and we must reject all hypotheses that in any way compromise the empirical character of sensory knowledge, or its veracity in that character. This is the only sound starting point for a realistic explanation of sensation. We can continue to make progress if we rely on the twofold certitude of the veracity of the senses as well as of the experimental, empirical nature of sensation. But we should also be aware that much more is needed to overcome the many obstacles along the way.

---

powers to activity, the seen, the heard, etc., are outside. The ground of this difference is that what actual sensation apprehends is individuals, whereas what knowledge apprehends is universals, and these are in a sense within the soul. That is why a man can exercise his knowledge when he wishes, but his sensation does not depend upon himself—a sensible object must be there." Cf. Thomas Aquinas, *Sum. th.* I, q. 78, a. 4; I–II, q. 15, a. 1; q. 17, a. 7, ad 3; *De pot.*, q. 3, a. 7; Sylvester of Ferrara, *In Cont. gent.* I, 53; John of St. Thomas, *Log.* II, q. 23, a. 1 (R, I, 734A37); *Phil. nat.* IV, q. 6, a. 1 (R, III, 170Aff.). In this last text there is a splendid dissertation on the problem we are concerned with, in answer to this precise question: "Is it within the power of God to produce an act of sensation in the absence of its object?" Suárez gives an affirmative answer: There is nothing to prevent God from preserving in the sense faculty the form of an object that is no longer physically present. But in this case sensation would have become an abstractive knowledge, even though still a true sensation. The argument of John of St. Thomas consists in showing that the presence of the object is part of the very definition of sensation, so that a sensation bearing on an absent object would be a contradiction. What the divine power can provide is the causality of the object upon the faculty (we shall see, p. 91, that this causality is but one of the means that make experimental knowledge possible); but that its object be an actually existing physical object is of the very essence of sensation. "All our knowledge has its origin in the external senses and is resolved into them. Thus the external senses must be moved by the ideas [species] received from external objects, and knowledge must terminate in the things themselves as they are. Now, God can take care of the first part, the being moved by the object, by infusing or producing the idea in the power in lieu of the object, so that there is no essential need of the presence of the object. But that would not take care of the second part, since it is of the essence of the specifying character of external sensation that it be external. The reason for this is that the external senses occupy the final place in the system of our faculties; it is impossible to go any further in tracing the origin of our knowledge or its ultimate resolution. If the soul is not in touch with the physically existing reality through the senses, all certitude must vanish, because there is no other source. It is clear that there is empirical knowledge in the external sense, because we have the closest experience of anything when we touch it with an external sense. Moreover, since experience is what ultimately confirms our knowledge by a kind of

Sensory Experience and the Passivity of Sense

The presence of the object that defines empirical knowledge is realized differently in different beings. In God, it is realized by the identity of the knower and the known. In the experience an angel has of himself, it takes place through the ontological union (compatible with a real distinction) of the known self and the knowing faculty. But when the ontological constitution of the knowing faculty in no way implies the actual presence of any object, empirical knowledge can come about only through the action that the physically present object exercises on the knower through the impression of its idea on the sense faculty.[10] *This is the case of sensory knowledge.* The sensible is not by its nature joined to the sense; they will be joined only if the sensible communicates itself by its activity with the actuality of its existence.[11]

---

induction, and is what introduces our knowledge into us, its object must be an object as it really is in itself. For if our knowledge were resolved into anything other than the thing itself, e.g., an image, resemblance, or some other kind of intermediary, we would still have to compare that intermediary with the thing itself, or with the object mediated, to determine whether it was true or not, and so the problem of confirmation would still be there. *And this is why for the sake of certitude and experimental evidence, we always return to the knowledge that of its very nature tends to things in themselves.* This is the knowledge of the external senses, which is our ultimate experimental knowledge, requiring its object to be actually physically present." Cf. also *Curs. th.* I–II, disp. 13, a. 2 (Vivès, VI, 261A).

[10] When it insists on the dependence of knowledge on its object, a realist philosophy often appears to maintain that impressing its idea on the knowing faculty belongs to the essence of the object. As we shall see farther on, the only truly essential function of every object of knowledge consists in its intentional participation in the immanent act of knowing. The idea may be present to the knowing faculty as a gift of nature, as in the case of the angelic intellect; the idea may also be provided by the activity of the knowing subject, as in the case of the human mind; or it is produced by the object, as in the case of the external senses.

[11] Aristotle, *On the Soul* II, 5, 416B33: "Sensation depends, as we have said, on a process of movement or affection from without." Ibid., 417B20: "the objects that excite the sensory powers to activity, the seen, the heard, & c., are outside." Ibid., 11, 423B31: "all sense-perception is a process of being so affected." Ibid., 12, 424A17: "By a 'sense' is meant what has the power of receiving into itself the sensible forms of things without the matter." Ibid., 424B16: "Smelling is a perception of the result of the odorous upon the air." Ibid., III, 2, 425B25: "The activity of the sensible object and that of the percipient sense is one and the same activity, and yet the distinction between their being

This passivity of the sense with respect to the external sensible is, of course, widely recognized and accepted. In the language of experimental science, the sensible object is designated as the stimulus acting upon a receptor endowed with a specific mode of response. But let us note that the action the biologist attributes to the sensory object, the one he records and measures, is an exclusively physical action that, by its nature, *alters* the receiver. Made to realize a physical union of the subject with the form communicated, this action cannot help but modify its subject accordingly. But as we have already established, *to know* is not to undergo an alteration; and so, if it is true that sensation in its very essence as an act of knowing requires the sense to be passive with respect to its object, we must hasten to add that beyond the physical action of the sensible on the sense *organ*, which is totally extrinsic to the essence of sensing, the sensible object also acts upon the sense faculty in a non-physical way, which results in the determination of that faculty by the *idea* of the object. The sensory form thus comes to exist intentionally in the sense, but not by virtue of the physical action of the sensible. The hand feels the roundness of the ball, but what the pressure of the ball produces is only a depression in the hand.[12] The *shape* of the ball, therefore, must be presented to the sense of touch by something other than just the physical action of the ball. This other type of action, which brings about not a physical union resulting in a composite of two natures but rather an objective identification of the receiver with the received, we call *intentional action*.[13]

---

remains. Take as illustration actual sound and actual hearing: a man may have hearing and yet not be hearing, and that which has a sound is not always sounding. But when that which can hear is actively hearing and that which can sound is sounding, then the actual hearing and the actual sound are merged in one (these one might call respectively hearkening and sounding). If it is true that the movement, both the acting and the being acted upon, is to be found in that which is acted upon, both the sound and the hearing so far as it is actual must be found in that which has the faculty of hearing, for it is in the passive factor that the actuality of the active or motor factor is realized." This last text illustrates perfectly the basic unity of the action−passion pairing (see above, p. 44) that allows the sensible object to make itself present to the knowing faculty with its actual existence.

[12] Cf. de Tonquédec, *La Critique de la connaissance*, p. 57.

[13] Aristotle's famous line, that *sense receives sensible forms of things without*

Stating the issue as precisely as possible, let us say that the thing considered to be an object of the external sense can be looked at as the principle of three kinds of actions. First, as a particular thing, the sensible exercises a *transitive material action* on the sense organ, considered as a physical receiver, and the result is a modification of the organ. Second, as an *object* acting intentionally upon the sense faculty, the sensible concurs in the *immanent action* of knowing. But this second kind of action, arising out of the intentionality of the object, is not enough to put the sense faculty in touch with the *physical existence* of the object. For this to happen, a third action is required, which, although it proceeds from the physically existing object, is not a physical but an intentional action, conveying not the object's quality but its existence. Beyond the immanent action of sensing, then, of which it is the co-principle along with the sense faculty (just as the object of thought is, along with the understanding, the co-principle of thought), the sensory object, to make itself present to the sense faculty in its existential reality and to cooperate with it, intentionally, in an act of genuinely experimental knowledge must also exercise on the sense faculty an *intentional transitive action*.[14]

---

matter (*On the Soul* II, 12, 424A18), expresses no more than this intentional passivity of the sense with respect to the sensible object. Thomas Aquinas, *Sum. th.* I, q. 78, a. 3: "Now, change is of two kinds, one natural, the other spiritual. Natural change takes place by the form of the thing that causes the change being received according to its natural being into the thing changed, as heat is received into the thing heated. But spiritual change takes place by the form of the thing that causes the change being received according to a spiritual mode of receiving the change, as the form of color is received into the pupil, which does not thereby become colored. Now, for the operation of the senses, a spiritual change is required, whereby an intention of the sensible form is effected in the sensible organ. Otherwise, if a natural change alone sufficed for the sense's action, all natural bodies would feel when they undergo alteration."

[14] Cajetan, *In De an.* II, 11 (B. 169A): "Know, then, that being passive to the sensible happens in three ways: materially, intentionally, and sensibly. For instance, when a hand is held over a fire, there is a *material passion*, by which the hand becomes warm; there is also an *intentional passion*, by which the organ of touch receives the species [idea, form] of warmth without matter; and there is a *sensible passion*, by which the sense receives the warmth, as the sensed is received in the sense." What we call physical action corresponds to what Cajetan calls material passion; what we call intentional transitive action corresponds to his intentional passion, and what we call intentional immanent action corresponds to his sensible passion.

But even among writers who are fully prepared to accept the existence of intentional forms in the sense faculty, some do not see it that way. Rather than acknowledge the paradox of an object's exercising in its physical existence two kinds of transitive activity, one of which results in physical change while the other produces a psychic identification, they prefer to attribute the intentional modality of these forms to the receptive power of the sense faculty.[15] Thus even though an intentional passion would be registered in the sense, this would not be due to intentional action on the part of the object. A seal depresses the flesh of the finger as it depresses the wax by physical action alone. But while the form of the seal is thus physically received by the flesh as by the wax, it is at the same time received also intentionally by the sense of touch. There is but a single action with two effects radically distinct in nature, the difference being due to the difference in nature of the receivers.

But is it not clear that, on this hypothesis, sensory knowledge completely loses its experimental character and is reduced to a dubious abstraction? A thing is not an idea; physical change produces things, but only ideas can determine a faculty of knowledge. Thus if the idea that determines the faculty does not come, as an idea, from the action exercised by the object, and if the experimental character of sensation can be guaranteed only by an efficient causality on the part of the physically existing object, then the intentional form has to be produced by the object, and it cannot be produced by a physical action. The alternative, again, is to imagine the sense faculty receiving but a single physical stimulus from which it would *extract* an intentional form on its own. But it is not simply that this would make ideas abstract

---

[15] Among them: A. Lepidi, *Elementa philosophiae Christianae* III (Paris: Lethielleux, 1875), pp. 211–12: "One may say that, as far as the external senses are concerned, the power of the sensitive soul uses the impression of the sensible object received in the animate organ as an instrument in order to produce in the faculty of the external sense a determined intentional idea [species]." Hugon and Gény express themselves similarly. Gredt (*Unsere Aussenwelt*, pp. 137–43; *Elementa philosophiae* I, nos. 379, 481) is not very clear on this point. But in opposing the interpretation of Pisters (*La Nature des formes intentionnelles d'après saint Thomas d'Aquin*, pp. 8off.), he seems to reject the production of the intentional form by the sense itself and appears satisfied to conceive, as we do, the physical influence of the object on the organ as the necessary vehicle of the intentional form produced by the object.

rather than experimental; it is by no means clear what the matter is on which the sense faculty would exercise this abstraction attributed to it. There is nothing there except a simple subjective physical alteration, which is not an intentional datum and thus is of no use to a cognitive faculty. The compromise that pretends to preserve the intentional passivity of the sense without acknowledging an intentional transitive action of the object requires us, then, to assume an interior production by the sense faculty, on the occasion of the organ's alteration, of a quality whose resemblance with the quality of the object can be guaranteed only by a pre-established harmony. Here not only does our sensory knowledge cease to be experimental, but we are pushed outside the conditions without which abstractive knowledge itself loses all reliability. When we abstract certain aspects from an *intentional datum*, our knowledge does not lose its essentially objective character because we leave other things behind, so to speak. But what can save abstraction from total arbitrariness if it is done not from the known, i.e., an intentional datum, but from the unknown, i.e., a physical matter that can never be a cognitive datum? Indeed, dismissing the notion of an intentional action of the sensible on the sense faculty strikes a twofold blow against the veracity of sense knowledge. Not only does it destroy its experimental character but it also deprives its abstractive function of all objectivity.

And so, no matter what obscurities this notion presents, we shall have to assume that the action the sensible object exercises on the sense is not just physical but intentional. To develop a satisfactory explanation of this notion, much preliminary work is needed, not the least because we have to contend with the heavy burden of three centuries of idealism. Moreover, while the best we can do is to take up the question where the Ancients left it, we must also recognize that their theory of the sensible forms is a mixed bag. We begin, therefore, with some brief remarks in which we try to sort out what is certain from what is conjectural and what is false.

(*a*) Just as there is a radical ontological difference and absolute irreducibility between intentional and physical existence,[16]

---

[16] Excluding the case where transsubjectivity is of the very nature of being.

i.e., between the idea and the thing, so, and for the same reasons, there is absolute irreducibility between intentional transitive action and physical action. Refine the notion of physical action as much as you like, by lightening it, making it invisible, calling it impalpable, and appealing to the unobservable (and often fictitious) entities talked about in modern physics, and you will still have an action that alters the subject that receives it, and that remains therefore, from the ontological point of view, infinitely remote from an action that in communicating an objective quality does not alter its subject. Between becoming *other* and becoming *the other*, the contrast is absolute, exactly as between physical action and intentional action.

(*b*) Does it follow, then, that the physical alteration of the sense organ is, as the Ancients thought, not at all necessary for the production of sensation, and that an intentional action can be produced even though no physical action is present?[17] Let us be

---

[17] What is essential in the doctrine of the Ancients regarding the physical alteration of the sense organ is outlined by St. Thomas in *Sum. th.* I, q. 78, a. 3: "There are two kinds of effects, the physical effect and the intentional effect (*immutatio spiritualis*), and only the second is needed in any kind of sensation. In the case of sight, the intentional effect is not accompanied by any physical alteration either on the part of the object or on the part of the subject. In the case of hearing and smelling, there is physical change, but only on the part of the object, and this change consists in local motion for hearing ('commotion of the air'), and a qualitative change for smelling ('to exhale odor a body must be in a measure altered by heat'). In taste and touch, there is physical modification of the organ itself, with this difference that the organ of touch receives physically the same quality which constitutes its object in knowledge, whereas the quality physically received by the organ of taste is one presupposed by its object; thus while the hand that feels heat becomes hot, the tongue that tastes bitterness does not become bitter, but moist." See also *In De an.* II, lect. 14 (P. 418); III, lect. 2 (P. 583).

The statement of the problem will become clearer if we compare sensation and emotion. In its intrinsic structure, emotion implies an intentional or psychic side (movement of desire), which constitutes its form, and a physical side (reflexes, secretions, etc.), which constitutes its matter. Sensation, on the other hand, is essentially an intentional act. Contrary to emotions, which are regularly accompanied by organic disturbances, the physical alteration of the sense organ, if there is one, remains but an extrinsic concomitant, not an essential part of sensation. *Sum. th.* I–II, q. 22, a. 2, ad 3: "The organs of the soul can be changed in two ways. First, by a spiritual change, in respect of which the organ receives an intention of the thing; and this is essential to the act of the sensitive power of apprehension. Thus the eye is changed by the visible thing, not by being colored, but by receiving the intention of color. But the organs

careful here not to confuse problems. Whether the physical action of the sensible on the sense organ bears *intrinsically* on the act of sensing is one question; whether it is the necessary condition for it is another. Rational analysis requires that we answer the first question negatively, but experience suggests a positive answer to the second. With only the data of common and macroscopic experience, the Ancients thought that, in most cases, sensation took place without a physical alteration of the organ. But the refinements of scientific research have taught us that sensation is always preceded by an alteration of the sense organ. This is why we can make an exact, if incomplete, account of animal behavior by restricting our study to action measurable by external standards and the equally measurable reaction of the organism, without having to decide whether this reaction is governed by knowledge or even if there has been knowledge. Does the auditory equipment of a dog do anything more than

---

are receptive of another natural change, which affects their natural disposition; for instance, when they become hot or cold, or undergo some similar change. And this kind of change is accidental to the act of the sensitive power of apprehension; for instance, if the eye be wearied through gazing intently at something, or be overcome by the intensity of the object. On the other hand, this kind of change is essential to the act of the sensitive appetite; and so the material element in the definitions of the movements of the appetitive part is the natural change of the organ; for instance, anger is said to be 'a kindling of the blood around the heart'" (Aristotle, *On the Soul* I, 1, 403A31).

St. Thomas, Cajetan, and John of St. Thomas are tireless in recalling that the object of sight emits nothing but intentional forms. Thomas Aquinas, *Sum. th.* I, q. 78, a. 3; *In De an.* II, lect. 14 (P. 418); lect. 20 (P. 493); Cajetan, *In De an.* II, 10 (B. 155A); John of St. Thomas, *Phil. nat.* IV, q. 5, a. 5 (R, III, 158B). As far as sound and odor are concerned, they are in agreement that a physical reality is produced in the medium, but they add that if the distance is great, the physical reality produced in the medium by the sensible object gets lost along the way, so that only the intentional forms reach the organ. Thomas Aquinas, *In II Sent.*, dist. 2, q. 2, a. 2, ad 5; *In De an.* II, lect. 20 (P. 494); *In De sensu*, lect. 12 (P. 172); John of St. Thomas, *Phil. nat.* IV, q. 5, a. 4 (R, III, 153B24ff).

Why is it that some senses operate only by way of change in their organs? The Ancients seem to answer this question with an unconvincing argument from expediency. Among the senses, there is a hierarchy of dignity, and the sense of sight, which contributes most to the enrichment of knowledge, is the noblest of all. Because of its nobility, it is fitting that the conditions of its activity be as far removed as possible from the ordinary conditions of physical activity, and so its operation takes place exclusively in the order of intentionality. At the other extreme, touch and taste, whose principal function is the preservation of the subject, are the humblest of the senses and closest to being

analyze physical impressions? Is the physical reception of sound waves a sufficient cause of the conditioned reflexes studied by Pavlov, or is it necessary, to provoke salivation, that the sound be associated by the dog with a previous experience of feeding? These are questions that the biologist, concerned more with establishing the laws of conditioning than with determining proper causes, has the right to leave unanswered. For even if the physical modification of the organ is not the sufficient or proper cause of the reaction provoked by the sense stimulus, it is still true that this physical modification is always there and that it does, in fact, condition the reaction.

---

apsychic faculties, and for this reason we can see that their operation is always accompanied by some kind of physical modification. John of St. Thomas, *Phil. nat.* IV, q. 7, a. 7 (R, III, 236A5ff.). The need for a physical alteration of the organ in the case of touch and taste seems to have been very puzzling to the Ancients, and harder to explain than the lack of physical alteration in the case of the other senses.

But why did the Ancients think they were justified in maintaining that there is no physical alteration of the organ in the case of sight, hearing, and smell? Primarily, it seems, on the basis of factual data, the sort of argument from expediency, like the one just given, being added only to make the explanation more intellectually respectable. Today, of course, their interpretation of experimental data seems extremely crude. For example, while the odorous body emits, in addition to intentional forms, also physical particles, Aquinas reasoned that it was not necessary for these particles to reach the organ of smell; his proof was that vultures, alerted by the odor, gather from great distances at the site of the carrion, even though it is impossible for physical particles to be diffused to such great distances in all directions. *In De an.* II, lect. 20 (P. 494). Similar comments are made on the subject of sound: it is admitted that the waves produced in the air by the motion of the sounding body do not necessarily reach the hearing, because it is inconceivable that these vibrations can be propagated over the great distances at which the sound is still perceptible. *In De an.* II, lect. 16 (P. 447); *In II Sent.*, dist. 2, q. 2, a. 2, ad 5; John of St. Thomas, *Phil. nat.* IV, q. 7, a. 3 (R, III, 217A). John of St. Thomas adds that when a sound made on the other side of a wall is heard, only the intentional forms pass through the wall (ibid.).

But this notion of the intentional forms traveling through a medium without the support of the physical forms presented serious experimental difficulties even for the Ancients themselves. Why, for instance, do the intentional forms of sound and odor not reach the sense organ instantaneously? Why should a gust of wind slow up their diffusion? Is it not a fact that only physical becoming is subject to the law of succession, as well as to negation by the action of opposed principles? John of St. Thomas, who studies these questions patiently, has only a few embarrassed answers to them. *Phil. nat.* IV, q. 5, a. 5 (R, III, 158B); q. 4. a. 3 (R, III, 120B).

Clearly, the theory of physical influences is the weakest part of the Peripatetic

But every factual constant implies a necessary relation, and so we are led to conceive the alteration of the organ either directly or through an intervening medium as the vehicle, the support, for the intentional influx. Thus in the case of hearing, the vibrations of the air and the motion impressed by them on the inner ear can be understood as also containing and transmitting the quality of the sound, not unlike the way in which the motion of the brush contains and transmits the form of the work of art that springs from the mind of the artist.

(c) For the Ancients, an intermediate space with a determined

---

doctrine of sensation, and displays for us the main faults that made the development of an experimental science impossible in the Scholastic period: namely, crude macroscopic observations, a childish confidence in the data of common experience, and measurements related to the scale of human practice.

But it is equally wrong to think that once the reality of a physical influence in every kind of sensation has been established, there is no longer any need for the object also to exercise an intentional activity upon the senses. As Gredt (*Unsere Aussenwelt*, p. 134) tells us, "even when the object of knowledge comes into immediate contact with the sense organ—and this is the case with all the external senses—the intentional form is by no means superfluous." What he does not seem to have seen very clearly is that what he said about the intentional form of the object also covers its intentional action, whose function is to produce that form.

That a physical influence undergone by the sense organ is the necessary condition for the intentional influence undergone by the sense faculty is a proposition that appears to be in profound conformity with the dominating Aristotelian view that a sense faculty is nothing else but the act of a corporeal organ. This conception is suggested by St. Thomas in his commentary *In De sensu*, lect. 4 (P. 51). Democritus, Aristotle tells us, confuses sight with the image formed on the polished surface of the eye. St. Thomas contends that the formation of this image, an exclusively physical event, cannot be identified with sensation. Nevertheless, he writes, since this act of the soul, seeing, takes place only with the help of a corporeal organ, it is not surprising that a physical influence is in some way its cause. The image formed on the surface of the eye is only a physical reflection that has little to do with the act of seeing as such, but as an antecedent encounter of the visible form with the organ of sight, it is clearly involved in the act of seeing.

There is no reason to think that when he wrote these lines St. Thomas was aware that he was contradicting what he said elsewhere about the purely intentional character of the influences determining sight (it is well known that for the Ancients the images on the surface of polished bodies other than the eye were also intentional forms). But as it turns out, his formula, whether or not he perceived its bearing, anticipates in a remarkable way the more modern theory of the physics of sensation: "For seeing is an act of the soul only through a corporeal organ; and so it is no wonder that it has some cause by way of a corporeal passion."

nature, a medium, always intervened between the sensible object and the organ of sensation, and any direct contact between what senses and what is sensed was only apparent. The reason for this theory, maintained with remarkable consistency in spite of the special difficulties it raises in common daily experience (where two apparently contiguous bodies are thought to be really touching),[18] seems to be as follows. The spiritualizing of forms takes place by degrees; the sensible form achieves the state of greater immateriality that it has in the perception only after it has passed through a state of lesser immateriality in the external sense. But between the completely material state it has in the thing, and the intentional and psychic state it acquires in the external sense, the sensible form has to undergo a stage of an intermediate immateriality, which can take place only while it is passing through a medium.[19] Now, the least one can say about

---

[18] Modern physics suggests to us a discontinuous image of the material world, one in which there are spatial intervals not only between individuals but even within individuals. If there is, then, as we are inclined to think, a compelling reason for insisting upon a medium between the sense and its object in every kind of sensation, modern physics gives us ground here for speculation not available to the Ancients, except that they thought they could claim it by sheer force of rational argument.

[19] Aristotle, *On the Soul* II, 7, 419A46, 421B9; 423B12; Thomas Aquinas, *In De an.* II, lect. 22 (P. 527), lect. 23 (P. 530ff.); *Q. De an.*, q. 10; Pisters, *La Nature des formes intentionelles selon saint Thomas d'Aquin*, p. 46.

J. de Tonquédec writes: "The reasons given (by the Ancients upholding the need for a medium) are taken mostly from experience. Things happen this way as a matter of fact: the colored object placed directly on the eye blinds it; the sound produced within the ear deafens it; and the aromatic body placed in the nostrils overpowers the sense of smell. But there is more here than simple observations. For when they have to decide which is the organ of touch and which of taste, they argue as follows: other senses require a medium between the organ and the object; consequently, the organ of touch and of taste *must* be located deeper than the surface of the skin, which comes in direct contact with external bodies. This argument from analogy involves an *a priori* principle. But which one? Neither Aristotle nor St. Thomas is very clear on this" (*La critique de la connaissance*, Appendix. III, "Milieux et organes de sensation," p. 470).

The various arguments used by Aristotle, St. Thomas, and John of St. Thomas to establish the need for a medium in the case of touch and taste certainly do not appear to justify the boldness of their conclusions. But Cajetan handles the matter with greater clarity. After he has shown that the experimental evidence is not decisive even for the sense of sight and, in any event, cannot have universal application, he states that, in his opinion, the theoretical

such a conception, considered as a general law of all sensation, is that it has some degree of plausibility. The existence of intentional forms in the inanimate medium appears inevitable when there is an obvious distance between the sensible thing and the organ of sense. If between the colored surface and the organ of sight there was only physical modification of the medium through which the light is propagated, there would be no way for the

---

argument has to be deduced, in the first place, from the conditions under which material being changes into spiritual and vital being (*In De an.* II, 6 [B. 133B]), and, in the second place, from the conditions of the union of the sense in act with the sensible in act. He writes: "It must be derived, as I see it, from the natural order of the passage from material being to vital spiritual being and from the natural linkage of the sense in act with the sensed in act. And it is from the natural order, since the sensory form in the object has a completely material being and cannot be assumed to be able instantly to reach the degree of spirituality possessed by the intentional species. This must be done step by step, from one degree of spirituality to the next, and then to the third, and so on. Now, it is evident that the species in the sense is not even at the lowest level of spirituality, so that, if the material sensory form has to undergo some change in order to become an intentional sensible species in the sense, there has to be some medium intervening in which this material form rises to that lowest level of spirituality. Again, the higher level of spirituality of its subject, i.e., the sense, shows that the sensible species is not, in the sense, at the lowest level of spirituality. The spirituality of the species is of so much higher degree as the sensitive soul is further removed from matter than the nature of the medium. Between these two there is this distance: the soul is as immaterial as it has to be in order for it to know, as Aristotle affirms, and we shall expand upon. In sum, and considering also that the natural order always advances gradually, because the sense cannot directly receive the sensory form in the completely material being that it has in the object, because the sense operates at a higher level of spirituality, the sense has to depend on the sensible form as it exists in the medium, where it is neither totally material nor totally spiritual.

"Moreover, a medium appears necessary also in view of the nature of the union of the sense in act with the sensible in act. For since the thing sensed is twofold, as we are told in *De sensu et sensato*, viz., primary and proper, i.e., remote and proximate, and since what is primarily sensed is the object itself, the proximate being its intentional form, then if there were no medium intervening, not only would it be impossible for a single thing to be seen, heard, or smelled at the same time by many, but what is to be sensed would also be obliterated. For if the object had no being in the medium, there would be nothing left to connect the sense with the primary object. This is a radical difficulty, because the sense in act is so spiritual that just as it cannot be directly affected by what is wholly material, so it cannot have its term in what is wholly material."

Cajetan's first argument, the only one we have thought fit to retain (based on the present state of our investigation), was clearly suggested by St. Thomas in *Q. De an.*, a. 20.

object to impress its unaltered quality on the sense faculty.[20] Consequently, we are convinced that there is an intentional and apsychic state that is intermediate, as far as materiality is concerned, between the state the sensible quality has in the thing and the state it has in the sense faculty. The whole problem is to know whether the passage through this first degree of immateriality is always necessary, so that one would have to affirm the existence of a medium even when it is impossible to be precise about its nature and limits. The existence of a law of progressive spiritualization of forms is not in doubt, and there is no reason why it could not include this stage of apsychic immateriality.

(d) But how are we to conceive this intermediate intentional and apsychic state of the sensible form in an inanimate medium? Would it be something like the instrumental intentional existence described earlier? No one will deny that the medium is the instrument of the sensible in its action on the sense; it is the transmitter of its efficiency.[21] But from the fact that the medium plays such an instrumental role, it does not necessarily follow that the intermediate intentional state the sensible form enjoys in the medium should be confused with instrumental intentional being.[22]

---

[20] Maritain, *Degrees of Knowledge*, pp. 114–15: "Examine everything entitative about the medium that transmits sensible quality and you will only find the properties and movements—the wave movements and others—that the physicist sees in them. You will no more find quality there than you will find the soul under the scalpel. Yet quality passes through it, *secundum esse intentionale*, since the sense will perceive it when the wave or vibration reaches the organ. It is like a dream of a materialistic imagination to want, with Democritus, to have quality pass through the medium entitatively, or, since it is not there entitatively, to deny, with the votaries of modern 'scientism,' that it could pass through it at all."

[21] Thomas Aquinas, *In IV Sent.*, dist. 1, q. 1, a. 4, sol. 2: "The power of affecting the sight is present in the air, which is an instrument moved by the external thing being seen."

[22] John of St. Thomas, *Phil. nat.* IV, q. 7, a. 2 (R, III, 212A). [Against the thesis that light is a physical, not an intentional, quality, some quote St. Thomas' saying (*De pot.*, q. 5, a. 1, ad 6) that light exists in the air, not as a perfect form, but in an intentional way.] John of St. Thomas explains: "St. Thomas speaks there of the intentional nature, or mode, not as it refers to the representative form contrasted with the object represented, but rather as indicating something transient in contrast with something permanent and fixed. For after all, the intentional species do exist in the air in the manner of something fleeting,

Physical action transmitted by an instrument has as its term no more than a physical effect, on the same ontological level as that of the effect produced by the principal cause prior to the involvement of the instrument. A belt transmits power that does not originate with it. The power that has its origin in the motor exists intentionally in the belt, but at the end of the belt there is only rotation, a physical movement existentially identical with the original movement produced by the motor. Thus if the sensible object exercised only a physical action, its efficiency would pass through a state of intentional existence in the medium entirely in vain, for the effect produced at the end of the transmission could never be anything more than a physical effect.

What has to be explained here is an effect belonging to an order higher than the whole physical order. As it exists in the inanimate medium, the sensible form, which obviously does not yet possess there an *Erkannt-Sein*, must already be at least an *Erkenntnisbild*, a kind of virtual idea destined to bring about an act of knowledge. And to explain this, we could assume that nature anticipates cognition by producing a universe of intentional forms outside the realm of the soul to provide the soul with what the soul needs to "become all things."

(*e*) But this brings up in an urgent way the all-important problem of the efficient cause of the intentional forms or, more accurately, of the intentional state which they possess before they are penetrated by the activity of the soul, and which they have for the sake of making that activity possible. If this intentional state of sensible forms is supposed to develop into the full-fledged intentional existence that alone makes knowledge possible, it seems clear that it cannot be produced by the things themselves, which, since they have only material being, possess of themselves

---

depending on the object for their origin and preservation, and any quality or power in this mode may be said to be in an intentional way, even though it is not an intentional representation. For instance, St. Thomas (*De pot.*, q. 3, a. 7, ad 7) calls the power by which God acts in inferior causes an intention, precisely because it is something similarly transient." Thus we do well to remember that when Thomists say that the color that exists physically in the colored object exists intentionally in the medium that transmits it, they have in mind something other than this fleeting and incomplete way of existing that one may attribute to the power of the principal agent passing through its instrument.

only a material efficiency. We shall have to admit that the production of intentional forms by the sensible objects, therefore, presupposes a participation on their part in some kind of a higher efficient power, a special motion or premotion, distinct from the ordinary physical premotion, and one which conveys with particular force the excellence of the first cause.[23]

And so we are led to recognize that after He has given material things a causal power proportionate to their nature, God communicates to them an additional efficiency, designed specifically to make them known to beings who are deprived of innate

---

[23] The problem of the efficient cause of the intentional state of the sensible forms does not seem ever to have been considered by Aristotle (Cajetan presents his own theory as being in conformity with Aristotle's thought, but he does not quote any texts); it is raised by Averroës (*In De An.* II, com. 60). St. Thomas is satisfied to say that the sensory object is a sufficient cause of the impression of sensible forms on the sense, most probably because he wants to eliminate the hypothesis of a *sensus agens* and safeguard the principle of the soul's passivity in the reception of the sensible form (see especially *Quodl.*, 8, a. 3). But he never explains whether this sufficiency is possessed by the sensory object of its own nature or through a participated power. Still, in a well-known passage from *De potentia* (q. 5, a. 8), St. Thomas expressly relates the intentional activity that gives rise to sensible forms to the object's participation in the power of the separated substances: "One should be aware that bodies exercise two kinds of action. One of them corresponds to the condition proper to bodies, viz., action by way of motion. Indeed, being moved to move and act is the condition proper to bodies. But bodies exercise another action inasmuch as they are in contact with the order of the separated substances and enjoy some participation in what properly belongs to the superior nature; this is manifest in some animals which possess a faculty akin to prudence, although prudence properly belongs to men. This action of the body is aimed not at the transmutation of matter, but at a certain diffusion of a likeness of the form in the medium in the likeness of a spiritual intention that is received from the thing in the sense or the intellect. This is how the sun illuminates the air, and *the color multiplies its species in the medium.*"

This text is far from clear, and the comparison St. Thomas uses lends itself to misinterpretation. When he says that some animals participate in prudence, which properly belongs to rational beings, what he means is this: while typical animal behavior is instinctive and fixed, that of rational beings is prudential, shaped by and always ready to adjust to new experiences. But we know that some animals are able to take advantage of their individual experience and to modify their behavior accordingly, and in this respect they resemble man and may be said to participate in the privileges of his nature. But is the participation in the ways appropriate to the separated substances that St. Thomas sees at work in the production of sensible forms no more than a simple resemblance? As we see it, there is more to it. The reason why St. Thomas attributes to bodies the power to produce higher intentional forms is that for him their

ideas and who are at once material and cognitive. This conception, which might have a certain romantic appeal for both the materialists and the idealists (often birds of a feather), also fits neatly with the theory of superabundance discussed in the first chapter. And the ultimate explanation we can give of the fact of knowledge, then, is the divine plan to communicate to some creatures an image of the divine infinity. The divine art was pleased to create some knowing creatures, angels, with innate knowledge of things. But it has also pleased God to extend the privilege of knowing beyond the pure spirits and to grant it to some

---

efficiency is actually penetrated by a higher efficiency. We must not forget that, in Thomism, the state of the intentional forms is invariably considered ontologically superior to the state of physical existence of corporeal things. And for a reality on a higher ontological level to issue from a reality on a lower ontological level, the latter's efficiency must be reinforced by a higher one.

The question we are dealing with is addressed at some length by Cajetan, *In De an.* II, 11 (B. 162Bff.). First of all, Cajetan develops two theses presupposed by the question. (*a*) There is a specific distinction between the sensible and its intentional form. But one should keep in mind that a specific distinction can result either from a diversity of nature (as whiteness is specifically distinct from sweetness) or from a difference in the *ways of being.* If two things are specifically distinct by reason of difference in nature, one of them cannot be produced by the other, for every agent produces something similar to itself. But if the specific distinction results from a difference in ways of being, one of two specifically distinct things can be produced by the other. It is in the second way, not in the first, that color and its intentional form are distinct. (*b*) Intentional being is in a certain way spiritual, and consequently it is nobler than physical being. But *since the less noble cannot produce the more noble,* Averroës rightly asks "What, then, is the cause of the spiritual state of sensible forms?" But his answer that the cause of the intentional being of the sensible forms cannot be the sensory object goes against the teaching of Aristotle, who holds that color is visible *per se,* which implies that it has in itself the cause of its visibility. Cajetan also notes that it is also contrary to experience, which shows that the visible object produces its intentional form in the mirror. To deny such facts would be as arbitrary as to deny that fire burns, and we would be in danger of falling into the error of the Mutācallimūn (the *Loquentes* in Moorish law), who denied things any causal power of their own. For Aristotle, Albert the Great, and St. Thomas (loc. cit.), Cajetan says, the cause of the intentional being is the sensory object, not inasmuch as it is material, but inasmuch as its form participates in the properties of the separated forms. For bodies and other natures have two kinds of traits (*conditiones*), viz., those that are proper to them, and those that they have by way of participation in the privileges of the separated forms. This is manifested by activities: bodies act in two ways, viz., as moved, and without motion. To act as moved belongs properly to bodies; to act without being moved belongs to the separated forms properly and to bodies only by participation. For example, the warm body exercises two kinds

corporeal beings, rational and even irrational animals, that have no innate ideas and must use as means of knowledge objects proportionate to their faculties. From this point of view, the endowing of things with the power of intentional as well as physical causality is but the counterpart to or the complement of the creation of animals and of man. It may well be paradoxical, but it is no more so than this participation in the divine infinity granted with the gift of knowledge to angel, man, and the lowest of the beasts.

THE PASSIVITY OF SENSE AND THE IMMANENT ACT OF KNOWING

Still, the notion of an intentional influence from physical objects raises additional serious difficulties. The sense, exposed to this influence, has to be absolutely passive because nothing moves without an idea to direct its activity, and insofar as the sense receives its idea from the object, it will not have a rule for its activity until after the activity to which it must submit passively

---

of activity, one by which it causes heat in physical being, the other by which it causes the intentional form of heat in the medium and in the sense. To sum up: the proximate efficient cause of the intentional being of the sensible form is the form of the object, but the primary principle by participation in which this causation takes place is a separate agent. Averroës' arguments do not disprove this, and Cajetan repeats: "If we look for the proximate agent, it is the form of the object; but if we look for the primary agent whose participation makes sensation possible, it is a separate agent." See also John of St. Thomas, *Phil. nat.* IV, q. 6, a. 2 (R, III, 188B30ff.).

Contemporary Thomists are no longer in the habit of calling upon the pure spirits to explain sensation, which is doubtless one reason why their interpretations of the theory of sensation are so unsatisfactory, even incomprehensible. This timid silence has had, among other harmful effects, the result of lending credence to the opinion that, according to Thomism, the material object acts directly on the mind, contrary to the Augustinian principle (which is also a Thomistic principle as well as a principle of common sense) that the inferior cannot act upon the superior. Thomism can never admit that an inanimate body, as inanimate, has the power to exercise any influence on the sensible soul. In genuine Thomistic thought, it is only by a kind of *participated animation* that bodies act upon the soul. For noteworthy remarks on this subject, see Réginald Garrigou-Lagrange, o.p., *Le Réalisme du principe de finalité* (Paris: Desclée De Brouwer, 1932), pp. 18off.; Maritain, *Degrees of Knowledge,* p. 188n1.

has been completed.[24] But have we not established that where there is pure passivity in the subject, the result can only be a physical or material union? An intentional action unaccompanied by any reaction is a contradictory notion. Passive reception of a sensible form would have to be then a material reception. But then it could never bring about an act of knowledge.

The solution to this difficulty undoubtedly lies in the previously established distinction between the two aspects of the idea, its physical or subjective aspect and its intentional or objective aspect. The idea must be physically united to the soul for the soul to have access to the object, somewhat in the manner of a bridge anchored at both banks. Thus the effect of what we have called the intentional action of the object on the sense faculty is indeed a kind of physical union of the faculty and the idea, which introduces into the faculty the idea as a physical reality and thereby affects and qualifies the faculty in its natural being.[25] It is important, however, to see that such an action, if the object is considered, or such a reception, if the faculty is considered, is at the same time both physical and non-physical. In one sense, it is an entirely physical event that, like any transitive action, can have no other result than the constitution of a composite; but in another sense, what happens here is an event specifically distinct from anything that goes on in things without knowledge and one that cannot be reduced to physical becoming. When the sense faculty and the idea unite their natures, the faculty is put into initial act, made perfect in its natural being; the influence of the object joined to the receptivity of the soul can produce nothing but this physical perfecting of the faculty.

---

[24] Thomas Aquinas, *Quodl.*, 8, a. 3 "[Things outside the soul] are related to the external senses as sufficient agents with which the patients do not cooperate, but from which they only receive. . . . The external senses are recipients from things only as patients, without contributing anything to being informed; but *once informed*, they have their own operation, which is a judgment about their proper objects."

[25] John of St. Thomas, *Log.* II, q. 21, a. 4 (R, I, 676B44); *Phil. nat.* IV, q. 6, a. 3 (R, III, 191B28). "And so, although the idea [species] informs the sense faculty by uniting with it physically, it informs it intentionally only when the faculty joins in the act being aroused by it. The informing by the object is for the sake of preparing for cognition. The idea as such inheres physically in the faculty; but in its intentional aspect it serves as a medium that connects the sense

But if we keep in mind that the *idea* differs from the *thing*, we shall also discern the other effect of its union with the sense faculty. The idea has physical being, and goodness, not for its own sake but exclusively as an intentional medium whose union with the faculty derives its entire *raison d'être*, with nothing left over, from the intentional union of the faculty and the object. And because of that, transitive action of the object on the faculty and the corresponding passion in the faculty in relation to the object are, by virtue of their essential purpose, something quite different from ordinary action and reception, which always result in the constitution of a composite. The immediate effect of the action of the object on the sense is simply to disengage from the potentiality of the sense a form that will determine that potentiality. But this is an intentional form affected to the very depths of its physical reality by what may be called its intentional vocation. Just as the physical being of the idea is what it is only for the sake of the idea's intentional function, so the influence of the object on the sense, with its immediate aim of determining the faculty by the physical being of the idea, is made what it is by what constitutes the goal of the idea and of the physical determination it exercises, viz., the intentional union of the soul with the object. The intentional union that gives its character to the influence exercised by the object on the faculty of knowing requires thus a special explanation to account for it. Because this union will ultimately be effected by the soul, this original influence that the object exercises on the knowing faculty cannot be reduced to ordinary causality. And so, even though it is a physical action, it deserves to be called *intentional* action because it is *essentially* designed to give rise to an intentional union. For what the action of the object impresses upon the faculty physically is only the idea in which the object itself is present in a sleep-like state and ready to awake as soon as the soul communicates its own vitality to it. The subjective reception of the idea thus fecundates the faculty and supplies it with everything it needs to move to its terminal act, which will coincide

---

to the object itself. And so, as we have said above, the physical effect of the idea is distinct from its intentional effect in that in the former the idea acts alone, whereas in the latter it is the object that acts to beget cognition, with the idea mediating, taking the place, so to speak, of the object that is contained in it."

with the awakening of the object present in the idea.[26]

But if we now say that in contrast with an initial phase of pure passivity, the soul becomes fully active, or reactive, in the act of sensible knowledge, the sensation properly so-called, we run the risk of oversimplifying the causality in knowledge by conceiving it on the model of physical causality and thus again confusing nature and cognition. Causality is measured by being; as being is, so will the causality emanating from it be. The heterogeneity of ontological valences rules out any univocal conception of causality. The basic difference between the modalities of the physical and the intentional existence entails a corresponding difference in the meanings of the notion of causality. As we have previously pointed out, the normal application of the principle of identity is upset when confronted by the act of knowing, considered as existence, because this act combines properties that are incompatible everywhere except in cognition, viz., being oneself and being the other. Considered as an activity, the act of knowing, for a reason immediately derived from the preceding, will similarly overthrow the normal application of the principle of causality.

It really makes no difference whether we are dealing with the senses or with the understanding, for causality in cognition presents universal properties that are verified, *mutatis mutandis*, in all creaturely knowledge at the moment when the intentional aspect of the idea, which is simply the object existing intentionally, comes forth from the faculty determined by the idea in an

---

[26] John of St. Thomas, *Phil. nat.* IV, q. 4, a. 1 (R, III, 104A46): "And so from this we can draw the obvious conclusion that the knowing power, while indeed always present in the order of knowledge, is formally passive and only capable of being made actual by the object. In fact, the knowing power depends on the object not only to be actuated, to be in act, but also for the specification of that act. And yet the act of cognition does not proceed partly from the object and partly from the faculty: it is a single emergence and emanation, in which the soul's vitality and the object's specification are fused together, an emergence which is necessarily from the power, because this is its vital role; and so, *whatever it has from the object must have first come into the power*, in order that the emanation arise from it . . . just as in a single birth from his mother a son is also the father's son because the mother had previously been impregnated by the father. And so, in the production of knowledge, the faculty and the object are related as mother and father, since the power is fecundated by the object as the mother is by the father."

act that has its vitality from the faculty and its determination from the idea. *The knower and the known, which are but one in existence, are also one in activity.* The distinction between agent and patient disappears here, because the distinction between the same and the other has also disappeared. If there is an activity of the soul, there is also an activity of the object; and the activity of the soul is the same as that of the object, because the soul and the object are one. Thus in its terminal act cognition is properly neither action nor passion but a surge of vitality that transcends the usual action–passion modalities, in a way similar to that in which intentional existence transcends the ordinary modalities of identity and otherness by uniting the same and the other.[27]

This joint activity that holds the known and the knower in intentional union is the only kind that can be attributed to the object of knowledge considered *as such*, rather than, say, as an

---

[27] Thomas Aquinas, *De ver.*, q. 8, a. 6; Cajetan, *In Ia*, q. 79, a. 2 (Whether the intellect is a passive power). In this commentary, which deserves a place of honor among the great texts on the metaphysics of knowing, Cajetan takes up two important questions: (*a*) "Is intelligence passive with respect to its initial act?" and to this he gives an affirmative answer; and (*b*) "What is the role of intelligence in its terminal act, the act of understanding?" For some, he writes, the naked intelligence is the only active principle in the whole of knowledge; for others, the naked intelligence is only a partial principle; for still others, the intellect is totally passive. But, finally, some hold that while passive *per se* (*ratione sui*), the intellect becomes active when actuated by the intelligible form. This last thesis is held by St. Thomas, but if the special meanings that these terms assume in the context of cognition are not carefully distinguished, it is open to serious misunderstanding.

"The intellect by its nature is in the genus of passive power, and it does not have, of itself, any explanation for its activity. . . . The latter must thus be explained with reference to the intelligible in act, for it is common to every form to be such a principle of action as long as it is not prevented from doing so. But because *the intellect does not receive the intelligible as matter receives form but actually becomes that intelligible*, it follows that this totality, viz., the intellect in the first act, understands not just by reason of its active part, although it is because of it that it understands. We must remember that the soul that apprehends belongs to a different order of being than do things of nature, and that its community with them in being, in power, and in receiving their forms is an equivocal one." Matter receives form in such a way as to produce a composite whose action nevertheless belongs to the form and not to the matter, except insofar as the matter sustains the form and is part of the composite. But the soul (as Averroës put it so well in *In De an.* III, com. 5) does not receive the knowable to make a knowing composite; rather the soul becomes the knowable

object of sensory knowledge. It is a way of acting that is infinitely delicate, infinitely respectful of the spontaneity of the living receiver on which it is exercised but only in order to bring about a joint performance. If we wish to conceive the action of God upon created things, this provides the least crude image of how it takes place. No force is involved here, no constraint; the independence and the transcendence of the object agree completely with the vitality of the act that reaches it. There is a single efficiency, as there is a single existence; in acting as in being, the soul and the object are identified.

This marvelous functioning of efficient causality in the immanent act of knowing requires nothing more than the intentional presence of the object; it is realized in thought as it is in sensation, in angelic thought as it is in human thought, and in abstractive knowledge as it is in intuitive knowledge. The soul here does not require the physical presence of the thing known, and it can

---

and, once actuated by the intelligible form, it is the soul that is the bearer of action. In other words, the intellect cooperates actively in the act of understanding, in contrast to the way in which material things are made to act; the way the soul in act becomes the knowable is totally different from the way matter is put into act. Moreover, the active cooperation of the intellect should not be seen as merely contributing to the understanding, as Scotus imagined against Aristotle; nor should we assume that the intellect's activity comes exclusively from the intelligible species [idea], as some contemporary writers would have it. This cooperation comes about because the human intellect is a vital power that when activated must act, and does so with action that belongs to it alone. A great many are mistaken about this, because they make judgments about the soul as if it were a physical thing, and they pay no attention to Averroës' rule that there is a far greater unity, including their operation, between the intellect and the intelligible than between the physical matter and form. *To understand, therefore, is not formally to be passive, even though, properly speaking, it is not, formally, to act either. Rather, understanding is a vital operation, part active and part passive, and the same is true of sensation.*"

Note that what Cajetan says here about the activity of the knower in the terminal act of sensation and thought seems to be as true of angelic thought as it is of human. In this respect, Cajetan's conclusion states a law that applies to all created knowledge. Cf. Bañez, *In Ia.*, q. 79, a. 2: "Once put in act by the idea [intelligible species], the human intellect cooperates actively in bringing forth understanding, just as the angelic intellect does, and in this respect there is no difference between them."

Cajetan's views on the activity of the sense are outlined, discussed, and compared with those of Aristotle, St. Thomas, and John of St. Thomas in Yves Simon, "Positions aristotéliciennes concernant le problème de l'activité du sens," *Revue de Philosophie* (May–June 1933).

know things that have no physical existence. But let us also realize that none of this applies to the intentional transitive action that we have established as the exclusive guarantee of the experimental character of our sensory knowledge.

What we must insist upon at this point is that the intentional transitive action, which is all that goes on in the preparatory phase of sensation, and in which the sense faculty is totally passive, *does not cease* when the faculty, stirred into initial act, joins with the intentionally present object in the full exercise of the act of cognition. What would happen if the action of the physically existing object suddenly stopped when, duly prepared, the act of sense knowledge was about to be exercised? If at the moment when sensation is about to take place the influence emanating from the physically existing object ceased, for whatever reasons, to determine the act of the faculty, the essential conditions for true experimental knowledge would clearly also disappear. And so, we have to conclude that the influence exercised by the physically existing object is necessary not just to produce the union of its idea with the faculty but also to preserve that union. The sensation will persist only as long as this influence is exercised. This is not like the case of the universal, whose form once impressed in the soul stays there and is forever ready for an intentional union with it. The singular sensible exists outside the soul, and the soul can be united to it only under the influence of its external reality.

That is why the notion of immanent action is realized only imperfectly in sensation. The immanent act of sensory knowledge remains tied, for its duration, to a transitive action exercised by the object.[28] Prepared strictly through an intentional passion, sensation does indeed become a vital activity, but it can last only as long as the transitive action of the object. For an example of a more genuine immanent activity, we must turn to thought, which enjoys the privilege of a different kind of freedom.[29]

---

[28] Thomas Aquinas, *Sum. th.* I, q. 27, a. 5: "Sensing is not entirely removed from the genus of external actions; for the act of sensation is perfected by action of the sensible upon the sense."

[29] Thomas Aquinas, *Q. De an.*, a. 5, ad 7.

The Birth of the Idea[30]

If we were given the power to sense as pure animals, even for a single instant, there is no doubt that the philosophy of sensualism would be totally discredited. Sensualism claims to explain the properties of thought by the evolution of the properties of images, and without reference to any higher ontological principle. But the image could not play its assigned role in this little charade if care were not taken to hide in it a germ of thought.

What the experience of pure sensation would be like, were it possible, is barely suggested by some psychological states attained under rather exceptional circumstances. A couple of contrasting examples would be the anguished torpor induced by ethylene-chloride intoxication, on the one hand, and the lethargic peace of the convalescent on a gentle spring afternoon. The emotional response in both these cases is an intense feeling of strangeness, unbearable and frightening in the first instance, and rather pleasant in the second. Indeed, when by either violent or peaceful inhibition, the presence of thought in our experience drops below a certain level, the whole universe of sensation invariably takes on a strange new appearance. For we can feel at home in the sensible world only to the extent that our sensations are penetrated by thought.

This can also be verified by considering something quite different from the state of torpor, namely, the way the sensible world appears to the scientist, who is alert and able to name and define the things presented in the flood of sensations. The nature walk taken by the scientist is accompanied by a feeling of familiarity. Pierre Termier is thus quite at home in the Grand Canyon. In fact, some people with strong imaginations, fond of colors, shapes, and odors, hostile to all abstractions, and lacking a scientific cast of mind, still develop an intense liking for natural science. For instance, Francis Jammes collects plants while he writes poetry; he loves flowers for their beauty, but his love includes also a keen sense of the challenge that vegetative spe-

---

[30] In this chapter we shall use the term *idea* not in the broad sense in which it covers every intentional form (cf. above, chap. 1, note 22), but in a narrow sense restricted to the spiritual intentional forms (in contrast to sensory), and especially to those that are at the starting point of thought (*species impressa*).

cies as such present to our understanding. In the same vein, André Gide certainly knows his insects. On friendly terms with the sensible world, we are unwilling to show up there as strangers, which happens every time our sensations are not accompanied by understanding. We are at home in the world, we are at ease, only when the data of sensation are closely associated with an object of thought, so that when we see colors and shapes (the sensible *per se*), we at the same time grasp essences and laws (the intelligible *per se* and sensible by accident). It is seeing ideas incarnate in the sensible things of nature that gives them, as it were, a human countenance. Still, there is a significant paradox involved here. The typical rules of their disciplines oblige the poet, the naturalist, the geographer to express their understanding of the world in terms related to sensations. But even though this represents a clouded intelligibility, it in no way prevents the scientist or the poet from experiencing an unmixed intimacy with the things of this world. By contrast, when he confronts nature, the metaphysician, who strives for complete intelligibility, cannot avoid a certain feeling of melancholy. Faced with a system of white, yellow, and green colors with a definite pattern, the botanist recognizes a daisy and has little doubt that he understands what he is seeing, which he does indeed on the level of empirical intelligibility. But even if he knows as much about the daisy as the naturalist does, the metaphysician is well aware that he does not understand what he is seeing—from the perspective of the higher intelligibility prescribed by the law of metaphysical thought. And he comes to realize that, to a great extent, the sensible world is closed off to him. Indeed, in order for the ontologist to experience the feeling of familiarity comparable to what the empiricist feels in the real sensible world, he would need to find himself in something like the Eden described by André Gide, which is a quasi-angelic universe of essences, presenting just enough objective sensibility and mobility to allow poetic imagination to appear convincing.

> Paradise was not very big, but it was perfect; each form opened up but once; a single garden held them all. Whether it existed or not makes no difference, but this is the way it was, if it existed. Everything was crystalized in an inevitable flowering, and everything was perfectly as it was supposed to be. Everything was

motionless, because nothing wanted to be better. A still gravitation was alone responsible for the revolution of the whole.

And since no impulse ends, either in the Past or in the Future, Paradise had never come to be—it simply always existed.

Chaste Eden! A Garden of Ideas, in which the forms, sure and rhythmical, revealed their number effortlessly; in which each thing was what it appeared to be; in which proof was futile.

Eden, where melodious breezes undulated in anticipated curves; where heaven exposed its azure to the symmetrical lawns; where the birds were the color of time and the butterflies on the flowers made providential harmonies; where the rose was rose because the beetle was green, which is why it came to rest there. Everything was as perfect as a number and was scanned in a normal way; a consonance emanated from the relations of lines; a constant symphony sounded over the garden.[31]

How strange the world when it is merely sensed! How familiar nature when it has become intelligible! If we pay attention to these convergent facts, we come to realize that the universe of pure sensation is an inhuman universe that becomes human only to the extent that sensation is penetrated by thought. The customary universe of human perception owes its appearance, its consistency, and its humanity to the presence of thought in human perception. The sensualist charade is exposed. What those who claim to explain the highest operations of the mind by reference to sensation alone are actually using is not pure sensation but the complex of human perception in which thought is already present. Pure sensation, even aided by the richest train of images, can never explain the slightest thought. And that is where we are now. Having accounted for the birth of sensation, we find that the problem of the birth of the idea remains untouched.

To continue, we propose an intuitive approach similar to the one followed at the very beginning of this inquiry. Then we needed to recognize and describe the object of knowledge in its form as object, abstracting from any content. Now we need to extend that intuitive method to examine and describe what

---

[31] André Gide, *Le Retour de l'enfant prodigue* (Paris: Nouvelle Revue Française, 1912), p. 13.

appear to be two basic aspects of that content. And just as we found that *being* is realized or expressed primarily under the forms of being in potency and being in act, it appears that the transcendental notion of *knowing* is realized and expressed as sensory cognition and intellectual knowledge. The content of the object of knowledge being thus primarily determined by the characteristics of intellectuality and sensibility, this is what we want now to concentrate on. We want to consider the object of knowledge not with respect to what makes it be purely an object of knowledge, nor yet to what causes it to express itself as a particular thing in a particular genus and a particular species; we want to examine it with respect to what causes it to be either an object of sensory cognition or an object of intellectual knowledge. Indeed, we want to concentrate on those characteristics of intellectuality or sensibility that, as the given content of its transcendental notion, remain forms in relation to every determinate object of knowledge, sensory or intellectual. And what strikes us first of all is the recognition that, unlike an object sensed or imagined, an object of thought necessarily implicates in its intellectuality the very *being* of the thing thought,[32] together with its identity, which absolutely refuses—and here the domain of the absolute begins—to be confused with what it is not. With all the firmness of the principle of identity, the thing thought demands to be everything that it is and to possess all the properties that derive from its nature by virtue of the identity of its being with itself. For instance, it is not the three narrow white lines intersecting on a black background that want every triangle to be inscribable in a circle; it is the idea of the triangle that will have it so. Similarly, there is no way of pulling together into one concept the quality of being blond and possessing a certain social status, except by declaring that this man, Peter, who is a teacher, has a fair complexion. And finally, while the sight of a box of

---

[32] Aristotle, *On the Soul* III, 6, 430B27; Thomas Aquinas, *De ver.*, q. 1, aa. 1, 12; *In Meta.* IV, lect. 6 (C. 605); IX, lect. 5 (C. 2211); *Cont. gent.* II, 83; *Sum. th.* I, q. 5, a. 2; q. 55, a. 1; q. 79, a. 7; I–II, q. 94, a. 2; II–II, q. 8, a. 1. There are many references in the *Tabula aurea* of Peter of Bergamot under the word *intellectus*, nn. 18–23. On the relation of thought to being and the irreducibility of the idea to the image, see also the classic pages of Garrigou-Lagrange, *Le Sens commun*, pp. 44ff., and *Dieu, son existence et sa nature*, pp. 121ff.

oranges may make one remember Spain, and the memory of Spain may bring to mind Primo de Rivera, that box of oranges would not stop being a box of oranges even if Primo de Rivera had never existed. But a diagonal would instantly cease to be a diagonal the moment we were to find it commensurable with the side of the square. Thus no matter how much one tries to purify the sensible datum when passing from the sensation to the image, or how ingeniously one manipulates the image, one cannot and will never come up with an idea. The idea clearly does not come from the senses; it comes and can only come from the mind.

From this conclusion, it might seem only natural to assume that the mind must be essentially independent of the senses with respect to what it needs in order to know. It might also appear reasonable to assume that ideas and the mind came to be together and that knowledge consists in the progressive awakening of the ideas present in the soul from the moment of its creation. Such an innatist spiritualism, however, quickly runs into innumerable difficulties. For instance, if the human mind were not restricted to acquiring its ideas from experience, and if sensations and images were not the objective requirements of thought, then the condition of the body would have no effect at all on the life of the mind, either in its substance or in its operation. But there is no philosophical fact better established than the concrete, existential dependence of thought on bodily conditions. The parallelism of intellectual and somatic development, drunkenness, dreams, the psychic consequences of cerebral lesions, the deliria of intoxication, mental illness—all these facts, even if they do not prove the materialist sensualist argument, certainly belie the teachings of innatist spiritualism. Indeed, if, by a simple gift of nature, the human mind had everything required for the knowledge in which its perfection consists, then sense and imagination would be only a source of obscurity for it, and the body an embarrassment, separation from which would be naturally desirable. In the course of its history, such philosophical idealism has been accused of many harmful effects, which include leaving genuine spirituality defenseless against materialist critique. But the most shocking thing about this doctrine is that it is so untrue to nature. For the conclusion it points to claims in effect that in order to expand its grasp of truth, the human intellect wants death as the indispensable condition of its perfection.[33]

What we need, therefore, is to preserve at all costs the double certainty (a) that ideas are spiritual in origin and (b) that they nevertheless come somehow from sensory cognition.[34] This clearly presupposes some kind of collaboration between the mind and the senses. But figuring out the precise modalities this collaboration may assume is by no means an easy task.

---

[33] Thomas Aquinas, *Sum. th.* I, q. 83, aa. 3, 4, 7, 8.

[34] The following passage from Dalbiez' "Saint Jean de la Croix d'après M. Baruzi" (pp. 27–28) is well worth quoting in full. The author is discussing a text in which Fénelon appeals, in order to explain certain mystical states, to the notion of a thought that, without having anything miraculous about it, would owe nothing to the experience of the senses or to the imagination. Dalbiez writes: "If our understanding does not depend upon the cooperation of the imagination, how is one to explain the parallelism between the development of the body and the development of the intellect, between somatic and mental infantilism, on the one hand, and physical and psychic senility, on the other? How is one to explain dreaming? If our understanding were totally independent of our body and senses, and if we possessed innate ideas, we should be able to think just as correctly when asleep as when awake. Anyone who has ever dreamed, even if only once, has experimental proof of the falsity of Fénelon's thesis. And if we move on from dreaming to mental illnesses, the proofs come even faster. Though not all cerebral lesions corresponding to psychoses have been identified, there are cases in which they are known. And so we find ourselves trapped between two difficulties. On the one hand, the idea of a pure, disembodied spirit being ill seems inconceivable, the simplicity of purely spiritual realities being so opposed to the disorganization implied in the concept of illness. On the other hand, it is absolutely certain that strictly material causes not only can provoke mental illnesses but can, to a large extent, determine the character of that illness. For instance, though delirium caused by alcohol brings up visions of animals, opium intoxication causes impressions of lightness and flight, etc. Now, most psychopathologists and psychiatrists, whose knowledge of spirituality is that of classical Cartesianism (which Fénelon refers to without naming it, and making St. Augustine its spokesman), draw from these facts the conclusion that a philosophy of the spirit is bankrupt and see no other choice but to subscribe more or less openly to materialist interpretations. They make thought a function of the brain. But in that case our understanding would be just like a sense faculty, a little more perfect perhaps than the others, but still not able to grasp a universal concept, indeed, unable to have a thought. Some try to get out of this difficulty by claiming that there are no universals, but that is a self-denying proposition since 'no' is a negative universal. How, then, does one escape this antinomy? There is only one way, and that is to go back to the Thomistic thesis of abstraction. From this point of view, which recognizes that the senses are faculties bound to an organism, not only is it easy to explain that they can be upset by organic lesions but also,

Prior to possessing the idea, the mind is incapable of knowing anything, and so the production of the idea can be on its part—at least as far as primary ideas are concerned—only a precognitive operation.[35] Once it has acquired ideas, the mind will use them to construct new ideas in the light of knowledge; but the formation of the primary ideas has to be the work of a faculty which, although wholly in the service of knowledge, is yet not destined to know. This active power by which the mind gives birth to the ideas is indeed a blind source of light. It works to produce intelligible forms without perceiving them itself; it is intellect improperly so called that causes thought by causing the idea in the intellect properly so called.[36]

---

since the object of the understanding is derived by abstraction from the object of the senses and the imagination, it stands to reason that sense disorders can produce difficulties for the understanding. The dependence of the intelligence on the senses thus satisfies what is true in the materialist thesis, while the extrinsic character of this dependence respects the spirituality of the soul and permits the knowledge of the universal. Thought is not a function of the brain, but its object. And this object, the universal, is derived by abstraction from objects whose production is the function of the bodily senses."

[35] Bañez, *In Ia*, q. 79, a. 3 (D, II, 296B); John of St. Thomas, *Phil. nat.* IV, q. 10, a. 1 (R, III, 303A35). (In favor of the Suarezian thesis that the *intellectus agens* and the intellect are one and the same, it is argued that the intellect has the power to construct new ideas with the help of ideas previously conceived.) "The answer is that the intellect can indeed form new ideas from those it already has, because it forms them by composing what it knows; but preconceived ideas cannot be used to form the original and primary ideas, because these are formed by a non-cognitive power; and this is enough to distinguish between these two powers." De Monléon, "L'Intelligence humaine," 549: "But the agent intellect, whose entire activity consists in *causing* the intelligible, can be called intellect only improperly and by analogy, since it has no power to *think*. It is both luminous and blind, like fish at the bottom of the ocean."

Keep in mind that Thomistic philosophy, contrary to a widespread caricature of it, is a long way from attributing the formation of our ideas exclusively to the precognitive activity of the so-called *intellectus agens*. The function of the precognitive abstraction is to actuate the intellect; but once aroused by the *intellectus agens*, it is the intellect proper that proceeds to elaborate its ideas.

[36] For the general theory of the *intellectus agens*, see Aristotle, *On the Soul* III, 5, 430A10; Thomas Aquinas, *In De an.* III, lect. 10 (P. 728ff.); *De ver.*, q. 10, a. 6; *Q. De an.*, aa. 4, 5; *De spir. creat.*, aa. 9, 10; *Cont. gent.* II, 76, 77, 78; *Sum. th.* I, q. 79, aa. 3, 4, 5; Cajetan, *In Ia*, q. 79, a. 3; q. 85, a. 1, ad 4; q. 87, a. 1; *In De an.* III, 2 (B. 207Aff.); John of St. Thomas, *Phil. nat.* IV, q. 10, aa. 1, 2 (R, III, 295ff.); Tommaso Zigliara, "De la lumière intellectuelle et de l'ontologisme," *Oeuvres philosophiques* (Lyons: Vitte and Perrussel, 1880); Etienne Gilson, "Pourquoi saint Thomas a critiqué saint Augustin," offprint from *Archives*

But what is the specifying principle of this activity that in fact produces the idea? You will recall that the form of an action can be predetermined in only two ways: namely, either by nature or by knowledge. The rule of action is always either an idea or a physical constitution, and we have to ask which is involved in the production of the idea. Now, the formal predetermination of the action that produces the idea cannot itself be an idea; and of course it cannot be the nature of the mind either, because until the moment an idea is actually formed in it, the intellect has no specifications whatsoever. Prior to the formation of an idea, the only form the mind has is its spirituality. What it makes will be spiritual, if it makes anything; and if this is a representation, it will be the representation of an intelligible. But in the limitless field of the spiritual, of the intelligible, of being, there is, in the nature of the mind, prior to the production of the idea, no pre-formation of any particular species, no actual relation to any particular object. The spirituality of the idea can come only from the mind, but its specific determination cannot come from it. The activity that produces the idea must thus depend upon the intervention of a factor that puts at the disposal of the mind the necessary preformation for that activity.

A mind without innate ideas has no recourse other than to produce it own ideas, for nothing from sensible reality or the sense can produce them in it. But since the mind does not have within itself any ideas to direct its activity, and since their production requires preformation, which it cannot provide for itself, the mind has to be supplied with that preformation in some fashion, virtual or potential, by a knowledge not its own. The mind will give the idea its spiritual character, but what that idea will be is determined by the image.[37] The production of the idea is an *abstraction* that disengages the intelligible from the image.

---

d'Histoire Doctrinale et Littéraire du Moyen Age, 1 (1926)—a remarkable study of the historical formation of the Thomistic doctrine of the *intellectus agens*.

[37] Thomas Aquinas, *De spir. creat.*, a. 10, ad 4: "And so if the intellect is considered in relation to the images, it will be in one respect in potency, and in another respect in act with regard to them. The image in act is a singular determined likeness, but that likeness is potentially abstractable from its material conditions. It is the other way around for the intellect. While the intellect in act does not have the likenesses of singular things, it has the immaterial power to abstract what is in potency abstractable from them."

By a unique act, the mind causes the intelligible to emerge from the image that contains it—the intelligible is there because nature is an idea of the divine art—and thus gives itself the means for thought. Risking a metaphorical description, we may imagine a space in which the mind, before the acquisition of experience, is eager to know but has no means of knowing, and, alongside it, the active faculty of the intellect ready to serve knowledge by abstracting ideas from images. Yet this faculty cannot act in a vacuum, as it were, to produce ideas that are not ideas of something. What kind of likeness could the active faculty set down in the mind if not the likeness of some particular object? Thus when all is said and done, we find that it is the potential intelligibility inhering in the image that provides the active faculty with the needed preformation that enables it to act in a determined way and deposit in the mind proper what we may call a concrete idea.

But what is not so easy to figure out is the type of causality exercised by the image. Since its sole function is to cooperate in the production of the idea by supplying its specification—that is, the intelligible outlines of the object which the mind cannot supply of itself—we might be tempted to credit the image strictly with formal causality and to make this type of causality also into a model for the entire working of the mind. To do so, however, would be to forget that the original production of the idea—I mean here the primary ideas—is a precognitive abstraction. In the postcognitive abstraction, performed knowingly and deliberately by the intellect, what serves as the matter for the abstraction does play the role of a model, and its causality is entirely formal; at work there is the knowing power in act, which is fully capable of stressing some features in this model while leaving others in the background. The image itself, however, cannot serve the mind as a model prior to the formation of the idea because until the mind is in actual possession of a specific idea, it is unable to know anything.[38]

And so we shall have to say that the cooperation of the image in the production of the idea belongs rather in the order of

----

[38] Cf. John of St. Thomas, *Phil. nat.* IV, q. 10, a. 2 (R, III, 307B29 and 312A11) for discussions on the Suarezian notion of the *intellectus agens*.

efficient causality. But is not the image a material reality, intrinsically dependent on corporeal functions, essentially related to an individual object, contingent, limited both spatially and temporally? So how can such a thing affect the intellect in such a way as to produce there an idea, an immaterial reality, bearing a relation to a necessary object, extraspatial and extratemporal? It is understood, of course, that there is no question of attributing to the efficient power of the image the spirituality of the idea, only its specification. But even in its specification the idea is spiritual, since its object is an intelligible, above space and time and contingency, and its exclusive purpose is to introduce into the mind the intentional spirituality of its object. If the function of the image, then, is to cause the specification of the idea, it must cause its intelligible and spiritual specification. And since no material agent is capable of producing a spiritual effect by its own powers, we must conclude that this causal power of the image is an instrumental efficiency, exercised in submission to a primary spiritual efficiency issuing from a mind.[39] As we pointed out earlier, the motion of the primary cause can raise the causality exercised by the instrument regardless of the powers inherent in the instrument itself, and when the principal cause itself is infinite, the elevation of the instrumental cause can be purely and simply infinite. Accordingly, there should be no problem in affirming that the image is the efficient cause of a spiritual reality, so long as it is understood that its efficiency, rather than primary, is only instrumental. The examples of instrumental causes contributing not only to the production of an effect (in the order of existence) but also to its specification are many and familiar. The material used by the painter cooperates not only in having the painting emerge from intramental to actual existence but also in causing the work to be the kind of work it comes to be. A sketch in ink, no matter what the subject, has a different quality from a sketch in charcoal, and this qualitative difference —delicate strokes and sharp outlines in one, blunt strokes and shaded outlines in the other —is due strictly to the nature of

---

[39] Thomas Aquinas, *Cont. gent.* II, 77; *Q. De an.*, a. 5, ad 6; *De ver.*, q. 10, a. 6, ad 7; *Quodl.*, 8, ad 3; Cajetan, *In Ia*, q. 79, a. 3; John of St. Thomas, *Phil. nat.* IV, q. 10, a. 2 (R, III, 306A11).

the instrument. In fact, the work cannot even be conceived until the sort of instrument to be used—pen, charcoal, pencil, brush —has been determined. The artist thinks in terms of charcoal, watercolor, or pencil just as he thinks about a landscape, a seascape, or a still life.[40] It is in this doubly instrumental way that the image specifies the idea and causes the mind to act; it itself proceeds from a mind at the same time as it brings to the mind the necessary predetermination for its action. At the outset, the activity of the mind has no specification other than its own indeterminate spirituality; but confronted with an image, the active faculty takes possession of that image as a specifying instrument with whose help the action is completed in the mind by the production of the idea.[41]

In our opinion, this is the most plausible explanation of the birth of the idea, although we admit that it does not dispose of all the mysteries. If we accept as certain (a) that the efficient cause in the production of the idea must be the mind itself and (b) that the specification of the idea has to come *somehow* from experience and the image, the causal role played by the image still needs to be explained. For even though the image serves here as a kind of instrument, the notion of the instrumental cause is not adequate enough to do it. It belongs to the essence of the instrument to perform, with respect to the recipient of the effect aimed at by the primary cause, an action that proceeds from its own capacities and is in some way prior to the action that the principal cause performs through the instrument and

---

[40] John of St. Thomas, *Phil. nat.* IV, q. 10, a. 2 (R, III, 309A11): "Just as the skill of the artisan is determined, say, by his cutting tool, and yet the tool is directed by his art so that the cut is straight or curved, so the power of the agent intellect while determined by the image to produce the idea of a given object or quiddity is able to produce that quiddity without the conditions due to matter."

[41] We share, on this point, the opinion of John of St. Thomas for whom the action of the *intellectus agens* is limited strictly to the formation of the idea. This is the opinion of most Thomists. Cajetan, however, hints at a prior illumination of the image distinct from and preceding the formation of the idea: "The light of the agent intellect produces the intelligible in act in the image by way of abstraction, before the intelligible species comes to be in the intellect" (*In Ia*, q. 79, a. 3; see also *In De an.* II, 2 [B. 213B]). This obscure theory of Cajetan's does not seem to stand up against the criticism of John of St. Thomas (*Phil. nat.* IV, q. 10, a. 2 [R, III, 306A37]).

that the instrument performs under the influence of the principal cause. A hammer may not be capable of driving in a nail by
itself, but it does have the requisite qualities of weight and hardness that the workman puts to use. Now, it is true that the greater
the power and the skill of the artist, the more independent he
becomes of the qualities of his instrument. Paganini proved this
when he gave a concert playing a violin with only a single string.
And when the active power of the principal agent is infinite,
anything at all can be used as an instrument for any sort of
action, just as any action can also be performed without any
instrument. But if this infinite power does use an instrument,
then, no matter what that is, it will perform an instrumental
function, or it is no longer an instrument.[42]

Now, if we conceive the image acting on the understanding as
moved by the divine mind as principal cause, can we attribute to
the image any efficient causal power of its own?[43] This condition
is absolutely essential to the notion of the instrument, and if it is

---

[42] Thomas Aquinas, *Sum. th.* III, q. 62, a. 1, ad 2: "An instrument has a
twofold action. One is instrumental, in respect of which it works not by its own
power but by the power of the principal agent. The other is its proper action,
which belongs to it in respect of its own form; thus it belongs to an axe to cut
asunder by reason of its sharpness, but to make a couch insofar as it is the
instrument of an art. But it does not accomplish the instrumental action save
by exercising its proper action, for it is by cutting that it makes a couch. In like
manner the corporeal sacraments by their proper operation, which they exercise on the body that they touch, accomplish through the divine institution an
instrumental operation on the soul; for example, the water of baptism, in
respect of its proper power, cleanses the body, and thereby, since it is the instrument of the divine power, cleanses the soul." John of St. Thomas, *Phil. nat.* I, q.
26, a. 2 (R, II, 524A22): "For an instrument to be elevated by God, it must
perform some operation of its own; if it were dead or without any action it
could not be elevated. . . . The reason for this is taken from what St. Thomas
teaches in *De potentia*, q, 3, a. 4: namely, that the action of anything, even if it
belongs to it as an instrument, must issue from its own power, and so some
action is needed on the part of such an instrument. For that action that issues
from its own power is its action as an instrument, for otherwise, if nothing
came from it, it would be doing nothing, and it would not be an instrument. If
nothing issues from it, and it remains inert, then the thing that is said to be
elevated by God as an instrument will be no more of an instrument than that
which is not elevated."

[43] John of St. Thomas, *Phil. nat.* I, q. 26, a. 2 (R, II, 529A15): "It is said that
in the production of the idea, the image is not properly the efficient instrument of the agent intellect, but an objective one; it provides what the agent
intellect needs to produce the idea. Thus though it determines the agent intel-

lacking, then, properly speaking, the role of the image in the production of the idea is not really an instrumental role. We call the image an instrument, writes an author who has sounded these problems in their depths, because in dealing with these mysteries we speak as best we can.[44] Accordingly, we must conclude that although the instrumental function very closely resembles the function performed by the image with respect to the mind, they are not exactly the same. Trying to be more positive and precise, we may, first of all, observe that although an instrumental function has to do more with the order of efficient causality, the actual function of the image is more in the order of specification and objective causality. An instrument, as happens in the examples we have given, may play a specifying role. But such a role is not of the essence of the instrumental function; in the supremely typical—and supremely pure—case of the instrument taken in hand by the divine Omnipotence, this specifying role may disappear completely. Thus rather than its possible specifying role, what defines an instrument properly so-called is an effective quality of its own for which it is used by the principal agent. The case of the image, however, is different. Its primary function is to contribute to the specification of the intellect, to put the intellect in touch with its object, and if in doing this the image has to exercise a certain efficiency on the mind, the sole reason for it is to specify the mind's own action. This primacy of the specifying role goes hand in hand with a reduction of its efficient role, since the image has, with regard to the intellect, no active power distinct from what the mind confers on it. And so, while for an instrument properly so-called

---

lect as objective matter, the image cannot produce the idea on its own, because it is not in itself an intelligible in act."

[44] Cajetan, *In Ia*, q. 85, a. 1: "Though the rule for instrumental agents is not entirely applicable here, in these mysteries we speak as we can. The image is not strictly an instrument, because it is the cause not so much of the idea as of the objective material for it." One will appreciate also the reservation with which John of St. Thomas formulates his own thesis on the instrumental role of the image in *Phil. nat.* IV, q. 10, a. 2 (R, III, 306A11): "Nevertheless, we have to say that the image necessarily cooperates in producing a determinate intelligible idea in the possible intellect, and there seems to be no better way of explaining this cooperation than saying that the image cooperates in this production as an instrument of the agent intellect. As St. Thomas says: 'in the manner of (quasi) instrumental agents' (*Quodl.*, 8, a. 3)."

efficiency comes first and specification second, for the image it is the other way around. In matters of knowledge, the main thing is not to produce an effect but to exist with a particular specification; efficient causality is regularly subordinated here to specification, which it serves as a condition or a means. A more precise understanding, then, of the causal function of the image in the production of the idea could perhaps be worked out with the notion of a *formal* or *objective instrument*, in which the principle of instrumentality would be transferred from the order of efficient causality to the order of formal causality and in which efficiency would remain only as a connotation.[45]

As for the transcendental nature of the activity that produces the idea, it is clear that this is a vital transitive activity. It consists essentially in the production of an effect, but this effect is by its nature destined to remain within the acting individual in order to contribute to his perfection.[46] What is so striking and what tells us so much about the wretchedness and the greatness of our mind is, then, precisely this: before we can engage in thought—which, because it is set above becoming and time from its first instant, is the act of a perfect subject, regardless of the possibility of further progress—our mind, in order to give itself that initial perfection, is obliged to perform a vital transitive action, which is a typical characteristic of an imperfect subject. Still, our mind's power to do so is an important feature that sets intellectual knowledge apart from sensory cognition. The sense is free from the worry of producing what it needs to sense, because it is the object that provides it with the necessary sensory form. Yet as so often happens in the social order, here, too, one less worry is paid for by a kind of servitude, a loss of autonomy. The initial act of the sense is in no way the work of the sense, which is completely passive when first exposed to the

---

[45] This interpretation is suggested, we think, by John of St. Thomas in *Phil. nat.* I, q. 26, a. 2 (R, II, 529A12); IV, q. 10, a. 22 (R, III, 308A and 312B). Though these texts offer useful directives for research, they do not contain a satisfactory definition of an "objective instrument." In the form in which John of St. Thomas presents it, this notion retains unresolved obscurities.

[46] John of St. Thomas, *Phil. nat.* IV, q. 10, a. 1 (R, III, 303B27): "The answer is that the action of the agent intellect is a transient and vital action, just as vegetative actions are transient and vital."

influence of something outside itself. By contrast, the initial perfection of the human mind is its own work; the mind gives it to
itself, and must give it to itself.[47] The angel possesses its ideas,
the initial perfection of its intellect, as a gift of nature as soon as
it emerges from nothingness; it has within itself that whereby it
may become all things; this divine-like power is given to it along
with its being. But man as he emerges into existence is a long
way from his perfection. To achieve it, he depends on two conditions: first, experience and the life of the senses, and second,
an active effort under the forms imposed by that experience to
acquire for himself the means for developing intellectual knowledge, for enjoying the immanent activity of thought.

THE INTERNAL EXPRESSION OF THOUGHT

What we need to understand now is that even though as far as
the mind is concerned, the formal conditions for thought are
completely realized once the intellect is in the possession of the
idea, this is not yet true as far as the object is concerned. Provided with the idea, the intellect has everything it needs, in the
order of specification, to perform its terminal act, and it only
awaits a call, so to speak, from either nature or the will to do it.
But the faculty of knowing is not the only thing involved here.
Once the problem of getting the knower ready has been solved,
there is still the problem of getting the object ready.[48]

As an essential prerequisite of cognition, as that which makes

---

[47] See Cajetan, *In De an.* II, 11 (B. 170A), and the interpretation of this text
in Simon, "Positions aristotéliciennes concernant le probleme de l'activité du
sens," 250–51.

[48] John of St. Thomas, *Phil. nat.* IV, q. 11, a. 2 (R, III, 356B16) (Some writers have maintained that it is in the nature of thought as an activity to produce
a concept; for these authors thinking consists essentially in the production of a
term): "On the contrary, for St. Thomas and his school, the [word] concept is
required in the intellect *not on account of its power* or of its productive operation, *but on account of the object itself.* If the object is absent, the concept renders
it present, or if present, suitably immaterial and spiritual as befits an intellectual term, something apprehended within the intellect itself and not simply as
the intelligible in the first act, the impressed idea. Finally, the concept is needed
to make the object manifest in some kind of representation as something said
and spoken."

thought possible and gets it started, the object must of course be present before cognition occurs. But it is important to realize that its contribution is even greater in the thought actually taking place, in the very act of knowing. It is in the thought in act that the object is more than ever present to the faculty, and it is only then that it attains its full character as object. Before it is introduced into the soul by the idea, the existing thing is an object only potentially. When the idea of a thing is first formed in the understanding, the thing has the character of an object in initial act, a modality intermediate between pure potency and pure act. The thing becomes the object in terminal act only in the thought actually exercised, where its existence as object, which is the knowing itself, becomes identified with the intentional act of existing in which the knower becomes what he knows. And since the object and the knower are now one, all the privileges of the knowing nature, intentionality, immateriality, spirituality, superabundance, become at the same time the privileges of the object considered in its being as object. We behold here one of the most astonishing aspects of the power of our thought. In the prayer of St. Francis of Assisi, base things such as animals, plants, and even rocks are raised to the same degree of spirituality as his soul. Likewise, the lowly potato we happen to think about is as spiritual a thing, in its existence as object, as the intelligence that thinks it. Now, as to the origin of this spirituality of the object actually thought, it appears that there are only two possible sources: either the existing being possesses the immateriality of the object thought, equal to the immateriality of the thought itself, by self-identity, or it gets it from thought. But only the being whose nature is identical with thought, the being whose nature is thought, can be the object thought by self-identity.[49] Only what is of itself *thought about in terminal act* is

---

[49] Aristotle, *Meta.* XI, 9, 1074B34. Thomas Aquinas, *Cont. gent.* IV, 11: "There are different levels to be found in the intellectual life; for though the human intellect can know itself, still it has the first beginnings of its knowledge from without, because it cannot understand without the image. . . . And so there is a more perfect intellectual life in the angels, in whom the intellect does not advance to knowledge of itself from anything external, but knows itself through itself. Yet the angels' life is not the most perfect, for even though what they know is wholly internal to them, *it is not their substance, because to know and to be are not the same thing in them.*" John of St. Thomas, *Phil. nat.* IV, q. 11, a. 2

also itself *thought in terminal act*. It is only if the being thought of possesses the nature of thought by identity with itself that it can be thought of as such. Thus only God possesses by identity the immateriality of things thought of, because only He possesses by identity the immateriality of thought. Everything else, i.e., every created thing, in order to become an object of thought, will have to receive from the thought the immaterial modality that elevates it to the level of thought and makes it intentionally identical with it. Indeed, our thought reaches out to the created reality by a kind of divine alchemy, immaterializing whatever it touches. But that also means that it is only in *the concept*, by which the thought expresses its object in order to grasp it and grasps it

---

(R, III, 358A22). If the object is absent, the term of the action of thinking can only be a representation; if the object is present but not spiritual, it must be raised to a spiritual state in a concept; if the object is spiritual of itself, but external to the intellect, as when one angel knows another, a concept is needed to bring it within the intellect; finally, if the object is spiritual of itself and naturally joined to the intellect (as in the knowledge an angel has of itself), a concept is still needed to give it the *esse objecti* it cannot have of itself. This is the extreme case showing the most profound reason for the need for an internal expression of the object of thought. (There are many reasons that render the production of the concept necessary or at least convenient, and our choosing the one that seems to us of the most profound and direct interest for the general metaphysics of knowledge does not mean that the others should be disregarded.) John of St. Thomas continues: "But even though the substance of an angel is most familiar to it, as the subject of its intellect, where it serves as an *impressed* species [idea], this is still not enough for a complete act of understanding, which requires also an *expressed* species [concept]. As St. Thomas proves in *Cont. gent.* IV, 11, since an angel's knowledge is not its substance or its being, but an accident, so its concepts must also be. The effectiveness of this proof consists in this: that the concept represents the object as known and understood, and not simply as intelligible, and so, if understanding and being understood are accidents, then the concept as understood must also be an accident and not a substance. Moreover, one and the same thing may be understood in a variety of ways, and so the act of understanding that is the result of an operation by the one who understands cannot be his substance or his being, because although operations are manifold and various, substance and being remain fixed and determined. It follows that if the term of the operations has to be manifold and various, since one and the same object can be understood in various ways, and the concept is the term that makes the object present as something understood, the operation has to have its term in something accidental and not in the angelic substance. But, of course, all this remains within the angelic intellect. The forming and the expressing of the object being an intermental operation, such a formed term is in no way external to the angelic intellect or to its power."

by expressing it, that the thing existing outside the mind in a mixture of potentiality attains to the state of being thought of in terminal act.[50]

We find the most striking manifestation of this activity of thought in the existence of logical beings of reason, where, within itself, thought grants to the thing thought of the status of an

---

Faith teaches us that the knowledge that God has of Himself brings forth a concept or a Word, the uncreated Word, the second person of the Blessed Trinity. It goes without saying that the generation of the Word is due to the abundance and the fecundity of the divine thought, rather than to any kind of deficiency in its object. In the Beatific Vision, according to the teaching of the best of the Thomists, thought takes place without producing a concept; a created concept would be incapable of representing God as He is, and it would also be totally useless, since God possesses in the highest degree, and of Himself, the immateriality of the object of thought in act and He makes Himself present to the intellect of the blessed by His essence. Thomas Aquinas, *Sum. th.* I, q. 12, a. 2; John of St. Thomas, *Curs. th.* I, disp. 13, a. 5 (Vivès, II, 197B). Although the angel and the separated soul are pure spirits and know their own substance directly without any prior representation (it is the very substance of the separated spirit that assures the initial actuation of the intellect joined to it), the knowledge that the angel and the separated soul have of themselves still requires the formation of the concept, for the created spirit is not sufficiently spiritual to be thought in act except in a product of thought. Citing St. Thomas (*De ver.*, q. 4, a. 2), John of St. Thomas points out that even if our thought always produces a concept, we should not conclude that a concept is also needed in the Beatific Vision (expressly denied by St. Thomas in *Sum. th.* I, q. 12, a. 2). The law that links the production of the concept to the exercise of thought admits of one and only one exception: namely, in the case in which what is thought of is pure thought in act. "The answer is that St. Thomas is speaking generally of everything that is understood by us, whether by likeness or essence, that is not pure act even though it may have its entire being in the intelligible order, as when an angel or a separated soul knows itself through its own substance and still forms a word or concept of itself." *Curs. th.* I, disp. 13, a. 5 (Vivès, II, 232B).

[50] Here is a summary bibliography on the general theory of the concept: Thomas Aquinas, *In I Sent.*, dist. 2, q. 1, a. 3; *De pot.*, q. 1, a. 1, ad 10; q. 7, a. 6; q. 8, a. 1; q. 9, a. 5; *De ver.*, q. 4, aa. 1, 2; *Cont. gent.* I, 53; II, 75; IV, 2, 11, 13, 14, 26; *Sum. th.* I, q. 27, aa. 1, 2, 3; q. 28, a. 4, ad 1; q. 34, aa. 1, 2, 3; q. 93, a. 7; q. 107, a. 1; Op. 13, *De differentia verbi divini et humani*; Op. 14, *De natura verbi intellectus* (the authenticity of these opuscula is suspect); Cajetan, *In Ia*, q. 27; Sylvester of Ferrara, *In Cont. gent.* I, 53; IV, 11; John of St. Thomas, *Log.* II, q. 22, a. 2 (R, I, 702Aff.); q. 23 (R, I, 722ff.); *Phil. nat.* IV, q. 11, aa. 1, 2, 3 (R, III, 344ff. [first rate]); *Curs. th.* I, disp. 13, a. 5 (Vivès, II, 244ff.). There are many references and citations in Maritain, *Degrees of Knowledge*, Appendix I, and M. T. L. Penido, *Le Rôle de l'analogie en théologie dogmatique* (Paris: Vrin, 1931), Part II, chap. 1; Pisters, *La Nature des formes intentionnelles d'après saint Thomas d'Aquin*, Part IV.

object of thought and marks it with all its characteristics. All the logical properties—to be a subject, to be a predicate, to be a genus in relation to a species, a species in relation to a genus —have their existence in thought only, as a function of thought,[51] and no matter what the thing is to which thought joins them, they remain for the mind completely dematerialized objects. The notion of subject or of predicate has no more sensory or material connotation than the notion of being or the notion of truth. Whether we say "The earth is round" or "God is good," the material status of these existing subjects has absolutely no effect on their logical counterparts in the mind. And that is why logic is so different from the psychology of knowing. The latter operates at the level of abstraction from *necessary* physical existence and thus belongs to the natural sciences. With its subjects completely *free* from dependence on physical existence, logic belongs in the same order of knowledge as metaphysics and theology.[52]

---

[51] John of St. Thomas, *Phil. nat.* IV, q. 11, a. 2 (R, III, 357A37): "We can only assume the necessity of producing the concept from [the need of] the object, which has to be formed in its being as object within the intellect and set within it in order to be understood, because the intellect is a power that in a perfect way attracts things to itself and unites them to itself by a union that not only tends to the thing as it exists outside but also understands it in all the relations and modes of which that thing admits as object: namely, prescinding, composing, comparing, dividing, etc. All these operations demand that the object be known and attained as it exists within the intellect, since outside of it the thing is not abstract, compared, divided, etc. Clearly, then, the power, which of its nature knows the object in all the modes this object admits of within but not outside of itself, must terminate at the object as it is formed within itself, and not as it remains outside. This is why it is not enough that the object be within the power as the impressed species alone. The function of the latter is merely to elicit understanding, and if the act of understanding were also to terminate at it, it would always have to be reflexive, turning back from the principle from which it is derived; besides, many concepts can be formed from the same impressed species."

[52] John of St. Thomas, *Log.* II, q. 1, a. 3 (R, I, 265A29): "The object of logic, which is a being of reason, enjoys a state of abstraction similar to that which characterizes metaphysics. It is an abstraction from all matter, achieved, not by purifying actuality from materiality, but by denying all matter."
It is well known that for John of St. Thomas many sciences can belong to the same order of abstraction (defined by an *initial* lumping together of the same material data) and yet be distinguished by different *degrees* of abstraction (defined by the difference in immateriality at the *term* of the abstractive process). For instance, such a difference distinguishes the philosophy of nature from medicine in the order of physical abstraction, and geometry from arith-

It is at this point that a problem arises which, unless we are very careful, leads straight to transcendental idealism. The thing thought is, in a certain sense, the work of thought. The intellect lives in a spiritual world that is its own creation, because it cannot live anywhere else. The intellect can deal only with what is like itself, and the actuality of what is known, the being of its object as object, which is at the same time its own knowing actuality, can only be the act of a spiritual subject. But does that not make the intellect a kind of divine ego open only onto itself? It is to the credit of idealism that it became aware of the difficulties involved in acknowledging the uncompromising spiritual nature of the object as thought. But what cannot be forgiven in idealism is the way it capitulated before this problem by cutting its critical inquiry short. For, after all, if the object of thought must be as spiritual as thought itself and is made such by thought, the problem becomes one of deciding how to reconcile this double spirituality, so to speak, with the fact that thought is in touch with things not at all spiritual in themselves. To conclude that thought reaches only to its own productions is not to solve this problem but rather to turn one's back on it the moment it is glimpsed.

The general theory of intentional forms outlined at the begin-

---

metic in the order of mathematical abstraction. "In logic, metaphysics, and theology, there is an abandoning of both sensible and intelligible matter on the part of the term *from which*, but the modes of immateriality attained by these sciences are different. Theology considers God Himself as known through the divine light of Revelation; metaphysics [considers everything it considers] under the first and supreme aspect of being, as abstracting both from createdness and uncreatedness. Logic considers [second] intentions as founded upon the objects known to our intellect; of themselves, these intentions have but a negative immateriality, since they are nothing real." *Log.* II, q. 27, a. 1 (R, I, 825B6).

The question of whether the psychology of the mind belongs to the order of physical or metaphysical abstraction has been a subject of debate in Aristotelian studies (see Zeller, *Philosophie der Griechen* II, p. 481). Generally, Thomists hold that the entire treatment of the human soul, apart from the study of the separated soul, belongs to the science of nature, for the reason, decisive in our opinion, that the mental life of man, as long as the soul and the body are united, invariably involves representations and images, or, more generally, the functioning of the senses. See Thomas Aquinas, *In Phys.*, lect. 4; Cajetan, *In De an.* I, 1 (B. 21A [the definitive statement]); John of St. Thomas, *Phil. nat.* I, q. 9, a. 2 (R, II, 180B21]; IV, proem. (R, III, 3B).

ning of this study provides, we believe, a better and more realistic solution. Since the existent thing lacks the immateriality required of it if it is to be grasped in an act of knowledge, it is represented to the knower by the idea, whose function is to lend the thing an immaterial *state* without in any way changing its *essence*. The intentional form impressed on the knowing faculty before it acts plays thus a subjective as well as an objective role. By introducing the object within the soul in a state midway between potency and act, the idea determines the faculty and gets it ready for action. The function of the concept, however, the intentional form expressed by the now fully active intellect, is entirely objective. Once past the stage of precognitive intentionality, the subjective determination of the faculty is completely subordinated to the objectivity of knowing, and in the postcognitive intentionality of the concept, objectivity triumphs absolutely. Subjectively determined by the idea, the knower here gives up all subjective claims and disappears purely and simply before the object. Thought does not produce the content of thought; what it produces is the state (the existential modality) in which what is thought is delivered to it. Thus while its term is indeed an ideal object (by which we understand an object existing in a state of immateriality), thought nevertheless keeps in touch with the extramental, material reality. For the thing that exists outside the mind as real, in the precognitive idea in the state of initial ideality or imperfect objectivity, and in the concept in the state of terminal objectivity, is one and the same thing. In fact, we could even say that the thing is nowhere more itself than in the concept, where its objectivity is disengaged from all potentiality and subjectivity, and where it finds itself at the farthest remove from all change.[53]

---

[53] Sylvester of Ferrara, *In Cont. gent.* IV, 14: "The concept of anything that is understood is not different in nature, as *concept*, from the thing that is understood as intelligible being in act. Thus the concept that the intellect forms of *man* is not different from the man who exists outside the intellect as a material being, but has immaterial and intelligible being in the intellect; for the man existing outside the intellect is the cause inside the intellect of the concept *man*, which contains formally the same indivisible nature as is intelligible in a real man." On the concept as a formal or intentional sign, see the profound analyses by John of St. Thomas and Jacques Maritain in the works cited in chap. 1, note 32.

If these views are correct, confusing thought with the production of concepts and failing to see its substantial identity with the cognitive acts that precede it seem equally absurd. Thought is being, not production; it is a pure quality, not a movement. To restrict it to the production of the concept is to disqualify it as an immanent activity. Considered in isolation and not *per se*, the internal expression of what is thought may appear as an efficient, transitive action essentially related to a term distinct from itself. It makes no difference that the term produced remains within. We do not consider activities involved in vegetative life as immanent actions, even though their terms remain distributed in their subject. Any action that produces a term distinct from itself is a transitive, not an immanent action, even if the term stays within the acting faculty itself. Thus no matter how much one refines, purifies, spiritualizes, interiorizes the notion of productive action, formally identifying thought with the production of the concept reveals a serious misunderstanding of the pure immanence of thought.

Taking a broader view, however, we come to realize that the expression of what is thought can never be an action really distinct from thought itself. For although the immateriality of the object of thought in act, which constitutes the conceptual state of what is known, *presupposes* the exercise of thought, thought can be in act only with an object brought to such a state. Any sort of dissociation between the act of thinking and the act of expressing what is thought would imply that there could be thought without an object or that becoming an object of thought could have its source in something other than thought itself.[54]

---

[54] Thomas Aquinas, *In I Sent.*, dist. 27, q. 2, a. 2: "The concept itself is an effect of the act of understanding." *Sum. th.* I, q. 93, a. 7: "But in our soul the concept *concept* cannot exist without actual thought." *Cont. gent.* IV, 4: "It is of the nature of the *concept* that it proceed from the one who understands by way of his act of understanding since it is, so to speak, the term of his intellectual operation; for in understanding, the intellect forms an intention of the understood given nature, which is the concept [inner word]."

On this subject, one should consult the splendid article of John of St. Thomas "Whether understanding belongs to the category of action or of quality and whether it is distinct from the concept of the mind" (*Phil. nat.* IV, q. 11, a. 1 [R, III, 344B]). The author summarizes his thought in five theses. (*a*) There is a real distinction between the act of thinking and the concept. (*b*) Thought, even when it is considered as distinct from the concept, is not a

Thus thought and the expression of what is thought are fused in a single act, at once immanent and productive—primarily immanent, since the production of the concept has thought for its end—in which immanence and productivity are distinct only as two modalities of that act. And if it seems difficult to accept that a pure quality—which is what immanent action is—may be confused with any kind of production, we should remember that bringing together in one and the same reality the antinomic pair of efficiency and quality is precisely the ontological privilege of immanent activity. An immanent action that produces no term distinct from itself, such as sensation, still includes a production from itself, which is what makes it an action. Thus there is no reason for excluding the efficiency within the immanent activity from serving to produce, beyond the activity itself,

---

predicamental action, i.e., an action constituted by the exercise of some efficiency, but a quality, whence it follows that it is formally distinct from the production of the concept, or the "saying" of the word. Here the best argument of John of St. Thomas consists in showing that if thought produces an effect, the ultimate justification and end of that effect is thought itself. Thus, whereas formally productive action exists only for the sake of its effect, the effect of the action of thinking, the concept, is on the contrary exclusively for the sake of the action of thinking and its perfection: "Understanding is not exactly like a passage, or the ordinary production of some term or effect. Rather, it is a perfection ultimately intended by the intellect, and if it does have some effect, that effect is ordered to its own good. The perfection of the intellect consists, not in producing an effect, but in attaining the truth; and if it produces any effect, e.g., the concept, it is for the sake of contemplating the truth in it, and so contemplation is what finally actuates and perfects the intellect. Thus beatitude, the supreme perfection of the intellect, consists in actual understanding and contemplation" (347A30). (c) The productive expression of the concept is not an action distinct from thought: "The expression that produces the concept, the saying of the word, is not an action distinct from the immanent act of understanding, for the thought itself is virtually the action that produces the concept. . . . The reason for this conclusion is that the utterance, the production of the word, expresses and reveals the thing not in some arbitrary way, but as it is understood and known, as the term of the understanding; a thing cannot be actually understood except in the act of understanding and being understood, and consequently the concept can issue from the intellect only through the very act of understanding" (348B1). (d) Between the act of thought and the act of expressing it, there is only a modal distinction; but the act of thinking and the concept differ as two distinct things. (e) "In the most formal sense, the act of understanding consists in an operation that is the ultimate act of the one who understands in relation to the object; in its form, therefore, the understanding, as distinguished from the saying, represents fulfillment rather than origination" (350A46).

a distinct term which satisfies the ultimate condition of its exercise and which that activity alone can deliver to itself.[55]

TO KNOW THE TRUTH

To recognize the conformity of knowledge and the real[56] is to know the truth. Now, all knowledge that conforms to its object is true, but it can be so in two ways. Like every reality that is totally faithful to its own law and is without defect, knowledge may be true simply as a thing. But when knowledge perceives its truth, it is true not just as a thing is true but also as knowledge is true: namely, expressing something over and above and irreducible to the common properties of being. Clearly, then, even though a relation to knowledge is implied in every notion of truth, it is in the truth of self-conscious knowledge, in the truth

---

[55] Note that the word *concept*, referring to the expression of that which is thought, needs to be taken here in a sense broader than that in daily usage. As a matter of fact, there is a concept, an intentional form expressed by thought, at the term of every completed act of the mind, not only, that is, at the term of simple perception or intellectual apprehension, but also at the term of a judgment. Thomas Aquinas, *Quodl.*, 5, a. 9: "There are two kinds of operation performed by the intellect. . . . One of them is called the understanding of indivisibles, by which the intellect forms within itself a definition, or the concept of something incomplex. The other is the operation of composing and dividing, by which the intellect forms a judgment. Both these operations of the intellect involve *concepts* [*verba*], the first constituting a definition, the second a discourse." Sylvester of Ferrara, *In Cont. gent.* I, 53; John of St. Thomas, *Phil. nat.* IV, q, 11, a. 3 (R, III, 372A16): "It does not seem that [Saint Thomas] attributes a distinct kind of concept to discourse, though it would seem that when we are thinking, which is a discursive action, we have not yet perfectly formed a concept. . . . Thus concepts are formed in the second as well as in the first operation, because in each there is a distinct object to be represented: in the first, the nature of a thing, the thing in itself; in the second, the truth itself."

[56] We know that this definition, made classic by St. Thomas, was attributed by him to Isaac Israeli, a Jewish physician and philosopher who lived in Egypt between 845 and 940 and was the author of a treatise *De definitionibus*. We should remember, however, that the grounds for this formula were prepared by Aristotle, who in *Meta.* IV, 7, 1011B26 put it this way: "To say of what is that it is not, or of what is not that it is, is false, while to say of what is that it is and of what is not that it is not is true." See also *Meta.* VI, 4, 1027B20; IX, 10, 1051B3, 6, 9, 17, 26; and *Categ.*, 5, 4B8.

of knowing as such, that we find the archetypal form of the polyvalent notion of truth.[57]

We possess this truth of knowledge only in the act of judging. In sensation, the sense is assimilated to the object sensed, but whether it is truly conformed or whether, owing to some accidental failing, it falls short, the sense itself cannot tell. Likewise, and barring accidents, in simple intellectual perception all that happens is that the intellect conforms to its object. But in judgment this conformity of thought and thing becomes itself an object of thought. Here the intellect compares what exists inside itself with what exists outside itself; it compares the idea in which the thing exists intentionally with the thing as it exists physically; and in doing so, the intellect can recognize whether its knowledge, in producing the thing in intentional existence, has preserved that thing's identity with itself.[58]

Indeed, this is what judgment seems to be in essence: an act of knowledge that by simply declaring a thing to be such and such bears directly on the relation of knowledge with the extramental real. A synthesis or composition when affirmative, and a division when negative, what judgment primarily deals with are not, as a superficial analysis might lead one to believe, mere ideas. Judgment composes or divides intramental and extramental; it compares knowing and being. And so, even as it necessarily deals with association and comparison of ideas, the syntheses and divisions exercised by judgment are those of the

---

[57] Thomas Aquinas, *De ver.* q. 1, a. 22: "Since truth is predicated of many things in a primary and a secondary sense, it ought to be primarily predicated of that in which the perfect nature of truth is found." John of St. Thomas, *Curs. th.* I, disp. 2, a. 3 (Vivès, III, 118Aff.).

[58] For Aristotle and the Aristotelians, truth, properly speaking, is a quality of the judgment and is found only in the mind that makes the judgment. Still, one speaks of the truth of things, and of the truth of sense knowledge and simple intellectual perception, all the while understanding that the word truth is used in these contexts in a weakened and derivative sense. See *On Interp.*, 4, 17A2; *On the Soul* III, 6, 430A26, 430B26; 8, 432A11; *Meta.* IV, 8, 1012B8; V, 29, 1024B17; VI, 4, 1027B20 (cf. Franz Brentano, *Von der mannigfachen Bedeutung des Seienden nach Aristoteles* [Freiburg: Herder, 1862], pp. 22ff.). Thomas Aquinas, *In De interp.* I, lect. 3; *In Meta.* VI, lect. 4 (C. 1227); IX, lect. 11 (C. 1898); *In De an.* III, lect. 11 (P. 747); *De ver.*, q. 1, aa. 3, 9; *Cont. gent.* I, 59; *Sum. th.* I, q. 16, aa. 1, 2; John of St. Thomas, *Curs. th.* I, disp. 2, a. 3 (Vivès, III, 122B).

mind that has become one with a thing existing outside the mind.[59]

Consequently, for a being to possess the truth of knowledge, i.e, know the truth in the full sense of the word, it is not enough to have the power of knowledge; a truly knowing being must also have understanding. When two things are absolutely the same, one cannot compare them. But even though knowledge and what is known are one, they differ in existential modalities, and this difference cannot be perceived except by a faculty capable of discriminating among the states of being. All knowledge that depends exclusively on some external quality, e.g., sensory cognition, exhausts itself in the quality known, identical with itself in its qualitative character, in nature, and in knowledge (the required actual presence of the physical thing makes no difference here). On the other hand, the knowledge of truth implies a reflection of the knowing faculty on itself, a consciousness of what is present in its act of knowing, and this reflexive return presupposes on its part the capacity to have itself for object. True, some knowledge of oneself necessarily accompanies every act of cognition;[60] a thing could hardly be an object for a subject if that subject, in perceiving the thing, did not perceive it as confronting itself. But the power of having oneself as object,

---

[59] This is clearly revealed by those texts in which Aristotle shows simultaneously that the truth of knowledge is measured by reality and that it is a property of the judgment. *Meta.* IX, 10, 1051в3: "he who thinks the separated to be separated and the combined to be combined has the truth, while he whose thought is in a state contrary to that of the objects is in error." John of St. Thomas, *Log.* I, q. 5, a. 1 (R, I, 145а12); *Phil. nat.* IV, q. 11, a. 3 (R, III, 370а43): "In an enunciation, the extremes are grasped as joined with each other, and there is a collation or comparison of one with the other; *what the judgment does is to compare or collate the proposition thus composed with what exists in reality* or with the principles on which the truth of the reality depends." *Curs. th.* I, disp. 2, a. 3 (Vivès, III, 125а).

[60] Cajetan, *In De an.* II, 13 (B. 174аff.) (on the meaning of sensation). "Now, when one hears, one obviously senses the sound causing a change in one's hearing, for otherwise one would not be hearing; to hear the sound causing the change, then, is to sense the action of the sound; but if the action of the sound is in the one who hears, and is the same as the hearing, it follows that when one senses the sound, i.e., the actual sound causing the change, one senses also one's own affection or passion. And you should know, further, that when we say that any sense senses its own sensation, or the action of the object, we talk only about facts, for all that we mean by it is that when we sense, we are

purely and simply, is the special privilege of the mind set free in its substance and operation from all the encumbrances by which materiality and extension restrict our knowledge. And this can never be the case in sensory knowledge, which intrinsically depends on a corporeal organ as its necessary instrument. Moreover, for the sense to have itself as an object, there would have to be an intermediate organ intervening between the sense faculty as the knowing subject and the same sense faculty as the object known, which seems absurd.[61]

What takes place when the mind turns from external realities to examine what is going on within itself is fundamentally different from the reflection implied in all knowledge of truth. For example, while it may not be possible to judge, say, the properties

---

affected by sound, light, etc. And if you consider these things carefully, you should no longer be bothered by various objections alleging that sensation is not sensed, or that the sense does not reflect upon itself, or that it does so by the same or another act, and so on. All these arguments spring from a basic misunderstanding, which assumes that what we are saying is that sight senses its own seeing as an object, or as a thing seen, as the intellect understands its own understanding as a thing understood, which never even crossed our mind. We do hold, however, that sight senses that it sees, and this pertains, as we said, to the question "Is it so?" It is no different from our knowing, when surrounded by total darkness, that we do not see. It is for the same reason that, when, seeing, the sight senses that it is seeing, as when not seeing in the dark, it senses that it is not seeing." See also John of St. Thomas, *Phil. nat.* IV, q. 4, a. 4 (R, III, 128A32).

[61] Thomas Aquinas, *De ver.*, q. 1, a. 9: "[Truth] is known by the intellect in view of the fact that the intellect reflects upon its own act—not merely as knowing its own act, but as knowing its relation to the thing, Now, this relation cannot be known without knowing the nature of the act; and the nature of the act cannot be known without knowing the nature of the active principle, that is, the intellect itself to whose nature it belongs to be conformed to things. Consequently, it is because the intellect reflects upon itself that it knows truth. But truth . . . is not in the sense as something known by the sense; for although the sense judges truly about things, it does not know the truth by which it truly judges. Consequently, although the sense knows that it senses, it does not know its own nature or the nature of its act or the proportion of this act to the thing. As a result, it does not know its truth. The reason for this is that intellectual substances, which are among the most perfect beings, are capable of reflecting upon their essence more fully, and they make a complete return to their essence. But all that the sense knows besides the sensible is that it is sensing; and this incipient reflection leaves it far short of knowing its own essence. Avicenna gives as a reason for this that sense knows only through a bodily organ, and a bodily organ cannot be a medium between a sensing power and itself."

of benzoic aldehyde without some sort of return to oneself, no one would want to attribute to chemistry the same kind of reflexivity as used in the science of the soul. With the soul as object, self-reflection is deliberate and explicit; in the study of nature, it is implicit in experience. In psychology, the question of how we know is always close to the focus of inquiry; in chemistry, it remains at the periphery. The primary concern in psychology is the self; in chemistry, it is the other. Since human thought is measured by reality, we may say that in simple presentative cognition the mind is like the eye or the hand that perceives some measuring instrument, a ruler, a bushel basket, without using it to measure anything. In simple reflective judgment, the mind is like the eye or the hand using that measuring instrument, but even though what is measured is the mind itself, what is seen and touched is still not the mind.[62] In the deliberate and explicit reflection appropriate to psychology, it is the mind as object that is seen and touched at the same time as the instruments it uses as subject to measure itself. Still, different though they may be, we need to realize that these two kinds of reflection have their origin in the same basic aptitude. For knowledge could not return upon itself and become an object to be measured by itself if it were not a faculty capable of taking itself and its principle for the object touched and seen, for its own self-measurement, and so on to infinity.

As experienced by the human mind, truth presents itself as a relation between two really distinct terms perceived by an act of synthesis.[63] Thus judgment bears upon something complex and

---

[62] Cajetan, *In Ia*, q. 16, a. 2; John of St. Thomas, *Curs. th.* I, disp. 2, a. 3 (Vivès, III, 120B): "In this (the knowledge of the conformity of the intellect with the thing) it seems that reflection takes place, inasmuch as the judgment presupposes the union of the extremes and forms an enunciation about it. But what in fact happens is that a simple judgment is passed upon the extremes composed and conjoined in the enunciation. . . . In the strict sense, there is thus no reflection, because the judgment is concerned only with what is represented in the enunciation and does not turn back either to the act of understanding or to the enunciation itself."

[63] John of St. Thomas tells us that some writers, contending that judgment does not consist in a synthesis of subject and predicate, refuse to recognize it as a synthesis. But those who say such things, he writes, have not read St. Thomas. In *De interp.* I, lect. 3, St. Thomas says that "to know the aforementioned relation of conformity is simply to judge things to be so or not to be so

is itself a complex act, even though indivisible. These conditions of human thought do not, however, express a transcendental necessity of thought. For in God, there is no real distinction among the knower, the act of knowing, and what is known, and the relation of truth is a purely logical relation between terms that are absolutely and in every respect identical. Nor is there a question of attributing any kind of complexity to the act that perceives this truth. The truth of the divine knowledge is an incomplex perceived by an incomplex act that is not really distinct from that truth or from the being of God.

For all created beings, however, the real distinction between the intentional and the physical makes the relation of truth necessarily a complex object. Yet there is no law inscribed in the essence of knowledge that requires it to share in the infirmities of its object—in materiality, mobility, multiplicity—and we do know that the divine thought goes out to all things in the unity of a perfectly simple glance. And so, what we still have to determine are the precise conditions that make this complex truth of created knowledge attainable only by an act that itself is complex, and that we shall call a judicative synthesis.[64]

To begin with, we need to recall as precisely as possible the

---

in reality, and this is to compose and divide," and in *Sum. th.* I, q. 16, a. 2, he again explains that "when the intellect judges that a thing corresponds to the form that it apprehends about that thing, then first it knows and expresses truth; and this it does by composing and dividing."

Thus judgment is a synthesis or division *per se* and not only by reason of the enunciation that it presupposes. "Although [judging] is not a composition in the manner of a union of a predicate with a subject, it is so with regard to what is in the intellect and what is in the real, which it composes and divides." John of St. Thomas, *Curs. th.* I, disp. 2, a. 3 (Vivès, III, 125A). This synthetic nature, however, does not prevent the judgment from being an indivisible act with its own unity in being. Ibid. (Vivès, 124B); Maritain, *Logique*, p. 114.

[64] We use the phrase *judicative synthesis* rather than judgment, because although there is judgment in every cognition of truth, judgment in an angel is only virtually but not really distinct from simple intellectual perception. Cf. Bañez, *In Ia*, q. 16. a. 2 (Whether truth resides only in the intellect composing and dividing). The commentator shows that St. Thomas's thesis applies only to the human intellect: "The composition and division by the intellect does not of itself prove that truth resides in it; as a matter of fact, some intellects have to resort to this procedure because of their imperfection, which requires that they proceed from potency to the act of judging only gradually and with the help of a great many things. But we do find truth in the judgment."

relation between the notions of *thing* and *object*. If we understand by "thing" the concrete reality whose act is extramental
being, made up of an essence joined to its properties, its contingencies, and finally its existence (actual or possible), and by
"object" whatever of that thing is made manifest in knowledge,[65]
we have to say, *first*, that there is no sense in which the object and
the thing make two—as if the object could be something other
than the thing—but also, *second*, that the thing and the object
do not necessarily coincide totally. Total coincidence of object
and thing is found only in an exhaustive knowledge, in which
the entire thing is constituted as an object. The object is always
identical with the thing, but this identity may be only partial,
and in every knowledge that is not exhaustive, there is more in
the thing than in the object. Now, it is this lack of total coincidence between the object and the thing, wherever such is the
case, that gives rise to the problem of the identity of the thing
and the object in our knowledge. It is not that this identity can
be ignored; it is the essence of the object to represent the thing
or, better, to be the thing as it manifests itself in knowledge. Thus
the skeptical position, which despairs of knowing whether there
is, beyond the phenomenal object, some reality identical with
what is perceived, goes contrary to the natural movement of the
intellect, and can be refuted by reduction to absurdity. In fact, it
is worth noting that despite the most systematic determination
to contradict the spontaneous certitude of the intellect concerning the identity of the object and the thing—of the phenomenal object and the thing itself—the skeptical doubt has never
been extended to the phenomenal object in its phenomenality.[66]
The skeptic gives up on knowing the truth because he does not
know where to go from there; namely, how to verify that the
phenomenal object is identical with the existing thing. And so
even though truth consists in the relation of conformity between
thought and reality,[67] rather than in the identity between the
object and the thing, knowing the truth certainly involves

---

[65] Maritain, *Degrees of Knowledge*, pp. 90ff.

[66] Victor Brochard, *Les Sceptiques grecs* (Paris: Imprimerie nationale, 1887),
pp. 137, 171–72, 361, 410, 426.

[67] John of St. Thomas, *Curs. th.* I, disp. 2, a. 2 (Vivès, III, 93B).

acknowledging expressly that identity, which a simple grasping of the object does not always provide. For how could the mind recognize its conformity to reality if it did not recognize that its object is identical with the real? And if the mind sees its object as identical with the real, how could it not see that it itself conforms to reality? The act of knowing the conformity of the mind to reality and the act of recognizing the identity of the object and the thing must go hand in hand. Simple perception contains truth because it lets us know that the object is identical with the thing. But fully demonstrating the conformity of the mind with the real requires a further act, because the identity of the object and the thing is not adequately expressed by simple perception.

In an exhaustive knowledge, the identity of the object and the thing is as fully manifest as the object itself. For a mind sufficiently penetrating to grasp immediately and without any remainder everything knowable in the thing, leaving no transobjective element, the recognition of the identity of the object and the thing does not require a distinct act, because such a mind knows that thing fully at the same time as it knows the object. There is no skepticism among the angels; the skeptical doubt that the human intellect cannot really live with cannot even be feigned by the angelic intellect. Regardless of the state of his will, an angel can no more feign doubt about the object–thing than the skeptic can feign doubt about the object–phenomenon, and for the same reason: the thing known exhaustively has entered wholly the order of phenomenality.[68]

---

[68] Thomists are agreed in saying that all angelic knowledge takes place by way of simple intuitions, and the reason they give is that the angelic intellect sees in its object at once everything there is to be seen in its object. *Sum. th.* I, q. 58, a. 4: "As in the intellect, when reasoning, the conclusion is compared with the principle, so in the intellect composing and dividing, the predicate is compared with the subject. For if our intellect were to see at once the truth of the conclusion in the principle, it would not understand by discourse and reasoning. In like manner, if the intellect in apprehending the quiddity of the subject were at once to have knowledge of all that can be attributed to, or denied of, the subject, it would not understand by composing and dividing, but only by understanding the essence. Thus it is evident that for the selfsame reason our intellect understands by discourse, and by composing and dividing: namely, that in the first apprehension of anything newly apprehended, our intellect does not at once grasp all that is virtually contained in it. And this comes

But in knowledge that is not exhaustive, the identity of the thing and the object, even though never in doubt, cannot be expressed by the mind to itself except through comparing the object with the thing. And this is where the skeptical doubt comes in. Because the thing extends beyond the perceived object, if our human, less than exhaustive perception is unable to express their identity, how, then, are we to get hold of the thing to compare it with the object and its idea? To the extent that it exceeds the object, the thing in itself, by itself, is something unknown. Therefore, comparing the object with the thing that does not totally coincide with the object would mean comparing the known with the unknown, which is something evidently impossible.

And yet it has to be done. We have to be able to compare the object with the transobjective thing in order to verify not only their identity but also the conformity of our thought to reality.

---

from the weakness of the intellectual light in us. Hence, since the intellectual light is perfect in the angel, . . . it follows that as the angel does not understand by reasoning, so neither does he by composing and dividing." Thus human thought is forced to use the complex modes of enunciation and judgment, because it is not exhaustive by its essence. Ibid., Ia, q. 14, a. 14 (Whether God knows enunciable things): "God has to know all enunciations that can be formed . . . [but] just as He knows material things immaterially, and composite things simply, so likewise He knows enunciable things not after the manner of enunciable things, as if in His intellect there were composition or division of enunciations; rather He knows each thing by simple intelligence, by understanding the essence of each thing, just as if we, by the very fact that we understand what man is, were to understand all that can be predicated of man. This, however, does not happen in our intellect, which moves from one thing to another by discourse, because the intelligible species represents one thing in such a way as not to represent another. Hence when we understand what man is, we do not understand from this all the things that belong to him; we understand them one by one, according to a certain succession. On this account the things we understand separately we must reduce to one by way of composition or division, by forming an enunciation. Now, the species of the divine intellect, which is God's essence, suffices to represent all things." See also ibid., I, q. 85, a. 5; *Cont. gent.* I, 59 (That the truth of enunciable things is not excluded from God): "The divine simplicity does not exclude any perfection, because it possesses in its simple being whatever there is of perfection in other things by an aggregation of perfections and forms. . . . When our intellect apprehends simple objects, it does not yet achieve its ultimate perfection, because it is still in potency with respect to composition and division, as, in the order of nature, simple things are in potency with respect to mixtures, and parts with respect to the whole. By His simple understanding, then, God has that perfection of knowledge which our intellect attains through two kinds of knowledge, that of

But because one cannot compare the known with the unknown, and since the object of the non-exhaustive perception is presented to the mind surrounded by an area of the unknown, somehow the object must be made to reveal more than what it is showing. We must find a way to use the certainty of its presence to get beyond it and to penetrate the transobjective thing in its very transobjectivity. And there seems only one way to do this. Comparing the limited object with the thing in itself directly being clearly out of the question, perhaps they can be compared as two objects, which could tell us what goes on in the transobjectivity of the thing and what causes it, so to speak, to pass into objectivity.

This is the roundabout way, unknown to the skeptic, that an intellectual realism has found to solve the paradoxical problem of comparing the object and the thing. We compare one object with another object, the known with the known, and if either

---

the complex and that of the simple things. But as our intellect in its perfect knowledge, when it has arrived at composition, has the truth, so God has it in His simple understanding." See also Sylvius, *In Ia*, q. 58, a. 4; John of St. Thomas, *Phil. nat.* IV, q. 11, a. 3 (R, III, 367A17) replies as follows to the question about the source of the distinction in the three operations of the mind: "The answer is that it arises from the lack of perfection in our intellect, which proceeds from the imperfect to the perfect, and from potency to act . . . in contrast to the angelic intellect which, because it is perfect in the intellectual order, penetrates everything as soon as it apprehends it. The angelic intellect thus relies not on discourse but on comprehension, and so it has a simple and unique way of operating, which is so powerful that it is the equivalent of our discourse and manifold acts. The rational soul, at the lowest degree of intellectual power and united to a corruptible body, attains its cognitive perfection gradually by discourse and composition rather than by direct and indivisible comprehension. The angels, by contrast, who are not united to a body and are free from all matter, have intellects that do not have to acquire knowledge gradually; they know things directly and comprehensively, penetrating by one simple act whatever is in the object."

For the notion of exhaustive knowledge, see John of St. Thomas, *Curs. th.* I, disp. 22, a. 1. The author shows that there are degrees of this knowledge and that a knowledge can be purely and simply exhaustive without being so absolutely and in every respect. Only the divine knowledge is exhaustive absolutely and in every respect: "For comprehension it is enough that something be grasped together with everything that is intrinsic and that naturally belongs to it. If, however, there is grasp also of everything that can happen to a thing from external causes, such a grasp will be due not just to simple comprehension but to its highest, perfect degree at the summit of exhaustive knowledge" (Vivès, IV, 789B).

rational analysis or experience shows they are necessarily identified, the problem is solved. If we find out that they are identical, we shall know that they cannot be so just within the phenomenal world—otherwise the two objects would be one—and the only other place for it is the transobjectivity of the thing.[69]

---

[69] As Maritain pointed out (*Logique*, p. 108n3), "The essential distinction between the act of the mind (the judgment) and the logical work constructed by it (the proposition or enunciation) has been obscured for many modern logicians, particularly under the influence of Kant." Also interesting is the following comment by John Stuart Mill: "[A]lmost all the writers on Logic in the last two centuries, whether English, German, or French, have made their theory of Propositions, from one end to the other, a theory of Judgments. They considered a Proposition, or a Judgment, for they used the two words indiscriminately, to consist in affirming or denying one *idea* of another. To judge, was to put two ideas together, or to bring one idea under another, or to compare two ideas, or to perceive the agreement or disagreement between two ideas: and the whole doctrine of Propositions, together with the theory of Reasoning (always necessarily founded on the theory of Propositions), was stated as if Ideas, or Conceptions, or whatever other term the writer preferred as a name for mental representations generally, constituted essentially the subject-matter and substance of those operations. . . . To determine what it is that happens in the case of assent or dissent besides putting two ideas together, is one of the most intricate of metaphysical problems. But whatever the solution may be, we may venture to assert that it can have nothing whatever to do with the import of propositions; for this reason, that propositions (except sometimes when the mind itself is the subject treated of) are not assertions respecting our ideas of things, but assertions respecting the things themselves." *A System of Logic* I, 5, 1. These few lines are sufficient evidence that John Stuart Mill was fully aware that the notion of judicative assent is irreducible to that of simple enunciation.

The notion of judicative assent is explained with unexcelled clarity by Franz Brentano. All his psychology is dominated by the division of psychic phenomena into presentations (*Vorstellungen*), judgments (*Urteile*), and affective movements (*Gemütsbewegungen*), from which there arises an urgent need to show in what way judgment is distinguished from simple presentative knowledge. What defines the psychic phenomenon, Brentano writes (*Vom Ursprung sittlicher Erkenntnis* [Leipzig: Duncker & Humblot, 1889], p. 14), is an intentional relation to something that may not exist actually but still exists internally as an object in the mind. ("The common feature of everything psychological . . . consists in a relation that . . . has been called *intentional* . . . to something which may not be actual but which is presented as an object" [*The Origin of Our Knowledge of Right and Wrong* (Westminster: Constable, 1902)]. The best division of psychic phenomena is the one that follows the modalities of the intentional relationship, which are three in number, according to whether the term of the relation is an object of simple representation, an object of assent or denial, or an object of desire or revulsion (ibid., p. 15). "[Before Descartes' time] judgments and presentations were grouped together as constituting a *single* funda-

For instance, the object *Socrates* is not identical with the object *man*. So, if I have to say that Socrates is a man, this can be only because of their identity in the transobjective realm. The thing that is Socrates, and that manifests itself in the object of thought "Socrates," is the same thing that is man, and that manifests itself in the object of thought "man."[70] But when I thus verify the identity of these objects in the transobjective realm, by an operation

---

mental class. [The same error has been made in more recent times; people have supposed that judging is essentially a matter of combining or relating presentations.] But this is a gross misconception of the nature of judgment. On the one hand, we may combine and relate presentations at will—as we do when we think of a green tree, or a golden mountain, or a father of a hundred children, or a friend of science—but if we have *only* combined and related, we have made no judgment. (To be sure, every judgment is based upon some presentation or other and so, too, is every desire.) On the other hand, we may make a judgment without thereby combining ideas or relating them as subject and predicate. Thus consider the judgment 'There is a God' as distinguished, say, from 'God is just.' What [then] is distinctive about judgment? It is this: in addition to there being an idea or presentation of a certain object, there is a second intentional relation that is directed upon that object. The relation is one of either affirmation or denial—either acceptance or rejection. If a man says 'God,' he gives expression to the idea of God. But if he says 'There is a God,' then he gives expression to his belief in God."

Thus not only would judgment be quite different from a synthesis of presentations, but synthesis as such could be left out altogether. This notion that *it is not at all necessary for judgment to rest on an enunciative synthesis* is developed at length by Brentano in his booklet *Von der Klassification der psychischen Phänomene* (Leipzig: Duncker & Humblot, 1911), pp. 35ff. For instance, when one says *A is*, one must not think, as is so often done, that this is a predication in which existence as predicate is joined to A as subject; the object of the assent is not this relation but the term A itself. "A itself is the subject that we are acknowledging" (p. 45). More than that, Brentano holds that all propositions are reducible, either immediately or mediately, to existential propositions of the type *A is*. It is in this way that the hypothetical proposition *If a man acts badly, he harms himself*, reducible to the categorical proposition *All men acting badly harm themselves*, is finally reduced to *A man acting badly who does not harm himself does not exist* (pp. 49ff.).

In spite of Brentano's criticism (and he does not hesitate to call upon St. Thomas [*Sum. th.* I, q. 3, a. 4, ad 2] in support of his position), we think that a proposition of the type *A is* is a genuine predication, one in which the verb *to be* plays the role of both copula and predicate, and that the assent given in this proposition bears not on the term *A* itself, but on the synthesis of A and existence. As we see it, a judgment that would not bear upon an enunciative synthesis could be nothing but a totally unspecified activity, a blind act.

[70] Thomas Aquinas, *Sum. th.* I, q. 85, a. 5, ad 5; Maritain, *Reflexions sur l'intelligence*, chap. 1; *Degrees of Knowledge*, p. 84.

that is strictly the work of my own mind, I know at the same time that my mind conforms to the real thing.

It is in this way that we come to understand the role of the enunciative synthesis, how necessary it is for the preparation of the judicative synthesis, and in what essential way the latter differs from it. Judgment consists in saying *Yes* or *No*. Yes, the thing is just as the thought presents it; no, it is different. An exhaustive perception requires no comparison between the mind and the real since it testifies directly to the mind that the thing is just as it reveals itself, just as the mind sees it. But lacking an exhaustive perception, we carry out the necessary comparison between our thought and the real by way of the enunciative synthesis, in which the mind both reflects upon itself and transcends objectivity to attain reality in its most distinctive otherness.

An assent given without reservations is like an oath. All knowledge is activity, but assertoric knowledge is presented to our inner experience as a superactivity. The one who gives his word, in serious and duly considered circumstances, feels that he is drawing upon the supreme energy of his being in an internal activity that is like a sober intoxication. Something analogous to this is experienced also in the most theoretical of judgments. Although farthest removed from affective influences, that judgment has the character and the weightiness of a moral commitment.[71] Think, for instance, of the conclusion of a scientific investigation carried on at great length. Thanks to the stratagems elaborated on its own initiative, the mind, now made fully self-conscious, has been able to penetrate into the transobjective and is in touch with reality. At last, the mind possesses the perfec-

---

[71] This superactivity of assertoric knowledge gives an apparent excuse to those who assign assent to the faculty of willing. "The doctrine of the *Meditations* that has the will judging and the will doubting is well known," writes Alain. "And it is certainly better than the version whereby a mechanical understanding produces thought the way an adding machine totals a sum, making it no longer either true or false but a simple product of nature. Descartes is the geometer who understood that geometry is not a product of nature and that a straight line is something willed and sworn to." *Préface pour Descartes: Traité des Passions* (Paris, 1928), p. 36. One has to admire the options given here: human judgment can be a mechanical product or it can be a product of the will. Such presumptuous oversimplifications will be easily avoided if one recognizes that knowing is an authentic activity that rises to its highest degree and perfect form in judgment, that is, the knowledge of truth.

tion, the truth that it was after. But in a very real sense it is its own truth, because everything that has been added to simple presentative, objective cognition has been the mind's own work.

THE PROGRESS OF THOUGHT

In the judgment, the mind makes two kinds of progress: it gets to know the truth, and, by completing the interobjective synthesis proposed but not made final by the enunciation, it has the object placed at its disposal.[72] The concurrence of the enunciation and the assent has this admirable result that the assent, in addition to the truth, the perfection it properly aims at—but which it could never arrive at without the preliminary formula of the enunciation—procures the mind another perfection: namely, the ability to develop its object, which the enunciative synthesis aims for but cannot achieve by itself. When I assent to the enunciation "Plato wrote the *Parmenides*," the object of thought "Plato" develops and expands before my mind in the order of objectivity at the same time as it presents itself as identical with the transobjective reality Plato himself. Whereas previously Plato had been for me the pupil of Socrates, the teacher of Aristotle, the prisoner of Dionysius, the author of the *Gorgias*, the *Phaedrus*, and the *Republic*, he is now for me also the author of the *Parmenides*. But he becomes for me the author of the *Parmenides* only when I perceive that the object "Plato" and the object "author of the *Parmenides*" are identical in the transobject. In short, while the enunciation is an *interobjective* synthesis whose function is to extend the knowledge of the object, the judgment is a synthesis of the mind and the thing, whose primary function is to establish the truth. But it is the interobjective synthesis that makes this possible, and it is the knowledge of truth that completes the interobjective synthesis.

---

[72] For these two directions of thought, see Thomas Aquinas, *De ver.*, q. 12, a. 7; *Sum. th.* II–II, q. 173, a. 2; John of St. Thomas, *Log.* I, q. 5, a. 1 (R, I, 144A25ff.); Maritain, *Logique*, pp. 110–12. The distinction indicated here corresponds roughly to that drawn by common sense between having good judgment and being intelligent. The error common sense makes, however, is to allow that one can be intelligent while not being able to judge well.

Here we touch upon a fertile analogy that links the metaphysics of knowing to the metaphysics of being. *What existence is to the thing that is, truth is to the object thought and to the thought identified with it in intentionality.* In nature, there are two orders of perfection, one of which rises from a thing's specific nature to the summit of actuality, whereas the other spans the ontological degrees of quality, quiddity, and the species of the thing. Existence is at the term of the first order; activity, at the term of the second.[73] Similarly, in knowing, one order opens up in which progress consists in becoming a *particular* object, while in the other progress is measured by the consolidation of knowledge through knowledge of the truth. Just as a subject in order to appear in existence must have a determinate possibility, which the gift of existence will fulfill without altering it, so a thought in order to know the truth must first have an object that specifies it. As nothing has value without existence, so no thought has value without truth. As a live dog, so they say, is worth more than a dead lion, so the truth from the mouth of babes, about even the least interesting object, is worth infinitely more then the most grandiose error from the mouth of a philosopher. As existence is the supreme good for a thing, desired by all things, the supreme good for the mind is truth. But just as for a thing it is not enough merely *to be*, because its perfection depends also on its qualitative development, so for a thought it is not enough just to be true. Indeed, the development of the breadth, depth, and plenitude of its object is as important to the perfection of a given thought as qualitative development is to the perfection of any existent thing. Thus although a boring philosophy textbook may well contain more truth than the works of Spinoza or Hegel, one wishes that all teaching of truth could display depth and richness at least equal to that of their erroneous treatises. The thing just born into existence is weak in its being, and so is the thought in its first instant of truth, when all it knows is that something exists and nothing more. Finally, comparing being and knowing, we find that just as the twofold potentiality of the thing derives from its not being identical with its existence, the twofold potentiality of creaturely thought arises from the fact

---

[73] See above, pp. 50ff.

that it does not conform, by self-identity, either to its object or to its truth.[74]

As soon as it knows, even by simple representation, the mind begins its perfection in the order of the object; as soon as it utters a true judgment, the mind becomes purely and simply perfect in the order of truth. Here we note a significant limitation with regard to the analogy between being and knowing. For whereas the thing must actually exist before it can be the subject of the least qualitative improvement, qualitative development of thought is a condition of its truth. Before receiving the gift of existence, a natural quality is merely a possibility present in the divine understanding, for there is nothing in the natural world to support it. Before expanding in truth, however, the object in act —the intentional *quod*—already has real, natural existence, ready to develop in intentionality. Truth is thus a *superexistence* rather than just existence. *Erkannt-Sein*, to be known, is a secondary existence superadded to a primary existence of just *to be*, and firmly grounded in it.[75] That is also why the possession of truth is not subject to the conditions of pure passivity that governs the acquisition of existence. The possible cannot do anything to emerge from nothingness; thought does everything in acquiring truth. *He Who has created you without you will not save you without yourself.*[76] As a superexistence actively produced by thought within itself, truth bears an infinitely greater resemblance to divine existence than could ever be suggested by any merely physical existence, which is necessarily received without any cooperation from its receiver. Indeed, when one is lacking perfection by identity, the next best thing is to give it to oneself by one's own activity.

There is another limitation on the proposed analogy between existence and truth: whereas the thing that has come into existence can develop only within the bounds of its specific nature, there is progress in truth over and above the assimilation of the object. By the gift of existence, the entire potential of the thing

---

[74] Thomas Aquinas, *Cont. gent.* I, 72; *Sum. th.* I, q. 16, a. 5.

[75] Just as judgment is a superactivity supported by the primary activity of simple representation.

[76] St. Augustine.

for its act of being is completely fulfilled. The material thing is brought into being with a contingent and corruptible existence, and it will never rise above it. A tree may live for centuries and provide shade for generations of people, but the synthesis of its essence and its act of being, separable at the first instant of its existence, will forever remain separable. Similarly, although from the moment of their creation angels and souls enjoy an incorruptible existence, they will never rise to necessary existence. A thing exists or does not exist; if it does exist, it may make progress as that particular thing; it makes no progress in existence. Now, in one sense, we have to say that the intellect, by its judgment, has the truth or does not have it, just as the thing has or does not have existence. But in another sense, we need to recognize that the mind, in possession of truth, may advance in a way roughly analogous to what would happen to a thing if it could, by its own activity, exchange a corruptible for an incorruptible existence, or a contingent existence for a necessary one.[77] The mind that affirms that it is raining at the time it is raining is true absolutely and without qualification, and its stops being true if it maintains its judgment an instant later when the rain has stopped. The truth of the mind that knows the contingent is a corruptible truth. But when the mind passes from the consideration of perishable things to the consideration of the laws that govern them, it rises from a corruptible to an incorruptible truth, which is the more incorruptible as the necessity of its object is itself less conditional, which is indeed the way our mind's truth comes more and more to resemble the Supreme Truth, Who is God. This progress in truth often takes place—at least that is when we notice it—through access to new objects that provide the basis for judgments more stable in their truth, and we normally distinguish this from the progress in the simple displaying of the object. When I learn that Plato is the author of the

---

[77] John of St. Thomas, *Log.* I, q. 5, a. 1 (R, I, 147A1): "The truth of a proposition as, formally, an adequation or conformity to being or non-being is indivisible, and is not susceptible of more or less; yet in terms of certitude and firmness, in which the conformity or adequation has some flexibility, truth may be more or less, one truth greater than another, and one proposition truer than another, i.e., more firmly and more certainly grounded in immutable truth."

Parmenides, the truth that I acquire is not qualitatively superior to the truth of the proposition "Plato is the author of the *Gorgias*." By contrast, when I rise from knowing things of this world to the knowledge of God, I know that I approach a superior order of truth. Yet there exists still another and not so obvious progress in the knowledge of truth. It consists in the mind's ever clearer awareness of the necessity of its judgment, which is also the source of the purest and least communicable joys of the life of study. Say that ten years ago I read for the first time a page from a certain great philosopher and, as soon as I read it, I gave my unqualified assent to his proposed conclusion. Since then, my rereading of this page many times has had no other result than to make me memorize it better; my judgment of it remained the same, the reasons for its conclusions fully convincing. But one day, in the course of still another reading, this page suddenly takes on a new and far more intense life in my mind. Though it is the same synthesis of subject and predicate to which I give assent, for reasons that remain unchanged, I nevertheless feel that there is no comparison between my previous and my new awareness of the force and clarity of the proposed conclusion. Indeed, it would do us all good every so often to relax our desire for amassing new knowledge and to try instead to deepen the knowledge of the truth we already possess.[78]

Now, whether it is a matter of having a clearer perception of the necessity of a judgment already made or of proceeding to establish new judgments, what is decisive for the entire theory of progress in the knowledge of truth are the *reasons for judgment*. By reasons for judgment I mean the light that compels the mind to assent to the identity in the transobject of the objects of thought that are not identical with each other in their being as objects. As we have maintained in the preceding, although the identity of the object and the thing is specifically *recognized* only in the judgment, it is never ignored. That the object and the thing are the same is assumed when the object

---

[78] Clearly, there is qualitative progress in the knowledge of truth when the mind rises from the level of probability to the level of certitude. But it is important to recognize that additional and most intensive progress takes place in the order of certain knowledge itself.

is first reached, and their identity continues to exercise an obscure efficacy in all our cognition. But what compels the mind specifically to identify two particular objects of thought cannot arise from the transobjectivity of the thing, which at that moment is not yet penetrated by the mind, any more than it can be derived from the objects themselves, which, as authentic, distinct objects of thought, resist being so reduced. By these qualities the objects resist identification, and from that point of view the Megarians would be right. And what that means is that this call for interobjective identification can come only from the objects themselves not as objects but strictly as *manifestations of the thing itself*. In other words, what gives any object of thought, non-exhaustive as it may be, the power to reveal to us its connection with other aspects of its transobjective reality is nothing else but its real identity with the thing it manifests in our knowledge.

Sometimes it is the sheer objective content of the concept that reveals its need to be joined in the mind to the objective content of another concept, and the judgment so determined is what we call a rational judgment. At other times, when their contents do not reveal the need for such an association, it is experience that shows us the need to associate one particular object with another. For example, although there is nothing in the concept of this man and in the concept of a flute player that compels my mind to assent to the proposition "This man is a flute player," I do so because I see and I hear this man playing the flute.

Empirical evidence is the prerogative of the experienced singular; rational evidence, the prerogative of certain axioms. Faced by an indefinite number of enunciations that put together objects whose identification is supported neither by an immediate datum of experience nor by a manifest requirement of related concepts, thought can find security only in doublechecking the synthesis proposed by the enunciation against another synthesis verified either in experience or by reasoning. What we call inductive reasoning is an operation by means of which the mind makes manifest to itself the necessity of joining a predicate to a subject, based on the assent given to a proposition verified in experience; and what we call deductive reasoning is an operation by means of which the mind makes manifest to itself the same neces-

of the intellect. This may not be the only reason for the fashionable mathematicizing noetic, but it is likely the most important.

Finally, concerning the mind's progress based on the exploration of the object, we note that progress in thought also takes place when thought exploits the content of a given idea in order to multiply concepts that illuminate various aspects of the thing itself.[83]

We see, then, that the activity of the mind assumes a variety of forms. The mind exercises a primary kind of activity, wholly transitive, in the precognitive abstraction of the idea; it exercises a second kind of activity, wholly immanent, in objective cognition, i.e., in the act of knowing; it exercises a third kind of activity, transitive in its nature but included in the immanent act of knowing, when it expresses the thing thought in a concept; the mind performs a fourth kind of activity when it enunciates a proposition; a fifth kind when it renders a judgment; a sixth kind when, relying on truth established antecedently, it provides itself through reasoning with new truth; and, finally, the mind exercises a seventh kind of activity, primarily transitive, when, with the help of known objects, it constructs new and original ideas entirely on its own initiative.

If we are right in these matters, a significant part in the life of thought is played by productive activities. Those engaged in scholarship in particular know very well that the preparation for knowledge, in which the mind is busy literally *working* on itself, takes far more time than the motionless and wholly immanent contemplation of pure knowledge does. But one would have to be blind not to see that the end and sole purpose of all this

---

nize that our intellect understands immaterial things and beings of reason through their proper ideas, which it acquires not from those things themselves, imperceptible to the senses, but by forming them from the likenesses and proportions of the ideas of corporeal things that are already present in it. And so we say that our intellect should not be called a purely passive power with respect to these ideas just because it produces them from ideas already possessed; for with respect to those it produces, it operates not passively but actively."

[83] John of St. Thomas, *Phil. nat.* IV, q. 11, a. 2 (R, III, 357A24): "Many concepts can be formed from the same idea because a thing can be considered from different points of view virtually included within a single idea, as well as through comparing one idea with another."

productivity in which the life of our minds is involved is precisely that immanent knowledge itself and especially the truth embodied in the superactive immanence of the judgment. We get ideas, we express concepts, we make constructs, we discourse —all for the sake of knowing the truth. When this is understood, one is secured against most misconceptions about the activity of the mind.

Appendix

Habitus

Of all the Scholastic words reputedly untranslatable into any modern language, *habitus* is the only one that we have decided to use as if it were fully anglicized. We simply had no choice. Translating *habitus* by *habit*, as some still do, is worse than inaccurate; it is anti-pedagogical. Between the characteristics of *habit* and those of *habitus*, the contrast is such that any meaning conveyed by the word *habit* is a heavy obstacle to the understanding of *habitus*. Again, there can be no question of changing the meaning of the word *habit* by frequently using it in the sense of *habitus*. According to derivation, *habit* might have meant the same as *habitus*, but at the time when modern philosophic languages were formed, the concept of *habitus* was absent from philosophic thought. The usage of Hume, constantly followed by British and American philosophers and psychologists, has forever obliterated the possibility that *habit* would take on the meaning of *habitus*.

A habitus is a quality characterized by *essential* steadiness. In the case of an operative habitus, steadiness is guaranteed by necessity in the object. The steadiness of a habit, on the other hand, is a mere effect of repetition. Steadiness resulting merely from multiplied acts—the steadiness of a habit—deceptively imitates the steadiness of objective necessity. Hume attempted to show that the causal interpretations of science have only the steadiness of a habit. In Aristotelianism, science, art, and moral virtues are habitus; their steadiness is guaranteed by objective

---

An earlier version of this explanation, by Yves Simon, of the use of *habitus* and *idea* appeared in his translation of *The Material Logic of John of St. Thomas*, pp. 611–12n5 and 613–14n4, respectively.

necessity. A stubborn opinion has but the steadiness of a habit; there is no necessity in its object. The virtuosity that resides in the fingers of the virtuoso is but a habit whose privilege is to act as the instrument of the habitus of art. There is a good reason for refusing to translate *habitus* by habit: what is at stake is the very notion of objective necessity.

The difficulties of the situation are increased by some irregularity in the use of the word *habitus*. Following the example of Aristotle, St. Thomas and his commentators are very particular about the precise meaning of technical terms whenever extreme precision is needed, but as soon as the context does not require so much precision, they relax and use technical terms in a broader sense. If the notion to be expressed is that of a disposition whose steadiness results from an essential necessity, a disposition whose steadiness is merely factual will be said not to be, by any means, a habitus. Science and opinion, for instance, will be set in sharp contrast as habitus and mere disposition. But there are many contexts in which it is not necessary to determine whether the steadiness of a disposition is essential or purely factual. This happens when the purpose is to distinguish a lasting disposition (e.g., science, opinion) from both mere ability (e.g., the intellectual power) and operation (e.g., the exercise of scientific thought or that of opinion). In terms of act and potency, what matters is not so much the ground of steadiness—a repetition of acts in habit, an objective necessity in habitus—as the property of *outlasting the actuality of operation*. Just as a mathematician remains actuated by his science when he thinks of no scientific object, so the man of stubborn opinion retains his opinion even in distraction or in sleep. Both opinion and science have the character of lasting "first acts," lasting "intermediary potencies." Very often the word "habitus" is used without any reference to the ground of the disposition's steadiness and designates, with no further specification, a quality that lastingly determines a power in relation to operation. In this sense, the expression "habitus of opinion" is used side by side with the expression "habitus of science."

Idea

The word translated by "idea" is *species*, in psychology and epistemology one of the most embarrassing expressions of the Scholastic language. Against the use of "idea" for *species* it can be objected that we have no other word than "idea" to translate the Latin *idea*, whose meaning will be hard to convey if the word to which that meaning is entrusted conveys also another notion of very frequent occurrence. In our opinion, this difficulty is inevitable and ought to be taken care of as best we can in each particular case. We have no choice, for "idea" alone can express with the needed vividness the meaning of the Aristotelian εἶδος and of the Scholastic *species*.

The Scholastic usage of *species* in psychological and epistemological contexts is fixed by Aristotelian sentences, the most famous of which is: οὐ γὰρ ὁ λίθος ἐν τῇ ψυχῇ, ἀλλὰ τὸ εἶδος (*On the Soul* III, 8, 431в29). J. A. Smith translates this, in *The Basic Works of Aristotle*, as ". . . it is not the stone which is present in the soul but its form." This is a perfectly accurate translation, but the word "form" is of no help in our endeavor to figure out precisely what is present in the soul when the stone is perceived. The theory of cognitive "forms," which, in Aristotle, involves much obscurity, has been greatly clarified by St. Thomas and his commentators. With particular reference to its treatment by Cajetan and John of St. Thomas, it can be outlined as follows.

Knowing is a certain way of being, primarily distinguished by the paradoxical ability of the knower to be not only what it is but also what other things are (*On the Soul* III, 8, 431в20: "Let us now summarize our results about the soul and repeat that the soul is in a way all existing things" [trans. Smith]). The mode of existence according to which the soul is all things is described as immaterial, spiritual, objective, *intentional*, transsubjective, in opposition to the mode of existence according to which things are just what they are, and which is called material, *physical*, natural, entitative, subjective. Here, as elsewhere, existence is intelligibly prior to what bears it, and the contrast between, say, the stone and its "form" must be understood in relation to an intelligibly antecedent contrast, viz., that between the physical and the intentional ways of existing. "Notice," Cajetan writes (*In Ia*, q. 55, q. 3), that there are two genera of beings. Some are primarily designed to exist, although, secondarily, they may happen to represent other beings, and these we call *things*. But some beings are primarily designed by nature to represent other beings; and these we call intentions of things, and sensible or intelligible *species*. The reason why it is necessary to posit these two genera is that the cognitive must be not only itself but also others, and the intellective, all things, as established [by St. Thomas' exposition] in I, q. 14 and by the consensus of the philosophers, who agree that like is known by like. Now, the natures of things cannot be present in the cognitive with their own entity. It is not the stone that is present in the soul. Again, the knower cannot, by its finite substance alone, be so excellent as to have in itself the means of assimilating the natures of the knowable things, distinctly and according to their proper features. Thus it was necessary for nature to establish the intentional being, by means of which the knower is the knowable.

The intentional form of Aristotelianism (εἶδος) has sometimes been confused with the simulacrum of the Epicureans (εἴδωλον). In the terms of Cajetan's exposition, it is clear that the Epicurean simulacrum remains a *thing*, i.e., an entity of the first genus, which is defined by the existential function of existing. The simulacrum is a small thing, which inconspicuously accomplishes feats that big things could not conceivably accomplish, viz., getting through the pores of the skin, reaching the subtle center of the body, etc. But just as the intentional "to be" of the Aristotelians is by no means a physical existence, so their "intentions" and "sensible and intelligible *species*" are not things. They are defined by their being related to "to be intentionally" as things are related to "to be physically." To designate such entities, there is only one word, the word "idea." The two systems described by Cajetan are the system of the things and the system of the ideas. We commonly use "ideas" not in its Augustinian and Scholastic sense of creative pattern, but in the sense of intelligible "*species*." Much can be learned about Aristotelian psychology and theory of knowledge by extending the use of "idea" to the *species* of all cognitive powers. There are ideas in the intellect and in the imagination and in the memory and in the external senses. Aristotelian views on sensation, so wretchedly expounded most of the time, become intelligible when we understand that Aristotelianism is the philosophy that posits ideas not only in the intellect and in the imagination and in the memory but also in sight and hearing and touch. Other philosophies know of ideas born in the soul, e.g., intellectual representation consequent upon images, images consequent upon sense impressions. But Aristotelianism knows of ideas that are initial in an absolute sense and are born not in the soul but in nature. The sensorial idea is the Aristotelian answer to the problem of the initial connection between physical nature and the soul. Those things are impossible to explain if we translate *species sensibilis* by sensible "species" or "form" or anything short of the thought-provoking power of the word "idea."

Index

Compiled by Joseph W. Sprug. Numbers in ( ) refer to footnotes.